ANIMAL TRAFFIC

ANIMAL
TRAFFIC

Rosemary-Claire Collard

Lively Capital in the Global Exotic Pet Trade

Duke University Press | *Durham and London* | 2020

Designed by Aimee C. Harrison
Typeset in Portrait Text and Canela Text by Copperline Book Services

Library of Congress Cataloging-in-Publication Data
Names: Collard, Rosemary-Claire, author.
Title: Animal traffic : lively capital in the global exotic pet trade /
Rosemary-Claire Collard.
Description: Durham : Duke University Press, 2020. | Includes
bibliographical references and index.
Identifiers: LCCN 2019058227 (print)
LCCN 2019058228 (ebook)
ISBN 9781478009894 (hardcover)
ISBN 9781478010920 (paperback)
ISBN 9781478012467 (ebook)
Subjects: LCSH: Wild animal trade—Moral and ethical aspects. |
Exotic animals—Economic aspects. | Wild animals as pets—
United States. | Wildlife smuggling. | Wildlife conservation—Guatemala.
Classification: LCC HV6410 .C65 2020 (print) | LCC HV6410 (ebook) | DDC
382/.439—dc23
LC record available at https://lccn.loc.gov/2019058227
LC ebook record available at https://lccn.loc.gov/2019058228

Cover art: Isabella Kirkland, TRADE, 2001. © Isabella Kirkland.

CONTENTS

A NOTE ON THE
COVER ART

"Taxis" is a Greek word meaning "order" or "arrangement." It is the root of "taxonomy": the science of describing species and fitting them into evolutionary order on the tree of life. Each of the six oil paintings in a series called TAXA explores one aspect or dynamic of conservation. Each species was carefully researched. Each of the six paintings took nearly a year to complete. All are painted to scale, at life size, and are depicted as accurately as possible. The image used here, TRADE, from 2001, shows species of plants and animals whose wild populations are depleted by collection for legal, illegal, and unregulated markets.

In-depth study of a single species can yield a world of information: each life cycle is deeply entwined with that of others in its community. The more we learn about the intricacies of one organism and its ecosystem, the more we see the limits of our current knowledge. The more we discover, the more we comprehend our responsibility for every other living thing.

Oil paintings can last for centuries. I use accuracy, attention to detail, craft, and research to send a snapshot of our current view of humans' relationship to the rest of nature into the future: a modern momento mori.

—Isabella Kirkland

ACKNOWLEDGMENTS

Like most academics' offices, mine has a wall of books. I used to look at it and marvel at the thousands of hours of authors' work represented on the shelves. Now I know about the thousands more hours of work behind those books—work by people named not on the book jackets but in the acknowledgments. So many people have shared their time, ideas, and energy with me as I researched and wrote this book.

The book would not exist without a crew of supportive, trustworthy intellectual heavyweights I am lucky to call friends, colleagues, and family (many who fit in more than one of those groups, and in the case of my sister, Juliane Collard, all three!). There are two people I need to thank first: Katie Gillespie and Jess Dempsey, who have been the most energizing, inspiring pals and collaborators to have in my corner. From listening to me debrief over Skype during fieldwork to reading multiple drafts of the book and generously giving round after round of feedback and encouragement, they've been instrumental to this whole process and have even made it fun, from the beginning, through the looooonnngg middle, until the end.

The rest of the crew is far-reaching—so I'll start with the farthest flung and work my way toward home. No one else is nearly as far as Beirut, where I send thanks to my cousin and lifelong friend, Rebecca Collard, a journalist who has spent years exchanging pep talks with me and patiently attempting to help me express academic ideas less dryly. In the United States, special thanks to James McCarthy at Clark University for reaching out to me years ago at one of my first conferences, supporting my work in all kinds of ways since, and generally making academia more human. In Lafayette, Indiana, thank you to my aunt and uncle, JoAnn and Norman Phillion, for their infectious intellectual curiosity and enthusiasm, for their mentorship, and for the more practical matter of recharging my nutrition levels and spirits during a cross-country auction research road trip.

To what feels like my second home, Montréal, I send thanks to Norma Rantisi for her friendship and for modeling a way of navigating the university with generosity, care, humor, and gentle rigor. Thank you to Jesse Arseneault, Bernard Lansbergen, and Julia Freeman for all the road trips, mountain walks, homemade dinners, and conversations over beer about everything from postcolonialism to pop culture. Jesse also started up the Society, Politics, Animals and Materiality (SPAM) group at Concordia University with me; thanks to all the members of that group, especially Kathleen Vaughan, Constance Lafontaine, Stephanie Eccles, and Rebekah Glendinning. I lucked out big time in having Stephanie, Rebekah, and Meghan Gagliardi as my first student supervisees—I learned a ton from them, and all of them also lent expert research assistance to this book. Thanks to the Political Ecology/Economy Reading Friends (PERF), especially Bengi Akbulut, Nil Alt, Hannah Brais, Noah Cannon, Piyusha Chatterjee, and Samiha Khalil. The students, staff, and faculty at the Department of Geography, Planning and Environment at Concordia set the gold standard in home departments. Thanks especially to Kevin Gould and Ted Rutland, friends with whom I was lucky to share departments in grad school and work; to Angela Kross, Pascale Biron, Marilyn Malofy, Craig Townsend, Sébastien Caquard, and Sarah Turner, regulars in the lunchroom for *l'heure sacrée*; and to Nalini Mohabir, who I wish I'd been able to share halls with for longer but still count on for Skype chats. Finally, thanks to valued friends and colleagues Mireille Paquet, Kathryn Furlong, and Amy Swiffen.

In Ottawa, huge thanks go to Emilie Cameron, Pablo Mendez, and Fiona Jeffries, three people I feel incredibly lucky to call friends and colleagues, who have heard their fair share about exotic pets over the years, and who still manage to seem interested. Emilie especially has for years been a trusted source of savvy advice and creative insights. In Toronto, Scott Prudham supervised my short postdoc stint at U of T and has since lent his vast theory chops to helping me puzzle through some of the ideas in this book over the years, including a memorable long Skype conversation about fetishism.

Acknowledgments

In Vancouver, where I did my PhD and now live again, I would first like to thank Trevor Barnes and Juanita Sundberg, as well as Gerry Pratt and Matthew Evenden, for doing so much work to steer me through the first years of this project. Trevor in particular steadily nudged me toward clearer thinking and writing over the years. This book bears each of their stamps in different ways—the best ways—which I hope they can see as clearly as I do. I thank them too for their ongoing mentorship, especially Gerry, who, sitting on Jess Dempsey's back deck, helped dislodge me from a years-long writing block. Thanks also to Jess and Sara Nelson for reading a draft of the book and, in another afternoon on Jess's deck, initiating the dislodging process that Gerry helped finish.

Also in Vancouver, huge thanks to Joanna Reid as a best pal and expert editor, for everything from endless support and encouragement to reading recommendations to nitty-gritty grammar revelations. Jo and Tony Massil, another great source of creative inspiration, also came along with me to Story Book Farm and Sanctuary to visit Darwin, where Tony took photos. Thanks also to Laura DeVries and Lara Hoshizaki for their ongoing friendship.

At Simon Fraser University, where I now work, Geoff Mann, Eugene McCann, Nick Blomley, and Michael Hathaway are generous, brilliant colleagues. Thanks to them for their high fives in the hall when I finally submitted this book, and then again a few months later when I *really* finally submitted this book. The feminist geographers are a bright light at SFU—thanks especially to Baharak Yousefi and Natalia Perez (who also translated the Spanish text in an ARCAS photograph for this book). And a final thank-you in Vancouver goes to a world-class group of grad students from whom I learned so much while we were all geography students at the University of British Columbia, especially Matt Dyce, Jono Peyton, Dawn Hoogeveen, Sarah Brown, Carolyn Prouse, Dan Cohen, May Farrales, Jon Leudee, Paige Patchin, Max Ritts, and Kelsey Johnson.

There are some key people to thank in Victoria, as I inch closer to home on Vancouver Island. At the University of Victoria, where I first caught the research and critical theory bug, several people shaped my approach to research, theory, politics, and academic life in ways I still notice today, especially Kara Shaw, Michael M'Gonigle, and Wendy Wickwire. I'd also like to give huge thanks to Nicole Shukin for the unmatched way she combines bigheartedness and sky-high intellect as an academic. She has supported and inspired much of my scholarship.

This brings me to Sooke, the place that still feels like the epicenter of home, where there are so many people to thank, including my longtime friends Allison Watson, Angela Jenkins, Maria Moran, Jessica Swinburson, Lauren Hutchings, and Jocelyn Lukow. Katie Rose McKenzie opened up her cabin on Gordon's Beach for a week of what ended up being the last push of book writing in front of a window with an eye-level view onto the Pacific.

The most important people to thank are the members of my small but formidable family. My sister, Juliane, has read countless drafts of this book over the years and listened to hours and hours of book thoughts. I can't believe the luck of having an endlessly fun and hilarious sister who is also a best friend and a brilliant academic—a feminist geographer to boot. Our parents, Francine Dagenais and Andrew Collard, have always seemingly effortlessly found a balance between being interested in what we're doing and encouraging us, but never dictating or pressuring us on any particular path. Each of them has their own distinctly grounded, open orientation to the world, always calling our attention back to the material world (which may partly explain how they ended up with two geographer daughters). Thank you to them for their love and for being so easy to love back.

There are a few final people to thank for their help and feedback: first, everyone who spoke with me, hosted me, and worked with me during the field research for this book, especially Rob Laidlaw, Juan Carlos Cantu, Alejandro Morales, Jose Luis Rangel, Peter Fricker, Sara DuBois, and Ernie Cooper. I'd also like to thank the people who have listened to presentations or chatter about parts of this book and given savvy feedback, including Juno Parreñas, Heidi Nast, Jody Emel, Richard Schroeder, Jenny Isaacs, Claire Jean Kim, and Tony Weis, as well as wider audiences in geography departments at Rutgers University, Clark University, the University of Toronto, the University of Victoria, Concordia University, and McGill University, the environmental studies school at UVic, and especially the Multispecies Justice group at the University of Wisconsin–Madison. Thank you to Liz Hennessy for inviting me to workshop this book's introduction with that group, to Laura Perry for showing me around Madison, and to the group members for their careful and helpful feedback, especially Matt Turner and Sainath Suryanarayanan.

Thank you to Jake Kosek and the Department of Geography at Berkeley for hosting me during my auction fieldwork, to Mark Kear for being such a fun colleague during that visit, and to the Department of Geography at the

University of Toronto for hosting me as a postdoctoral fellow while I was writing the proposal for this book. At U of T, in addition to Scott Prudham, mentioned earlier, special thanks are due to Sue Ruddick, Alexis Mitchell, Emily Gilbert, and Mike Ekers for their generous intellectual engagement.

At Duke University Press, my deepest thanks to Courtney Berger, an editor extraordinaire, for patiently and intelligently pushing me to make this a far better book, and to three reviewers for helping me get there with their clear guidance and sharp insights. I would also like to thank the rest of the editorial, production, and design team at Duke, especially Sandra Korn, Liz Smith, and Aimee Harrison and my copyeditor, Susan Ecklund, for steering and improving this book in its final stages. Finally, thank you to Isabella Kirkland for her inspiring artwork and her permission to use one of my all-time favorite pieces of art—her evocative painting *TRADE*—for the cover of this book.

INTRODUCTION

A small black sign attached to the cage wall warns in bright yellow capital letters: KEEP BACK FIVE FEET! Inside the cage, canvas ropes hang a few feet off the ground, and brightly colored plastic toys meant for kids—balls, a child-sized playhouse—lie on the rocky dirt floor. The walls and ceiling of this outdoor cage are made up of thin metal bars that crisscross to form squares just big enough to slip slender fingers through. A solid wall separates the outdoor cage from an attached inner cage, and a small window—no more than a foot and a half square—about three feet above the ground allows passage between the two cages, controlled by a metal grate over the window that can lift and lock into an open position. Today, the grate is up. The cage's resident, a young monkey, spies out the window from inside. When he sees us looking at him, his head disappears back into the dark.

"He's really shy," says Sherri Delaney, one of the monkey's caregivers and founder of Story Book Farm Primate Sanctuary, two hours north of Toronto, Canada.

You would not know it by his web presence. This monkey is one of the world's most famous. Named Darwin, but more widely known as the Ikea Monkey, on a cold winter day in 2012 the at-the-time foot-tall, months-old Japanese macaque escaped his crate and his owner's parked car outside a Toronto Ikea. Wearing a diaper and a miniature shearling coat, Darwin wandered the parking lot and attempted to enter the store. Eventually, Toronto animal services confiscated him in the lot, but not before a cluster of shoppers circled him, taking photos that launched him to momentary global fame.

In the next days, while Darwin's image circulated at lightning speed around the world, animal services delivered the caged monkey to Story Book. He quickly became the center of a storm of media attention, controversy, and legal action. Although the city of Toronto bans the ownership of primates as pets, Darwin's owner at the time, forty-three-year-old real estate lawyer Yasmin Nakhuda, claimed he was purchased in a Montréal borough, where he was captive-bred and where monkeys are legal pets. Nakhuda called herself Darwin's mom and posted YouTube videos of the two of them hanging out around her house, brushing their teeth and bathing together. In an effort to regain possession of Darwin, Nakhuda moved outside of Toronto to where she could legally own primates, and sued Story Book. She argued in court that Darwin was not her pet; he was her son.

But after hearing the case, Superior Court justice Mary Vallee denied Nahukda's claim. The judge stated that "callous as it may seem, the monkey is a chattel . . . a piece of property" (Ontario Superior Court of Justice 2013). Nakhuda, the judge ruled, lost ownership of this particular piece of property when she lost possession of it. The judge's apparent ambivalence about Darwin's legal status as property, glimpsed in her words "callous as it may seem," belies the inescapability of this designation—all animals are property under Canadian law. But the ruling about ownership was less straightforward and hinged on a distinction between domesticated and wild animals as different kinds of property. If Darwin had been a domesticated animal, Nakhuda would not have lost ownership when she lost possession because domesticated animals are considered absolute property. Nonnative wild animals, in contrast, are property only when in their owner's possession.[1] As such, Nakhuda lost ownership of Darwin when he escaped his cage and her car.

So Darwin remained at Story Book, where he still lives today, by himself in his cage. Around twenty other primates of various species also live at the sanctuary, for the most part also individually caged. You can read about them on Story Book's website (Story Book Farm Primate Sanctuary 2020). Boo and Gerdie, two rhesus macaques who are among the sanctuary's only residents to live as a twosome, were both born in 1996 and spent the first seventeen years of their lives as test subjects for neurological research at an unspecified lab in Ontario, until they arrived at Story Book in 2013. Many other monkeys at Story Book were former pets, petting zoo or roadside zoo residents, or actors for film and television. Others have spent time in all of these roles. For example, a spider monkey called Mr. Jenkins was born in 2002 and as a baby was purchased as a pet. Shortly after, he was sold into film acting, where he reportedly did not perform adequately. He was then sold to a petting zoo to work in educational programs for children. He was too "unpredictable" for this work and was sent to an auction, where he failed to gain the desired price and so returned to the petting zoo before "retiring" at Story Book.

Stories like Mr. Jenkins's are not unusual in the global exotic pet trade, where animals are frequently purchased as small infants and then become unwanted by or unmanageable for their owners after they grow and mature. Thousands of transactions like these—animals being purchased as exotic pets, animals being re-sold—are happening as I write these words, and thousands more as you read them. But while stories from the exotic pet trade occasionally make the news—when animals like Darwin escape, for example—much of this multibillion-dollar trade goes unremarked upon, under the radar of everyday people, media, governments, and academic study. In this book I try to shed light on this shadowy trade. Through participation in and observation of embodied multispecies encounters in the nooks and crannies of the global exotic pet trade, I investigate the often hidden processes through which exotic pets are produced and traded as lively capital.

Darwin himself has grown into an adult macaque—at least three or four times the size and strength of his younger self—and no longer wears clothes. A volunteer at the sanctuary describes him as mischievous and hopes that he will be introduced to two new Story Book residents, another pair of former scientific test subject macaques who arrived from a Canadian university lab in 2015. When I visited Darwin, I mostly spotted him out of the corner of my eye—a blurred gray shape flitting behind a cage wall; an arm reaching out of the dark window, hairless fingers curled around the ledge. Having outgrown the curiosity and fearlessness of his younger days, Darwin now seems to prefer to stay out of sight, at least to strangers.

Staying out of sight has become more difficult for wild animals. Report after report, study after study, headline after headline signal the dwindling amount of space left in the world for wild animals to inhabit. Habitat loss, coupled with other factors, among them the global exotic pet trade, have induced what James MacKinnon calls a "ten percent world," a planet with a fraction of the diversity and abundance it once had, a world of paltry salmon runs and dead-quiet forests. This is not a scientifically precise term— MacKinnon is a writer describing the decimation of nonhuman life within his lifetime. But scientists are busily studying defaunation, a term that refers not only to the extinction of species but also to the loss of populations and abundance. A grim picture is emerging. Vertebrate populations are undergoing a "biological annihilation," declining by an average of 60 percent since 1970.[2] Systems biologists have generated a mind-boggling model of total animal biomass on earth, which shows that today, domesticated birds constitute 70 percent of all bird life, almost entirely broiler chickens. The picture is even more dire for mammals, of which only 4 percent are wild, and 60 percent are domesticated—with the remainder made up of humans.[3] These numbers signify how defaunation is tethered to the ascent of commodified animal life, the vast majority in industrial livestock production, leading Tony Weis (2018) to coin the term "commodi-faunation."[4] For wild animals, too, the dramatic rise of exotic pet keeping and zoos over the past centuries and especially the last few decades would suggest that more wild animals than ever before live enclosed in cages, as Darwin does, where they have little option to go unseen. But this can be the case whether or not these animals are commodities.

Darwin, like the other monkeys at Story Book, is no longer a commodity; he will no longer circulate in markets and will, barring the unforeseen, die at Story Book. But, as Justice Vallee's decision makes clear, Darwin is still property, a "thing" or object that is owned. Darwin thus embodies a tension within the pet form—exotic or not. Pets are constructed and encountered as intimate companions; they are valued for their energy and creativity, their aliveness, even their sentience—although all within limits. Animals who are pets are viewed, in this sense, as beings: lively subjects who engage in their own world-making practices. At the same time, pets are legally and materially property, even commodities. They are in this sense treated as things or objects.[5]

Arguably, all propertied and commodified animal life embodies this tension. Living commodities like farm animals are also sentient property. But their sentience is largely denied; it is not typically a valued or prerequisite quality of the commodity or property form. Within the pet form, however, sentience is not only admitted but valued. Expressions of animals' personalities, will, responsiveness, and feelings are part of what make them beloved companions and sellable commodities. Yet pets live subject to limits that attend their property status, including limits on movement, reproductive choice, and generally the extent to which they can express their will. Exotic pets are arguably especially controlled. Unlike domesticated pets like cats and dogs, who have adapted over time to life alongside humans, particularly in a manner that provides companionship, exotic pets are often wild-caught or only one or two generations captive. They are not adapted to captive life and are often unruly, even dangerous, and consequently subject to tight control and enclosure. As I document in this book, exotic pets are removed from their families and social groups, bought and sold as individuals, for example, at auctions, kept enclosed in cages, and controlled on leashes. The effect is that exotic pets are alive, but their lives are profoundly circumscribed—socially, spatially, ecologically, behaviorally—such that in most cases their pet lives are starkly divergent from their lives before capture, or from the lives of their uncaptive counterparts.

This tension between being valued as a lively subject and being controlled as a propertied object can be expressed in more economic terms. Part of what animates an exotic pet as a "useful" object and as property, and what propels an exotic pet through trade circuits and into markets as lively capital, a living "thing" with economic value that is realized when it is exchanged, is its very *not* thing-ness: its liveliness and sentience, its capacity to respond to and interact with humans, its ability to be *encountered* as a living being, as a companion. This tension expresses itself sharply in an animal like Darwin, whose sentience is at odds with his property status. His nearness to humans—his human-like hands, his familiar tiny coat and diaper—makes Darwin's sentience undeniable, even within a conventional humanist frame. Perhaps more than most pets, he forces a confrontation with the tension they all embody. Darwin makes his own designation as "property" tremble; his anthropomorphic, "son"-like qualities strain his object status, prompting the judge's tempering clause, the "callous as it may seem," revealing a degree of anxiety around the construction of Darwin's property status. This legal case exemplifies how a pet is a sentient, dynamic, emotional being who is *made* thing*like* when it is made a commodity, made property, through markets, the law, the state, and other institutions and mechanisms.

This book sits in the middle of this tension and process of making thinglike. My primary concern is to track how animals are made thinglike, lively capital in the global exotic pet trade. The process of making lively capital is related to but broader than commodification, which refers to the more specific process of making something a commodity, or an object that is exchanged. Not all forms of lively capital, exotic pets included, are commodities, strictly speaking—some, like Darwin, may even be prohibited from being bought and sold. But they are all capital in the sense that they are a stock of possessions generating value or potential future value.[6] For exotic pets, this means they are also captive, living in enclosed spaces, and rendered dependent on their owners. And they are "useful" to these owners, generating what feminist science studies scholar Donna Haraway (2008) calls "encounter value": value produced through multispecies meetings, here between people and exotic animals, whether as companions, entertainment, or attractions for visitors, where they may form an important part of profit generation or economic exchanges and activities. Exotic animals do not necessarily generate encounter value as commodities, but often more akin to how unpaid or informal laborers form the economy, as I explain later. So while in this book I track the formation, reformation, and deformation of commodities, I am also interested in processes of enclosure and control that form the exotic pet but cannot be reduced to commodification. In general terms this means I am interested in how this economy works: How are animals captured? How are they exchanged? What embodied encounters and interactions form these actions and impel animals along trade circuits?

My second main concern is to capture the effects of this process of making lively capital in the exotic pet trade. This trade's reach extends into nests in sky-high canopies in the world's most remote forests; into equally high skyscraper apartments in the world's biggest cities; into fenced suburban backyards, rural farms, and roadside petting zoos. It is a trade that transforms animals from free-ranging forest and desert residents to captive property in someone's living room or backyard. What kind of life does this transformation produce for the exotic pet? I call this life "object life": the life that is the target of and reinforced through commodification and maintenance of the exotic pet, a life that precedes commodification in all cases and succeeds it in most. This object life for an exotic pet is individual, encounterable, and controlled—and this has high costs. Captured animals are rendered dependent on human-provided shelter and sustenance, often including binding captured animals to the lives and deaths of a wider network of animals in industrial meat production. And the captured animals themselves suffer extremely high mortality rates, as well as stress, trauma, and ill health. This exposes another iteration of the tension within the exotic pet form—that the processes of enclosure, individuation, and control that form the exotic pet as capital are driven by the pet's value as a lively, encounterable being, yet these very processes diminish and often even end life for exotic pets.

Although animal being is constrained in the exotic pet trade, the process of making thinglike lively capital is never complete; it cannot be—this is why I use the term "thing*like*" to describe an exotic pet, as opposed to "thing." The only way for an animal to be fully reduced to a thing is through the complete extinguishment of life and being, and yet death also necessarily ends the exotic pet form, because being alive is a necessary characteristic of a pet. Dead pets might still circulate as different kinds of commodities or property, but liveliness and sentience are no longer the valued qualities driving this circulation. So all exotic pets retain sentience and a degree of life. And their lives exceed attempts to manage them, in all sorts of daily, mundane ways—by refusing to eat, defecating in unwanted places, making noise, self-harming, escaping. When alive, exotic pets continually reassert their creative sentience and remind us of their persistent *being*, as Darwin does. A third main goal in this book is to be attuned, as much as possible, to the animal being that is never fully extinguished.

My final aim in this book is to look beyond the exotic pet trade to capitalist socio-ecological relations more broadly, to shed light on how capitalism functions in relation to animals—how capitalist socio-ecological relations include and have effects for nonhuman animals, whether or not they are directly commodified. Within capitalism, human-animal relations have acquired particular forms and patterns. Capitalist socio-ecological relations are primarily characterized by widening inequality not only between humans but also between humans and nonhumans, who receive less and less of their share of global space and sustenance.[7] In parallel to a siphoning off and funneling of surplus toward some humans, an intensification of domesticated animal life and an emaciation of wild animal life is underway, as alluded to earlier, producing MacKinnon's "ten percent world," or a world of what Weis (2018) describes as "ghosts and things."

Human-animal relations under capitalism are thus unequal and characterized by rising domestication and declining wild life, with animals in both those groups experiencing escalating violence. Yet while animal studies has made important interventions in the social sciences and humanities, it has not adequately grappled with capitalism as an organizing structure for human-animal relations. And theorists of capitalism and inequality, whose work is more important now than ever, have largely eschewed nonhumans. There are important exceptions across the social sciences and humanities, including work by Nicole Shukin, Donna Haraway, Tony Weis, Kathryn Gillespie, and Dinesh Wadiwel, among others—scholars who have for the most part focused on the largest segment of directly commodified animal life: industrially farmed animals. Looking to wild animals made lively capital complements this work in a broader project of developing an understanding of how capitalism drives ecological problems like extinction and biodiversity loss. A central starting point of this book is that these problems, in which the exotic pet trade is centrally implicated, stem in part from the making thinglike of animals, the denial of their being, that an animal like Darwin forces us to confront.

This paradox between valuing liveliness and loving a pet as one's child, and owning one's pet as an object, is not limited to the exotic pet trade. The exotic pet trade is one site where the dynamics of the relationship between capitalism and animal life are especially potent and visible. The arguments and conclusions I develop are made with an eye beyond this trade to the operation of capitalism more broadly, especially as it concerns animal capital. So while some people may read this book with a distanced curiosity about the wacky world of exotic pet ownership, I want to use the apparent oddity of the exotic pet case to illuminate the strangeness of our more ordinary relationships with animals—mainly, the strangeness of a familiar idea that is basic to most of the world's political-economic operations: that an animal is a resource, a piece of property, a commodity. This idea is central to capitalism. Paralleling the work of feminists who describe how capitalism relies on and requires uneven gender difference under patriarchy, I develop an understanding of how capitalism similarly draws on and perpetuates anthropocentric modes of human-animal relations.[8]

To accomplish these aims I follow global exotic pet trade flows and markets as they unfold in real time, on the ground, in specific places. I draw on moments of observation and situate them in broader power relations and socioeconomic processes to figure out and then describe how the economy works, from the specific practices that create mobile commodities and then drive their circulation, to the broader ideologies and ethico-political norms that enable and govern the trade, as well as how it affects individual animals.

Through these observations, I build an understanding of the global exotic pet trade, a booming, world-transforming activity that has largely circulated under the radar of critical scholarship, even within the recent and welcome rise of animal studies. In my attempt to peer into the exploitative practices that underpin the production of the exotic pet, my work is one of many such "follow the thing" studies of recent years by geographers, political ecologists, and others. What is unique about this study is that the "thing" I am interested in is alive, and I take this as an important ethical, intellectual, and political difference from nonliving things.

In the next section I paint a preliminary picture of the global exotic pet trade, its history, regulatory dimensions, and its stakes, before introducing some of the key theoretical ideas I draw on and develop in the book. This theory is in subsequent chapters brought into conversation with several years of fieldwork tracking the exotic pet trade, which I describe at the end of this chapter, as well as how this fieldwork forms the chapters of the book.

The Global Exotic Pet Trade

Of all the forms that animal capital takes, an exotic pet is especially peculiar. Anything from a bird to an alligator, a turtle to a tiger, its defining characteristic is that it is out of place. Either an exotic pet was born elsewhere—beyond the arbitrary borders that form nation-states—or its recent ancestors were. It is also generally thought to be wild, or undomesticated, although domestication is itself not a clear-cut term or practice. Most experts will tell you that an animal is only domesticated after centuries, if not millennia, of selective breeding and proximity with humans.[9] Exotic pets, in contrast, are often wild-caught or at most captive-bred, a designation that can be used for an animal after two generations of captivity, for the offspring of any captive-born parents. Although captive-bred animals are raised around and often reared by humans, their genetics, bodies, and behaviors have not yet been shaped by sustained domestication techniques. Exotic pets are, then, wild animals kept incongruously in spaces often thought of as the domestic domain: tigers in suburban backyards, snakes in condo bedrooms, birds in bungalow parlors.

Exotic pets may be incongruous, but they are more and more common, especially in wealthy countries. Legal and illegal trade in exotic pets has become big business over the last few decades. It is difficult to measure the size of either trade: the legal trade goes unregulated and unmonitored in many countries, and the illegal trade is by definition clandestine. Experts estimate the legal global exotic pet trade is worth at least US$5 billion, and the illegal global exotic pet trade is part of a broader illegal wildlife economy that is estimated to be worth US$5 billion to US$20 billion.[10] What is certain is that at any given time, hundreds of thousands of animals are in circulation. Sacks of monkeys, boxes of reptiles and turtles, and crates of parrots are being smuggled across borders with false papers. Geckos and snakes strapped into the underwear of airplane passengers; a baby primate hidden in a fake pregnant stomach; and drugged baby leopards, bears, monkeys, and panthers crammed in suitcases—all are recorded instances of actual animal smuggling. Sensational stories like these belie the routine reality of millions of animals entering and leaving national borders legally. From ordinary household pets like parakeets, ornamental fish, and turtles to fierce kinkajous, diapered spider monkeys, and spectacular wild cats like Siberian tigers, millions of exotic pets now live legally, but largely unregulated, inside private residences around the world. More than twenty million exotic birds live as pets in the United States alone—America's third most popular pet after cats and dogs—as well as more than nine million reptiles. More tigers are estimated to live in cages in the United States than live uncaptive worldwide.[11]

The high number of privately owned exotic pets in the United States and worldwide is unprecedented, but the practice of exotic pet keeping has long roots—particularly extending back to the height of early empire building and colonialism. For thousands of years wild animals from around the world have been captured, collected, and displayed, animating assertions of and claims to power. In early empires like Greece, Egypt, and Rome, wild animals were frequently gifted to kings and other rulers; the more distant and unknown the animal, the more value and power it conveyed on display in the royal courts as a testament to monarchs' might and reach.[12] Greeks and Romans kept exotic pets such as monkeys and birds, especially peacocks, and exhibited them in religious festival processions. Some animals, such as so-called war-elephants, were kept for military purposes but also likely doubled as show and hunting stock. The gladiatorial Roman games were an especially bloody spectacle in which imported live wild animals, including elephants and wild cats, with many from North Africa, were put to death before huge crowds.[13]

With the onset of European imperial expansion and the so-called Age of Exploration, global animal trade escalated. The trade at this time was primarily tied to natural history collecting and the concentration of animals from the colonies into royal menageries and zoological gardens in Europe.[14] Colonial expeditions caught and hunted live and dead animals in the colonies, amassing extensive collections for classification and study at the museums, botanical and royal gardens, libraries, universities, learned societies, and private storehouses that emerged in Europe during the colonial era. The knowledge that was produced in and through these collections parsed the world's regions and their inhabitants (plants, animals, people) in classificatory systems that reflected and fed a racialized humanism in which certain humans—white, European, male—were (re)produced as properly human subjects "naturally" dominant over all other forms of subordinate life, especially human and nonhuman life indigenous to the colonies. Exotic animal keeping during the colonial era was enrolled in these racist constructions of other places, people, and the nonhuman world.

Exotic animal keeping was also an opportunity to perform colonial power for audiences in colonial centers. In an imperial system that entailed domination over colonized territories, people, and animals, captive animals and colonized people were put on display in colonial centers, standing in for conquered distant territories, a demonstration of the "spoils of empire" and a testament to modern colonial power.[15] What is now known as the Tower of London functioned during the 1200s through 1500s as the Tower Menagerie; over the centuries, it contained a procession of wild animals, including elephants, lions, kangaroos, and polar bears. In neighboring France the eighteenth-century royal menagerie in Versailles was constructed under Louis XIV's direction. It had a circular layout with a large pavilion in the center, around which was a walking path. Outside the path were enclosures and cages of exotic animals, bounded on three sides with walls but with only bars on the side facing the pavilion, leading Michel Foucault (1977) to speculate that the menagerie inspired Jeremy Bentham's famous panopticon prison design.

In the Victorian era, exotic animal keeping moved into private homes, bringing a wave of exotic animals into England. Owning an exotic animal became less exceptional and not restricted to monarchs. Aristocratic naturalists, painters, and officers also owned private menageries containing animals ranging from panthers to elephants to lions. The rise of private exotic pet keeping paralleled a growth in pet keeping in general at this time. American historian Harriet Ritvo accounts for this rise in her book *The Animal*

Estate. She ties the rise in pet keeping to a shift in Europeans' understanding of animals from agential and powerful to "objects of human manipulation" (Ritvo 1987, 2)—a shift led in large part by the same scientific methods of knowledge acquisition and application, born of the Enlightenment, that also drove flows of exotic animals into colonial centers as objects of scientific study. As Enlightenment ideas built among Europeans a sense of control and mastery over nature, feelings of fear toward the nonhuman world gave way to affection—expressed as "sentimental attachment" to individual pets (Ritvo 1987). Early forms of exotic pet keeping were in these ways a direct product of colonialism and the Enlightenment; exotic pets must be considered, like other forms of animal capital, "colonial subjects" whose existence is tied to the attempted displacement of Indigenous knowledges and emptying of Indigenous lands (Belcourt 2015).

Some of the captured animals who arrived in Europe eventually ended up in North America, especially the United States, which has long maintained a thriving zoo and aquarium trade. The industry there boomed at the turn of the nineteenth century, during which time US zoos grew in number from four in 1880 to more than a hundred by 1930 (Hanson 2004, 79). But by the second half of the nineteenth century, zoos constituted only half of the United States' lucrative wild animal business, as animals were also delivered into circuses, laboratories, and, increasingly, the pet trade. By the beginning of the twentieth century, demand also emerged from Hollywood.[16] Just as today, many of the same animals circulated through these various arms of wild animal trade, moving from zoos to private ownership to film acting to circuses.

While the twentieth century marked a steady increase in private exotic animal ownership, live wild animal imports have especially spiked in North America since the 1990s. Escalation in exotic pet demand is attributed to a broader rise in international shipping and trade under economic globalization, as well as to the growing role played by the internet in facilitating endangered and rare species trade, leading conservationists to claim that the internet is one of the biggest threats to endangered species for the role it plays in fueling trade.[17] Popular films and video games can also have a significant effect on the demand for particular species of wildlife.[18]

As a result, the scale, reach, and breadth of popularity of the global exotic pet trade are at record levels today. But the vast flows of animals move in patterns that largely still mimic the historic colonial trade flows I briefly traced: animals are traded out of biodiversity-rich, capital-poor countries to nations wealthier in capital than biodiversity. Globally, wildlife export zones are primarily located in Asia, especially the Southeast, followed by South and Central America, Eastern Europe, and Africa.[19] As for top importing countries, blame and attention are often directed toward China and other Asian countries—Vietnam, Thailand, Indonesia. These nations frequently feature in news reports of large wildlife confiscations, especially as sources of demand for wildlife.[20] But by most estimates, it is the United States that has long held the top spot in imports of legal and illegal wildlife and wildlife products, partly due to the United States' enormous demand for ornamental fish in the aquarium trade.[21] The United States is followed by the European Union as a top importer, as well as Japan and China, with several Middle Eastern countries also emerging as key markets.[22]

The United States legally imports hundreds of millions of live animals each year, with around half of the individual specimens being fish for the aquarium trade. Tens of thousands of the imported animals are live mammals, hundreds of thousands are live birds, millions are live reptiles, and tens of millions are live amphibians. More than half of these live animal imports into the United States originated in Southeast Asia.[23] More than 90 percent of the imported animals are designated for the pet trade, and almost 80 percent are captured from wild populations (K. Smith et al. 2009; K. Smith et al. 2017). Although many of these wild-caught imports are likely fish, many species of which do not reproduce easily in captivity, a review study of internationally regulated species worldwide found that, surprisingly, 20 percent of birds and 10 percent of reptiles traded internationally for personal use were officially declared wild-caught or of wild parents, including some species whose international commercial trade is prohibited due to declining populations (Bush, Baker, and Macdonald 2014). Another review study reports that of animals traded legally and whose trade is monitored and regulated internationally, more are from captive populations than in decades past, but for reptiles, mammals, some bird species, and invertebrates, the majority of this internationally regulated legal trade is still in wild-caught animals (Harfoot et al. 2018). It is likely, too, that many wild-caught species are traded under falsified captive-bred papers (Nijman 2010).

Governing and keeping track of this geographically wide-ranging, complex, massive trade is challenging.[24] Exotic pet trade regulation can exist at every formal governance scale, from municipal to state/provincial, national, and international. It is a complicated political sphere, and this plays out in ways that often disable effective monitoring and enforcement in the face of uncertain regulations and responsibilities. Regulations are also in flux at all scales, as will become clear in later chapters. At the international level, the Convention on International Trade in Endangered Species of Flora and Fauna (CITES) is the primary regulator of the exotic pet trade and wildlife trade more broadly. The convention, which came into effect in 1975, is an international agreement "to ensure that international trade in specimens of wild animals and plants does not threaten their survival" (CITES 2013). Currently, 178 governments ("parties") adhere voluntarily to its resolutions, which establish what species are legal to trade and in what amounts.

Meanwhile, at the national level, there is no coordinated strategy, legislative authority, or funding devoted to oversight of the live wildlife trade in either the United States or Canada.[25] In both countries, municipalities and provinces/states provide their own exotic animal regulation if they so choose—and they are so choosing, more and more often. As will be discussed in chapter 2, several US states and Canadian provinces, as well as innumerable municipalities, have recently established or are in the process of establishing stricter exotic pet trade and ownership regulations—including outright bans on owning and trading many species. The primary impetus for this burgeoning state and provincial regulation is human health and safety concerns. Exotic pets escape, attack people, and carry potentially serious zoonotic diseases.[26] Other sources of public alarm over exotic pets concern the introduction of "alien" species into local environments.[27] The charged debates surrounding these new regulations, as well as ambiguity around what specifically the new regulations are or will be, and how they will affect the industry, are all evidently engendering anxiety for economic players in the trade. They are also exacerbating tension between animal owners and traders and animal welfare advocates, which affected the degree to which I could access interviewees and research sites and carry out conversations, the tenor of these conversations and sites, and the actions and behaviors I observed.

In these debates around exotic pet bans, human and environmental health, and human safety and security concerns predominate. Little to no exotic pet regulation is motivated by or targeted to address the conditions of life for animals kept as exotic pets. Yet exotic pets, as subsequent chapters will show, are formed through a series of wrenching separations from their homes, families, and societies, depriving them of the most basic life require-ments. They experience widespread health, emotional, and psychological problems in captivity, especially if they are receiving inadequate care.

Local exotic pet regulation is not alone in ignoring these conditions by focusing nearly exclusively on human health and safety concerns. CITES, too, does not consider animal welfare. CITES, arguably circumscribed by its founding function—"to track and regulate trade"—is in my observation more of a trade organization than a conservation organization.[28] This man-date goes some way to explaining the enormous numbers of CITES-listed animals traded around the world: 11.6 billion individual live wild animals between 2012 and 2016 (Can, D'Cruze, and Macdonald 2019). There is little to no room within the CITES framework to consider ethical or animal wel-fare dimensions of trade, and no conversations about whether or not trade should even exist at all. Nondetriment findings, the mechanism that CITES uses to decide if a species trade should be restricted, account for whether or not the trade can be sustained at its current levels, not for the effect of trade on individual animals, even though it is increasingly acknowledged that ani-mal welfare is compromised along all stages of the global exotic pet trade.[29] This puts CITES in step with a broader conservation community that is more concerned with sustaining aggregate populations than with the health and experience of individual animals.

The costs of the exotic pet trade are indeed glaring at the aggregate scale. The extraction of animals from the wild for the pet trade is widely acknowledged as a major drain on wild populations.[30] Animals have been exported so rapidly out of Southeast Asia to be pets in countries like the United Kingdom, the United States, and Japan that experts have coined the term "empty forest syndrome" to refer to the concomitant loss in biodiver-sity.[31] The steep rates of extraction of animals from wild populations stem not only from high demand but also from extreme mortality rates within the trade. For every ten birds or reptiles who are captured, as few as three make it to the pet shop. For fish, the mortality rate between capture and purchase is even higher, as much as 80 percent. The chance of a new exotic pet living through its first year after purchase is just over 20 percent. This can drive a perpetual motion machine of demand. And mortality rates also extend beyond trapped animals. For example, the capture of birds as chicks, a process I will describe in the next chapter, often destroys nests and kills breeding adults. For each animal captured, then, several others often die.[32]

The worldwide expansion of the exotic pet trade that I have just outlined is thus deeply implicated in the global reordering of life I have already described, and which serves as the chief context for this book. The global exotic pet trade has especially driven the decline in wild animal abundance—what I earlier referred to as a process called defaunation. The defaunation tragedy is a story, then, not only of extinction and endangered animals but also of a more general loss of wild animal life—a story of emptied forests, of "ghosts and things" (Weis 2018). The exotic pet trade is a key, if proximate, driver of the diminishment of animal life at this aggregate scale as well as for individual animals, by engendering both mortality and confinement.

The contemporary exotic pet trade also reflects a broader capitalist political economy that is my interest. In this book I track a particular set of capitalist interspecies relations—those that form and are embodied by the exotic pet—to understand how precisely capitalism shapes or constrains nonhuman life. The global exotic pet trade exerts lethal and violent effects for animals but is largely perceived as trade motivated by *love* for animals. Darwin, the "Ikea monkey," experienced extreme trauma in the process of becoming commodified and kept captive, but Yasmin Nakhuda refers to him as her son. This is a common refrain among pet owners. How is this seemingly paradoxical entanglement of love and violence justified? This is a key question of this book, one answerable through consideration of how the exotic pet is fetishized not just as a commodity but also as an animal.

Beyond Commodity Fetishism:
Animal Fetishism and the Doubly Fetishized Exotic Pet

Animals are not born, but made commodities. In this, they are not exceptional.

No commodity magically sprouts into fully formed being. It has to be crafted in a place or several places, by a person or many people, according to specific laws, ideas, norms, and political-economic forces—all of which are connected in dynamic, crisscrossing networks. The book, computer, or sheets of paper off of which you are reading these words, the desk or table on which these objects rest—none of them simply fell out of the sky. They were all fabricated through processes that cannot be separated from the social relations of which they are a part. Equally, none of these objects is automatically or inherently a commodity—something that can be bought and sold. Particular socioeconomic relations and legal designations uphold their status as commodities—property law, trade agreements, market processes, and so on.

Karl Marx observed this more than 150 years ago. When he insisted that social relations underlie all commodities, he was referring to social relations of human labor. He argued that when objects enter into exchange, and come to be seen as equivalent to each other, or to a money price, the social relations of labor that actually made those objects become obscured. Through exchange, commodities come to be treated as if they have a "life of their own," he says, when they are actually created at every stage through these social relations of labor.[33] For Marx, the origin of value is also obscured through capitalist exchange. Value appears to inhere in the object itself—this object with a life of its own. But value, for Marx, is actually produced through uneven labor relations in which workers are paid less than their labor is worth. Marx referred to this erasure of labor relations as "commodity fetishism": the concealment of "the social character of private labour and the social relations between the individual workers, by making those relations appear as relations between material objects" (Marx 1976, 168–169). The social relations at the heart of the production process—who labors for how much pay, who works for whom, in what conditions—are mistaken as economic relations among objects, becoming a mere question of how valuable a specific commodity is when compared with another commodity.

Generations of commodity scholars have taken on the task of recovering these obscured relations, of defetishizing commodities, for the most part working with this fairly strict Marxian version of the fetish. Their work focuses on a specific segment of social relations of commodity production that the fetish conceals: human labor relations—namely, class. They defetishize by conducting commodity chain analyses, or tracing commodity "biographies," or following the "lives of things."[34] The objective of these studies—of cut flowers, of furniture, of fruit—is to demonstrate how the "lives of things" do not belong to them intrinsically, but rather are the result of particular socio-ecological arrangements. In this contemporary literature, then, commodities are generally understood to be made by rearranging relationships. These relationships are spatial, energetic, social, ecological—loggers fell trees, timber is milled into boards, woodworkers build chairs and tables. These relationships fall away when the table appears alone in exchange, when it appears as if it is in a relationship with other commodities (e.g., money), as if value is attached to its physical form. The commodity is thus alienated from the relations that exist around it, allowing the commodity to seem like an independent, mobile, immutable object that exists on its own—as if it had a life of its own—and as if it has value and properties inherent to it.

My project in this book is inspired by and in conversation with these Marxist politics and analysis, and by this key political point that we should not treat commodities as if they have lives of their own, when they were actually produced by laborers and through uneven social relations of labor that generate surplus value, or profit. But I also nudge past this argument because it presupposes that commodities are *not* alive. And theorists of commodities have similarly largely rendered commodities mute and inert in a manner mimetic of their treatment under capitalism.[35] This is unhelpful especially when trying to understand the economies that traffic in "things" that are alive. Think of a rodeo bull, a circus elephant, a pet snake, or the crickets sold to feed that snake. These living commodities may be unexceptional in being made (not born) commodities, but they are unusual in other ways. Unlike other commodities, animals are actually born. They do have lives of their own—lives that cannot be reduced to their commodity biography, lives that are not produced only, or at all, through human labor. These lives are also or even instead produced through animals' own labors, families, societies, emotional connections, and the complicated ecosystemic networks of which they are a part.

Since these lively commodities are my interest here, and my political project is to recover the processes by which an animal is made thinglike, my departure point is in a way the reverse of Marx's. Where Marx was interested in how commodities come to appear as if they have lives of their own, my overarching questions in this book are, How do living things, including some commodities, come to appear as if they do *not* have lives of their own? Through what mechanisms are their lives made not their own? I develop the concept of animal fetishism to refer to this denial of a life-of-one's-own, as I explain later. My argument is that exotic pets and animal capital are subject to a double fetishism, which extinguishes two sets of relations—although never completely: a commodity fetishism that, through exchange, erases the socio-ecological relations of commodity production; and a second fetishism of the animal, an erasure of the socio-ecological relations and networks that produce living commodities as living, social beings in the first place.

Nicole Shukin (2009) first sparked my interest in considering fetishism and animal capital alongside each other. She describes the fetishistic quality of both "animal" and "capital"—the former which functions as a naturalizing "generic universal" in Western modernity (as others like Derrida have shown), and the latter which is treated as having intrinsic properties as opposed to being produced through specific historical social formations, such as class (as Marx describes). In animal capital, these two fetishisms form what Shukin (2009, 18–19) describes as a "redoubled" or "tautologous species of fetishism," a "metafetishism." Like Shukin, I track this powerful formation. I empirically investigate the embodied ways that both fetishisms are enacted on the ground, for particular animals, and how this shapes the way they can live. To do so, I engage in a commodity chain methodology (as I explain in the next section), but I also go beyond a strictly commodity focus and direct much of my attention to animal fetishism and how it is enacted. Animal fetishism cannot be explained only through commodity fetishism; exotic pets are still subject to animal fetishism (i.e., are made "thinglike") even if they are not commodities, and the relations that are hidden by the fetishism include the socio-ecological relations of animal being, the relations that produce the animal as a world-making subject—not just the human social relations that produce the commodity.

How, then, is animal fetishism enacted, if not through commodification? I suggest animal fetishism is enacted spatially and bodily, in particular through enclosure; and it is enacted discursively, through the assigning of a use value that comes to mask animals' own use values and their own life-making practices. The latter is particularly distinct from commodity fetishism, which in Marx's formulation is enacted through exchange and the assigning of exchange value. In what follows I develop this argument more fully. To do so I first explain the importance of moving beyond a commodity focus in work on animal capital. Here, I draw on the work of feminist political economists who show how unpriced work is functional to capitalism, an insight I—and others—suggest is crucial to understand the role of uncommodified natures in capitalism. These ideas help me build my argument that exotic pets are lively capital or capitalist natures even when they are not commodified directly. Second, I turn to feminist and postcolonial scholar Sara Ahmed's more expansive conception of fetishism to construct my notion of animal fetishism, which allows me to consider how exotic pets are subject to a fetishism not only of their commodity form but also of their animal being.

A key starting argument of this book is that nonhuman life is subject to human domination and control, and is potentially productive for capitalist economies, even if it is not commodified directly. This is a different starting point than the one with which I began my research into the exotic pet trade. At first, I was interested centrally—even resolutely—in the exotic pet as a commodity, and in the commodification processes that form exotic pets. But fieldwork and new (to me) readings in feminist political economy changed my mind, revealing the limits of my initial commodity focus. In the field, I was repeatedly confronted by animals like Darwin, who are no longer commodities but who still live much like commodities do. Darwin's enclosure and his forced dependency on humans—spatial and social processes in which I am centrally interested—cannot be reduced to commodification. This does not mean that animals like Darwin are somehow outside of capitalist social relations, either. While the Story Book sanctuary, where Darwin lives, is a nonprofit organization, it is tied up in all kinds of ways with money flows: donations, purchases of food and equipment to support Darwin and the other animals, and so on. In some cases, animals like Darwin are an actively productive aspect of profitable enterprises even though they are not commodities—for example, animals that cannot be bought and sold because of regulatory prohibitions but are grandfathered into ownership arrangements and are featured in for-profit roadside or petting zoos. It is for this reason that I refer to Darwin and other noncommodified exotic pets as lively capital— a living stock of objects from which value, especially encounter value, is (or could be) generated.

Feminist political economists have long made arguments along relatively similar lines, although in a different context. Early socialist feminist arguments in the 1960s and 1970s urged political economists to consider the largely unpaid work of social reproduction—the daily labors required to reproduce individual and collective human life, including child-rearing, household chores, and the maintenance of social bonds—as fundamental to the operation of capitalism.[36] Feminists critique how this reproductive work is devalued and naturalized as women's work, conceived of as work that is performed out of an innate biological drive and capacity, rather than free labor necessary for capital accumulation and delegated to women within exploitative patriarchal relations. In this way, feminist political economists show how patriarchy—a particular organization of social relations in which men assume positions of dominance over women—is useful for capitalism, even as it cannot be reduced to its function under capitalism, given that it does not just benefit capitalists or the owners of the means of production, but also benefits men. This also allows feminists to undertake a more nuanced analysis of something like commodification—of labor, for example. In some cases, as feminist political theorist Nancy Fraser (2014) points out, commodification can be emancipatory—for example, when women are able to sell their own work as a commodity, for a wage, rather than do it for free. Similarly, what precedes commodification should not be romanticized, as social processes that are not commodified—that is, unpaid work—can still be shot through with uneven power relations, such as patriarchy.

These arguments prove insightful for understanding the realm of the nonhuman and its relationship to humans and capitalism. Nonhuman nature is also often unpriced and does not labor for a wage. Yet it is still useful for capitalism in all kinds of ways—as even the stunted language and common conception of ecosystem services seeks to acknowledge. This is not to say that nature and women are equivalent within capitalism; this would dangerously slip back into a discourse about women as "closer to nature" that naturalizes women's role as social reproductive workers. But much of humans' social reproductive work and nature's work can be said to occupy similar structural positions within capitalist social relations—both are "super-exploited," to borrow Maria Mies's (1986, 48) term: they produce materials and energies for "the general production of life, or subsistence production," and this subsistence production is appropriated by capitalists; it "constitutes the perennial basis upon which 'capitalist productive labour' can be built up and exploited." The appropriation of this general production of life is referred to as "super-exploitation" because, unlike wage exploitation, it is not even compensated by a wage. Similar to how patriarchy positions women as devalued social reproductive workers, power relations between humans and animals, what we can think of broadly as anthropocentrism, position animals in devalued but useful positions within capitalist socio-ecological relations—even, again, when these animals are not directly commodified.

Accordingly, in this book I adopt and adapt feminist political economists' powerful concept of social reproduction: the everyday work of caring for others and oneself, of building and maintaining social bonds, that reproduces individual and collective human life. Here, I project this concept into the world beyond humans, and refer to *socio-ecological* reproduction and socio-ecological reproductive networks. Like the feminist political economists whose ideas I borrow, I do not mean reproduction in a strictly biological sense, as in the reproduction of species or even populations; rather, I mean the daily work and complex networks through which animals reproduce themselves and their communities. This work is, like social reproduction, useful to capitalism even if it is often not directly commodified. And both this work and the capacities it enables are disrupted through enclosure and animals' entry into exotic pet trade circuits.

The preceding insights direct attention beyond the commodity form—to processes that precede and succeed the living animal commodity. When it comes to the exotic pet trade, what comes into view with this more expansive lens? I argue that commodification in the exotic pet trade requires animal fetishism prior to the act of commodification. Before being commodified, animals must be made "thinglike"—alienated, individuated, controlled (chapter 1). Animal fetishism, or the designation of an animal as thinglike—the denial of its complex life history—is a condition of possibility for commodification of the animal. What this suggests more broadly is that anthropocentrism is a key logic and structure within capitalism. Capitalism did not invent anthropocentrism, but capitalism taps into it, channels it into a site for accumulation on multiple fronts. Anthropocentrism is incredibly useful for capitalism, making available a pool of devalued living "things" that can provide cheap or even free work, energy, material inputs, commodities, and waste absorption. In turn, I suggest capitalism deepens and extends anthropocentrism. In particular, in this book I argue that the act of commodification propels and intensifies animal fetishism (chapter 2); commodification heightens the extent to which animals appear as if they have no lives of their own. The two fetishisms thus entangle. The exotic pet is *doubly* fetishized: as animal and as commodity. But, importantly, the commodity form can end and animal fetishism remains in place (chapter 3). This state of being "thinglike" cannot therefore be reduced to commodification— it both precedes and in most cases persists after commodification in the exotic pet trade.

As I suggested earlier, the process of being made a thing is also never complete. An animal can never be fully reduced to a thing while it is alive; its life will always exceed the state of a "thing." An animal's life is also a quality necessary for the exotic pet commodity form or its possibility. We arrive again at the tension inherent in the exotic pet and many other forms of animal capital—commodification depends on the life of the animal but also depends on making the animal thinglike, which impinges on, constrains, and threatens that life. In the exotic pet trade a balance is sought in which animals are made just thinglike enough to control but not to kill. So although a living animal cannot be made completely into a thing, the attempt to make an animal thinglike is dangerous; the life that is made thinglike persists but is stretched so thin it barely resembles itself. The high costs of this will become clear over the course of the book.

But how precisely is an animal *made* thinglike? I argue that the overarching mechanism is through animal fetishism, which operates in conjunction with but cannot be reduced to commodity fetishism. We need a broad conception of fetishism to proceed, where to fetishize is essentially to mistake a social process for a thing, and where the political implications of fetishism are at the fore. Haraway (1997) provides an open entry point with her suggestion that fetishism can be considered to be operating any time the seemingly inert, ahistorical, or apolitical nature of an object or thing hides power's operation. Haraway is here already urging us beyond the commodity in our consideration of fetishism. Ahmed is a key thinker as we do so. She argues that not only commodities are fetishized, and not only social relations of labor are erased when fetishism is in place. For Ahmed, objects (2006) or figures (2000), such as the figure of the stranger, are also fetishized, meaning they are abstracted from the encounters, relations, and processes that produced them. Fetishized objects and figures, like commodities, are assumed to contain their signification, or value, within themselves, as part of their nature, "within the singularity of [their] form" (Ahmed 2000, 143). This is accomplished through an erasure of relations, a cutting off from complex histories, a "radical forgetting of the histories of labour and production that allow . . . a body to appear in the present" (Ahmed 2006, 53–54) as if it is a simple object.[37]

To fetishize something—object, commodity, animal—is then at base a failure to "account for [the object's] conditions of arrival, which are not simply given" (Ahmed 2006, 41). Ahmed is asking us to undertake a kind of historicization that is thick and specific. It is thick in the sense that it means not only to consider the past, or the question of events that deliver the present, but also to identify the social and political-economic formations that form the "conditions of arrival" of the present. It is specific in that it must be pursued in relation to specific figures, forms, objects: for her, the stranger, but we can equally consider the animal—in this book, the exotic pet. Combining the thick and specific, Ahmed's mode of historicization entails relentlessly digging under ostensibly self-evident, pregiven forms. It means considering "the history of 'what appears' and how it is shaped by histories of work" (43). For my purposes here, in relation to the exotic pet form, these histories of work include, most crucially, the socio-ecological reproductive work of multispecies collectives, sometimes but not always including humans.

Accordingly, in this book I do not take the exotic pet as a pregiven form, as a commodity or a bit of capital that contains its value in itself, inherent in its form. Instead, I aim to recover the exotic pet's "histories of arrival" and histories of production within the exotic pet trade to uncover how the exotic pet is made—not just as commodity but as thinglike: a living object that is not necessarily bought and sold but is nonetheless property, individuated, severed from its relations of being and world-making. An essential first step in doing this recovery of "histories of work" and the "history of what appears" is to orient the analysis not only to the productive or reproductive work of humans but also to the work of socio-ecological (re)production of animal life: the energies, relations, and metabolic exchanges that bring an animal life into existence and sustain it—the general production of animal life, to spin off of Mies. The animal is fetishized precisely through a forgetting of and severing from this production and the relations that underpin it. Animal fetishism thus involves the *cutting off of the animal from the complex history of its own being.* It operates not by conjuring a "life of its own" for inert objects but instead by denying a life of its own to the animal, rendering it a passive "resource" and covering over the intricate socio-ecological relationships that produce this life.

How is animal fetishism enacted? How is animal being erased, denied, forgotten? How are animals "cut off" from or dispossessed of their own histories of being and networks of world-making? I suggest that in the exotic pet trade this occurs in two main ways, which are discussed across the book. First, animal fetishism is enacted through spatial and bodily mechanisms, namely, enclosure, which is an act of animal dispossession in which animal being is individuated and alienated and the animal is placed in a state of forced dependency on humans, unable to provide for itself. Both commodity fetishism and animal fetishism are deeply spatial, depending on the movement of things across and between spaces in a way that obscures production. Enclosure—or captivity—in particular is a key spatial mode of individuating and controlling animals, and enabling their circulation across borders, through auction houses, into houses and yards on different continents. Second, animal fetishism is mobilized discursively, specifically, I suggest, through the designation of usefulness, or the assigning of use value. Different from commodity fetishism, which Marx suggests sets in at the moment of exchange, animal fetishism occurs in part with the designation of an animal's usefulness to humans. Jacques Derrida's and Ahmed's critiques of Marx are helpful here. Derrida (2006, 188) critiques Marx for his lack of interest in use value, for implying that "use-value has nothing mysterious at all." Derrida points to how use value is "always very human, at bottom"; it is always related to "men's [sic] needs"; it is, in a word Derrida does not use, anthropocentric.[38] Building from Derrida's short critique, I want to suggest that the properties of exotic pets that are seen as "useful" or as having use value—their encounterability, controllability, individuality—are not inherent in them, are framed in relation to human usefulness, and are part of forming animal fetishism, or the treatment of animals as thinglike.

There are two reasons I specifically refer to this as animal *fetishism*. First, I want to invoke commodity fetishism alongside animal fetishism, as they combine with each other potently in the exotic pet. Commodification can intensify more long-standing racialized, gendered, and colonial practices and relations. Commodification compounds animal fetishism in this way. It extends and deepens the manner and degree to which animals are made thinglike. It is important, then, that we hold the two fetishisms together but without collapsing them. The importance is analytical, demanding an examination of both the commodity and object form—of commodification and objectification. But the importance is also political. The dual fetishism of the exotic pet suggests that a politics in response must resist commodification but also something more.

This leads to the second reason I use the term "fetishism," which is to construct and offer a relevant political response. The point of identifying and describing fetishism is to defetishize, to see what the fetishism covers over—and this is a distinctly political project. Commodity fetishism led Marx to a particular politics: broadly, alerting commodity producers to their shared exploitation within capitalist social relations, leading to worker collectivization and ultimately revolution. To what politics does an acknowledgment of animal fetishism lead? It leads to a politics that is more modest than worker revolution, but is still largely novel in that it is distinct from existing dominant political responses to the exotic pet trade, including animal rights, animal welfare, and conservation. Animal fetishism leads, I suggest, to a politics against enclosure and against anthropocentric framings of use value—the mechanisms of animal fetishism I identify. It leads to what I call a wild life politics, where wildness is understood to be a condition of relational autonomy that allows animals to live lives of their own, as worldmaking beings. A step in this direction is to shrivel the market for exotic pets. The exotic pet trade is a demand-driven economy, yet demand management responses to the trade are scarce. As part of a broader politics of wild life, I join others in advocating for efforts to reduce demand for exotic pets.[39]

Following Multispecies Encounters and Their Conditions of Possibility

The global exotic pet trade is an incredibly diffuse and decentralized economy, a complicated swirl of captive animals crisscrossing the globe. There are no major corporations, no headquarters, no CEOs, no unions. Trade flows are dispersed, often clandestine. Tracking an economy like this is challenging. It is difficult to know where and when to jump into these flows as a researcher. In this research project's early stages, my intention was to trace the commodity chain—production, transportation, exchange, disposal—of one or more specific species: I had a long list, topped by scarlet macaws, dolphins, and/or orangutans after meeting with Canada's TRAFFIC national representative, who helped me draft a list of species for which significant research gaps existed (there are many). But I realized that focusing on specific species would be limiting and frustrating in the field. I envisioned being at a wildlife trade market and being able to focus only on a single species, having to ignore the multitude of other animals being bought and sold. So instead I decided to focus on the flows of multiple species in and out of specific bounded space-times—nodes—where the otherwise diffuse trade comes together, even if only momentarily; as a geographer, this seemed apt, and still does. I refer to this approach as "multispecies" in part as a simple recognition that my research is concerned with many different species of animals. Of course multispecies is also a signal to the multispecies ethnographies currently emerging from social science and humanities disciplines.[40]

A multispecies research approach is one that pays attention not only to multiple species but also to how they shape one another.

In this sense, my research is multispecies in that it is concerned with encounters between humans and exotic pets. The encounter is in a way my scale and unit of analysis—over the years for this project I studied, tracked, and observed innumerable encounters between humans and exotic pets, and I entered into my own encounters. But I also strive, as Ahmed encourages, to situate those encounters in more general political-economic, socioecological conditions that make those encounters possible—that lubricate them, drive them. I do this situating work out of a broader commitment to picking apart animal fetishism, to recovering exotic pets' histories of arrival to the encounter. Considering the histories of arrival to an encounter means never taking the encounter as a single, timeless moment or interaction, but instead always inquiring into how the parties locked in encounter got there. As Ahmed (2000, 144–145) writes: "We need to complicate the very notion of the face to face by discussing the temporal and spatial dislocations that are implicated in the very possibility of being faced by this other. Certainly, this is partly about locating the encounter in time and space: *what are the conditions of possibility for us meeting here and now?*" This is precisely the question I ask about the encounters I observed and participated in as part of the research for this book.

The majority of the encounters I track here took place between 2010 and 2013 in three prominent nodes within the exotic pet trade's circuits: capture in biosphere reserves in Mexico, Guatemala, and Belize (chapter 1); exchange at exotic animal auctions across the United States (chapter 2); and the attempted rehabilitation of former exotic pets at a wildlife facility in Guatemala called ARCAS (chapter 3). I complemented this more sustained research with smaller fieldwork trips in various places in Canada and in Geneva, Switzerland, to visit exotic pet sanctuaries and attend a CITES meeting, respectively. In each of these sites, I used a different combination of methods. I conducted more than forty interviews—ranging from semistructured to unstructured—in Canada, the United States, Mexico, Guatemala, and Belize. Most of these were expert interviews with people who have advanced knowledge of the exotic pet trade—with people engaged directly or indirectly with the exotic pet trade and its regulation, including regulators and trade enforcement and government officials; nongovernmental organization (NGO) and university scientists and researchers; veterinarians; people who own exotic animals; exotic animal auction attendees, participants, and owners; exotic animal sanctuary owners and volunteers; and wildlife rehabilitation owners and volunteers. I also employed both participant observation and spectator observation. For the latter, I worked as a wildlife rehabilitation volunteer at ARCAS; this research forms the basis of chapter 3. My spectator observation (a term coined by Jan Penrose to describe her research at US rodeos) occurred primarily at exotic animal auctions across the United States; this research features in chapter 2. This observation research allowed me to immerse myself in the action and to experience events in a multisensory fashion, and to derive a sense of my animal research subjects' situatedness within broader networks.

What did my attention to encounters and their situatedness mean for my research practices in the field? It meant that I sought to attend to the interactions between beings, and how these interactions combined to generate performances or effects. This included being attentive to my own interactions, most critically with the animals with whom I worked the most closely, such as at the wildlife rehabilitation center. It meant I conducted extended observation of animals' locations, living conditions, and movement through space. It also meant that I attempted to foreground nonhuman animals' experiences, insofar as this is possible given the challenges of communication across species. I did not consider animals as "good to think with" (as Lévi-Strauss famously commented) or as mirrors for reflecting back some truth about human existence.[41] Instead, in my research practice I tried to foreground animals as subjects in their own right, beings with their own outlooks, motivations, feelings, and affairs, beings who, while intimately entangled with each other and human beings, are—or can be—creatively independent, who are not just looked upon but also look back. Often, though, the animals in my company were incredibly controlled and constrained in their capacity for movement and expression—in cages so small their bodies could only be scrunched, or their bodies actually modified so that they could not bite or fly. These spatial and behavioral controls made gaining a sense of the animal difficult. The constraints also meant that I myself was enrolled in the uneven power dynamics of my research contact zones.

The book itself unfolds as an adapted "following the thing"—in this case, following the making, remaking, and attempted unmaking of a thing-like bit of lively capital: the exotic pet. The following three chapters build from the research I have just described to track how animal fetishism is enacted, how it interacts with commodity fetishism, and how attempts are made—and could be made—to undo it. Chapter 1 examines how wild animals are captured for the pet trade, focused on parrots, especially macaws, and monkeys, especially spider monkeys, who are captured in and around biosphere reserves in Mexico, Guatemala, and Belize. I describe capture as a onetime act that severs the animal from its socio-ecological reproductive networks, makes the animal dependent on a system of human-provided supports, and produces the animal as lively capital: individual, controllable, and encounterable. I thus interpret capture as a mode of bodily enclosure that dispossesses the animal of the ability to provide for itself and its community. Animal fetishism is, I argue, materially enacted through this capture, after which point the enclosed animal can appear as if it does not have a life of its own, cut off from the complex history of its own being. The conditions for commodification are, too, put in place through capture.

Chapter 2 picks up where chapter 1 leaves off, with commodification. Based on observations of repeated exchanges of animals at exotic animal auctions across the United States, I argue that the auction process performs lively capital anew, as individual, encounterable, and controllable. Animal fetishism and commodity fetishism intersect potently here, at the auction. Animals appear only in relation to their human use value (animal fetishism) and exchange value (commodity fetishism). In exchange, as commodities on the auction block, exotic pets' commodity histories are erased—who trapped them in the forest, whose labor brought them across the border to market, and so on. In this way exotic pet commodities are like other commodities whose value appears to be a property of their physicality rather than a property of the social relations of labor that produced them. But unlike other commodities, as I have been suggesting, the animals in exchange are not only products of a commodity history; they are also products of the history of their own being. But on the auction block, animals appear divested from the socio-ecological relations that gave birth to and supported them, and to which they contributed.

In chapter 3, I examine the attempt to undo exotic pets as lively capital, to rebuild lives of their own, in a rehabilitation facility, ARCAS, in northern Guatemala. The chapter documents the extraordinary amount of material inputs and energies required to sustain animals who are dependent on humans, and the immense challenge of attempting to rebuild their capacities to provide for themselves. I also show how although ARCAS's animals are no longer commodities, their enclosure persists, and so does a degree of animal fetishism.

For this reason, in the final chapter, I conclude by highlighting the necessary centrality of an antienclosure dimension to any political response that meaningfully resists the global exotic pet trade and the wider reordering of life in which domesticated, confined natures are ascendant and wild natures are deteriorating. I suggest the need for a wild life politics in which animals live as relationally autonomous beings whose own use values are respected and who live unenclosed lives in which they can work for themselves and their communities. This is an admittedly broad and far-reaching destination—so I suggest that demand management is an intermediary step in this direction, to at least contract the demand-driven market for exotic pets, so that fewer animals enter trade circuits. Some jurisdictions are curbing demand through bans on exotic pet ownership, but for the most part, demand management is underfunded at the national and international levels.[42]

How is an animal made to appear as if it does not have a life of its own? How are animals made thinglike, made lively capital, in the exotic pet trade? These are the overarching questions that I set out to answer in the following chapters, which track the making, remaking, and attempted unmaking of the exotic pet through capture, exchange, and rehabilitation, respectively. I engage in this analysis to draw attention to an understudied economy and its embodied effects, and to understand the operation of animal fetishism, or the denial of animal being, within the exotic pet trade and beyond. In so doing, I offer an analysis of capitalism that goes beyond wages, profit, commodity fetishism, and humans to examine one of its lesser-acknowledged conditions of possibility: the objectification of animals, the denial of animal being, and how this is achieved through the mechanism of animal fetishism, a cutting of the animal from its complex histories—even in an economy animated by a "love" for animals. Animal fetishism extends far beyond the exotic pet trade. Think of the adage loved by animal advocates, that if slaughterhouses had glass walls the whole world would be vegetarian. This assumption is based on the idea that defetishizing the commodity is enough, showing the violent relations underpinning meat or exotic pet production is enough. But what if those violent relations involve beings who are already devalued, who appear as "things"? It does not matter if walls are glass and violence is exposed if the "thing" being violated is not considered a being with a life of its own. The ultimate aim of this book is to challenge this notion, to suggest that animals like Darwin do have lives of their own, and that this should be the basis of a political response to the exotic pet trade as well as the reordering of life on earth of which it is a part.

An Act
of Severing

1

So far there is no rustling in the trees. I am on a stone ledge above the forest canopy, perched on the side of the tallest Mayan temple in Tikal National Park, one of the "core zones" of the politically contentious Maya Biosphere Reserve. I am nearly alone—in the early morning, you can beat the crowds. The forest stretches out in all directions, fading green to dark blue before disappearing into the mist. Three temples straight ahead rise uncannily clean-lined out of the canopy. But my eyes are on the near, still trees, scanning for spider monkeys.

It is a pleasure to read about spider monkeys, whom scientists writing in the thick, definitive text, *Spider Monkeys: Behaviour, Ecology and Evolution of the Genus* Ateles, describe as casting "a distinct morphological silhouette" (Rosenberger et al. 2008, 19): long, spindly limbs and a snaky prehensile tail arching from a narrow pot belly, a short neck supporting a small, round head and blunt face. Their diet of little other than rapidly metabolized fruit (supplemented by leaves, flowers, seeds, and roots) affords them an "unmatched high energy lifestyle" (19). The monkeys' lithe skeleton suspends and hurls their body weight, enabling them to "deftly fly and lope through the trees as if gravity and substrate did not matter and hands, feet and tail were octopus tentacles" (19) in search of ripe fruit in the upper canopy of a stratified tropical rain forest. Each monkey limb ends in four long, thin fingers (absent thumbs) that can hook around tree branches, foods, and locks. Spider monkeys' long, prehensile tails, ending in a flexible, hairless tip with skin grooves like fingerprints, are equally nimble and serve, for all intents and purposes, as a fifth limb.

Spider monkeys challenge scientists as study subjects because they are fast-moving and wide-ranging and live high in the canopy.[1] Researchers rarely encounter spider monkeys face-to-face in the forest, although the sounds of them often drift down from the treetops. While not as noisy as the aptly named howler monkey, spider monkeys do communicate using combinations of what scientists have named "whinnies," "trills," and "tweeters."[2] Wild spider monkeys also live in amoebic social clusters that are difficult to track. Almost always found in small subgroups, spider monkeys exemplify what scientists call a "fission-fusion" dynamic common to primates: individuals from the same community spend little time together as a whole group but form temporary subgroups that continuously merge and split with the larger community (Aureli and Schaffner 2008). Neither females nor males are aggressive with each other, and both genders often form close same-sex relationships. Spider monkeys sleep in large subgroups or even entire communities, pressed close into what I once heard called a "monkey ball."

Maternal bonds are significant in the lives of spider monkeys. Mothers only give birth every three to four years. A spider monkey gestates in its mother's womb for at least seven months, and once born it does not stray far from its mother for the first three years of its life (Campbell and Gibson 2008). This is an "exceedingly important period in the life of primates" (Vick 2008, 289), during which immature monkeys learn the complex social organization and behaviors with which they will live for the rest of their lives, usually more than twenty years.

This three-year period of development is what capture and commodification usually interrupt. Baby monkeys are easier to capture, and they are in far greater demand, as is true for most pet species. Common wisdom within the exotic pet trade holds that in order to form a bond between pet and owner, a pet should be obtained as young as possible. Infant animals offer the promise of intimacy, malleability, and obedience—all qualities of lively capital that are central to the exotic pet trade. This kind of life is unavailable for many adults, who tend to be too recalcitrant or reticent to submit to controlled encounters.

What are the characteristics of lively capital, and how is it formed in the first instance? These questions are at the heart of this chapter. Nature's commodification has long been a preoccupation of scholars across disciplines. How biophysical nature is enclosed, chopped into discrete bits, and worked into standardized units that are made property, circulated, bought, and sold—this process has been critical to deconstruct and characterize because nature's commodification is understood to be central to capitalism (N. Smith 2008). This is also the process under examination here. As studies of trees (Prudham 2004), water (Bakker 2003), and industrial farm animals (Boyd 2001; Weis 2013) show, the nature of the commodity—including whether or not it is alive—shapes the commodification process and can pose a barrier to production. For example, biological interventions to speed up production can be impossible to achieve or can breed disease outbreaks. My interest here, though, is less in how the nature of the commodity shapes its commodification, and more in the consequences of being made a commodity—an interest I have in common with Kathryn Gillespie (2018a) in her exemplary multisited tracing of cows' lives in the dairy industry.

The commodities I am interested in are specifically *lively* ones (Collard and Dempsey 2013)—by this I mean not only that they are alive but also that their value depends on actively demonstrating their liveliness. In the case of exotic pets, this means being made, and performing, companionability. How is this accomplished? To answer, this chapter borrows from political ecological and socioeconomic scholarship on commodification, but it is also necessarily in conversation with emerging work on biocapital and bioeconomies that is taking seriously the idea that life's commodification is unique and ascendant under modern capitalism (Rose 2006, 2008; Sunder Rajan 2006; Cooper 2008; Shukin 2009; Parry 2012). Feminist theorists especially are emphasizing the role of intimacy and encounter within such economies (Zelizer 2005; Haraway 2008). Haraway is a clear guide in this thinking, offering as she does the notion of "encounter value" to highlight how affective, multispecies meetings generate value—particularly, for her, ethical promise. But I see less promise here than Haraway. The capitalization of encounter is embodied in the pet. Nowhere are the costs of this more glaring than in the birth of lively capital through capture.

Capture is an act of severing, a sudden, explosive rupture, an abrupt, dramatic cleaving off of the animal from their socio-ecological reproductive networks: the kin and ecologies that support them and to which they contribute. Captured animals will likely again experience upheaval—as they are bought and sold, for example—but this original moment is crucial.[3] I argue capture can be understood as a onetime act of bodily enclosure—the confining and private ownership of individual bodies—that is the first and arguably most profound material separation of animals from their ability to provide for themselves. Bodily enclosure has parallels with the land enclosures—the privatization of land with previous common access—that have received more attention in critical scholarship. Land enclosures have since Marx been recognized as crucial to the development of capitalism.[4] Enclosure and its consequences have for the most part been studied in relation to agrarian societies whose common lands have been systematically enclosed under colonization and capitalism. These enclosures dispossess people of their ability to provide for themselves and their communities, for example, through grazing animals on common land or collecting fuelwood there. As a result, people lose the ability to reproduce themselves without reliance on waged work, which may or may not be available to them.[5] If the landless class can work for a wage, they enter an exploitative relation with the capitalist class, who scoop up surplus profits by not paying workers what their labor is worth. The relations of dependence that are established after enclosure are thus understood to empower capitalists, and disempower waged workers, who rely on capitalists to supply a wage because they can no longer produce for themselves what they need to survive.

There are some parallels with bodily enclosure.[6] Whether of land or bodies, enclosures are inescapably spatial interventions that rearrange, order, and fragment space in certain ways that control and constrain movements, orienting bodies in certain directions and empowering some while disempowering others. Enclosures, as Alvaro Sevilla-Buitrago (2015, 1003) writes, are a spatial means of dispossession, of "deprivation of autonomous capacities for self-valorization." Before capture, animals provide for themselves and their communities; they engage in the collective work of socioecological reproduction. As an act of enclosure, capture, like the privatization of land, achieves the establishment of private property rights over the animal: the animal (like the land) is now owned by someone with exclusive rights to that animal. As a result of animals' bodily enclosure, it is they, animals, who lose the ability to provide for themselves. A wage does not wait for them on the other side—but they do enter into relations of dependence on their human owner to provide their basic needs. While land enclosure empowers capitalists, then, who gain more control over laborers when their laborers are dependent on them for a wage to get by, animals' bodily enclosure empowers humans, who gain more control over animals when those animals are dependent on them for survival. As a mode of bodily enclosure, capture dispossesses animals of their ability to provide for themselves and their communities.[7]

Capture is not an act of commodification in and of itself, and not all captured animals end up as commodities, but capture is a necessary step to commodification; it puts in place conditions of control and alienation that are required for commodification in the pet trade. In this sense, capture is the first act that begins to form the exotic pet as lively capital: an encounterable, individual, controllable animal—the key characteristics of lively capital within the global exotic pet trade. Capture forms these characteristics. In so doing, capture also spatially enacts animal fetishism—capture strips the animal of a "life of its own" by severing the animal from the ability to provide for itself and its community. After capture, the animal appears divorced from the complex histories of its own being, disconnected from the socio-ecological relations that produced and sustained the animal until capture. In this chapter, I detail and discuss this act of severing, as well as the new relations of attachment that are necessary to maintain the animal's life and its status as lively capital. My aim is to attend to the enclosure process that spatially enacts animal fetishism, forges lively capital, and sets up the conditions for commodification, a process examined in more detail in the next chapter.

Swishing branches catch my eye. Below me, two brown bodies flicker through the leaves. They move so quickly and fluidly they give the impression of being blurred. These are the first spider monkeys I have seen outside of an enclosure. Here their movements can achieve full expression, and it is something to witness. They zoom through the air acrobatically, by turns "leaping and dropping" (the technical terms; see Youlatos 2008, 187) from branch to branch, soaring like they have wings. It is easy to imagine them covering several kilometers daily and hard to see how they could ever be captured. But they are regularly caught and brought down to the ground—a territory to which they rarely venture—and placed in a cage from which they will almost certainly never be permanently released alive. Finding out how precisely this capture is accomplished led me to two more biosphere reserves nearby: Reserva Integral de la Biósfera de Montes Azules (RIBMA, or the Montes Azules Biosphere Reserve) in Chiapas, Mexico, and Chiquibul National Park, in Belize. These three reserves are part of a network of protected areas constituting the region that conservation organizations have begun calling the "Maya Forest," though the name—and the reserves—remain controversial for reasons I will explain. Over the course of three months of multisite fieldwork on capture, I also spoke with governmental and nongovernmental officials and researchers in Mexico, Guatemala, and Belize.

In these places I learned how spider monkeys, scarlet macaws, and other animals are transformed from free-living forest dwellers into caged and leashed pets living halfway around the world. I also learned about the more strictly human politics of the reserves from which the animals are captured, about the powerful conservation and capital interests that are reconfiguring the region. The place and its politics are an uneven and active terrain shaping social, political, economic, and ecological relations and also the traded animals themselves.

CARRETERA FRONTERIZA,
THE "BORDER HIGHWAY" (HIGHWAY 307), MEXICO
October 28, 2011, 3:00 p.m.

When the van nears Playon de la Gloria (often known simply as "Playon"; map 1.1), a settlement in the south of the state of Chiapas, Mexico, bordered to the west by the Lacantún River and RIBMA and to the south by Guatemala, four women stand on the side of the narrow road carrying nets on long poles.

It has been at least a five-hour trip, and the van's passengers—Mexicans and *indígenas* young and old, single and as families—have been embarking and debarking in a steady stream. Now we're just two passengers—a young woman in enormous sunglasses sits just ahead of me—as well as the driver and his partner, who calls out the stops. The drive through Chiapas has been beautiful and varied. From San Cristóbal de las Casas southeast to Comitán, the landscape was treed with perennials, steeply undulating. Eastward from Comitán the land spread out in grassy-looking clearings dotted with the occasional long-trunked tree. Near Lagón de Montebello, I transferred vans at

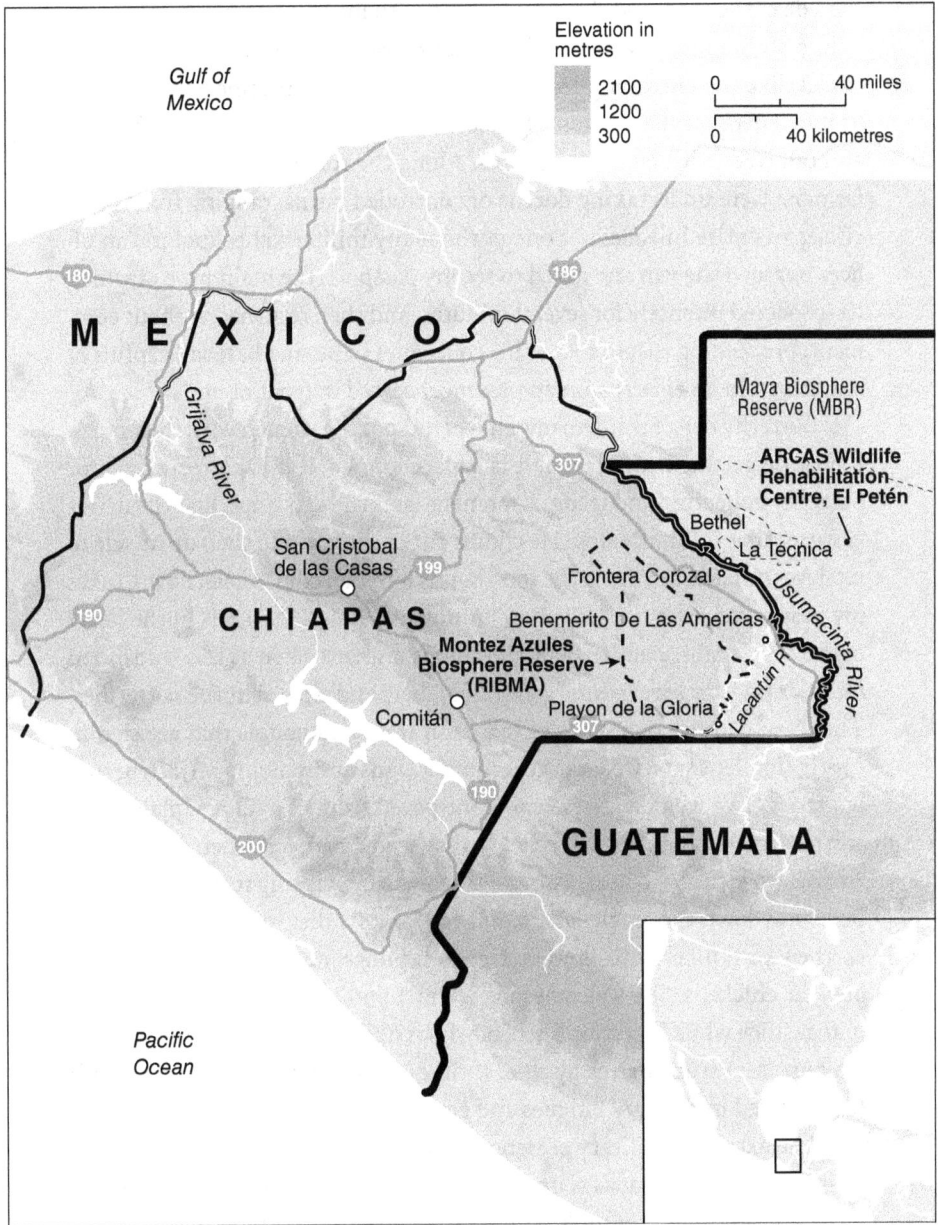

MAP 1.1 Chiapas province (map by Eric Leinberger).

the side of the road, and the driver waited with me for the next van to arrive. While we waited, few personal vehicles drove by; most were public vans, *combis*, like the one that idled beside me. The next van came and delivered us into a dense tropical forest of torso-thick vines, brilliant shades of green, and tall trees with fat buttress roots. Along the route campesinos (peasant farmers) were undertaking dozens of controlled burns, ranging from small circles to entire hillsides. At one of the many military checkpoints, an officer boarded the van and asked to see my passport, the main page of which he inspected intensely for several minutes, and then returned without comment, proceeding to join two of his colleagues in buying baseball capfuls of oranges from an elderly woman passenger seated in front of me.

Butterfly nets, I think to myself when I spot the women with their poles. I must be getting near Playon. It is a place known, if it is known at all, for butterfly collecting and trade. A moment later the van stops, and the driver gestures that this is my stop. He climbs out of the van and then up its side to retrieve my backpack from the roof, hands it to me, climbs back down, takes my pesos, and drives off. It is hot, humid, and quiet. Playon is in the heart of the Sierra del Lacandón, a mountainous region known as the "Lacandon forest," and I am here to interview researchers and check out the butterflies. The town consists of a series of tall palm trees and houses that are significantly smaller than two large government signs announcing infrastructure upgrades. Two women are sweeping the paved front of a square, plain Jehovah's Witness church; I ask them if they know Señor Rueben and Señora Anna, two locals who host, assist, and accompany visiting researchers. They point me down the single-lane paved road onto a dirt road. Anna is in her earthen yard filled with flowers, trees, and dogs, and with a cordoned-off area for chickens. She welcomes me warmly and gives me freshly squeezed orange juice while I wait for Rueben, who is out. While I sip the juice, a new white pickup truck drives by several times, cab and box both packed with men dressed in military fatigues and carrying machine guns.

The extensive military presence I encounter at checkpoints and on patrols in southern Chiapas is unsurprising. Mexico's southern border region is the site and subject of multiple conflicts. The United States has long pressured the Mexican government to stem drug and human trafficking across this border from Central and South America. The region is also host to decades of conflict over Mexico's natural and biological resources, in which the Mexican government, US-based and international conservation groups, and powerful corporations are pitted against Indigenous residents and a revolutionary movement, Ejército Zapatista de Liberación Nacional (the Zapatista Army of National Liberation, hereafter referred to as the Zapatistas). But even following militarization, the border was, according to an expert interviewed in the *New York Times,* "open sesame for illegal migrants, drug traffickers, exotic animals and Mayan artifacts" (Thompson 2006). Some interviewees corroborated this idea of the border's ongoing porosity but noted that the military presence may be partly responsible for a recent decline in wildlife trafficked in and out of Mexico. At the same time, some military personnel themselves reportedly buy and sell animals (Naranjo 2011; also see Kretser et al. 2012).

If size and frequency of wildlife seizures are any indication, though, wildlife trafficking in Guatemala and Mexico has declined significantly since the turn of the century, especially international trade out of these two countries. All interviews confirmed this trend, which is especially pronounced in Mexico, a country that now, legally at least, imports far more animals than it exports, a reversal of trends in the 1980s (Benitez 2011).[8] Not all interviewees were in agreement about the causes of decline in wildlife seizures, though; one interviewee explicitly speculated that it could be due to government funding cutbacks to conservation programs and enforcement, which would yield fewer seizures even if the number of traded animals stayed the same (Morales 2011). Other explanations include, most commonly, this increased military and police presence along the borders and also, simply, a reduction in the volume of available wildlife to capture and traffic.

Wildlife trade does continue, however, and is often linked, at least discursively, to other illegal trade flows in the region. NGO and government officials regularly claim that political instability opens the door for trafficked wildlife to move freely across borders. As one NGO interviewee expressed, northern Guatemala and southern Mexico are "anti-governed," a "black hole of governance" (McNab 2011). This narrative is politically charged. As geographer Megan Ybarra (2012) argues, this characterization of "wild" places where drug traffickers work with *narco-fincas* (drug-cattle ranches) inside parks, moving drugs north through the "cocaine corridor," has legitimized escalated "Green Forces" in Guatemala: army presence dedicated to policing drug trafficking in protected areas. In her extended research in the same region, another geographer, Jennifer Devine (2014), likewise observes that ecotourism is serving as a major impetus for militarized conservation, as tourist sites are created and maintained through the expulsion of peasants and their vilification as predatory on local fauna, as well as the army's increased presence through the creation of military outposts and their enrollment in enforcing conservation laws. The discourse of an "ungovernability" problem in the region, then, is implicated in an enduring trend toward greater state and military control over lands from which Indigenous and local residents are excluded, often along racialized lines.

Soon Rueben comes home, clad in high rain boots, sweatpants, and a dirty T-shirt. Two people join us for a tour of the Playon butterfly center: a professor from El Colegio de la Frontera Sur (ECOSUR), a university in Chiapas, who assesses ecosystem health by recording and analyzing forest sounds, and Rueben's older brother, the center's caretaker, building manager, and key master. The air is still thick with heat when, just before dusk, the four of us set out to the center, which, thankfully, sits in the shade of a stand of tall *caoba* (mahogany) trees on the bank of the Lacantún River. Several prominent signs boast the butterfly center's sponsors, which include WWF, the Carlos Slim Foundation, and Mexico's state-owned oil corporation, Petróleos Mexicanos (PEMEX), all of which partnered with the Mexican government to implement this butterfly ecotourism project in Playon. The project is two-pronged: in a large workshop space, Playon residents make art—prints, cards, bookmarks—out of locally wild-caught and captive-raised butterflies; and two large, lofty cages hold hundreds of live butterflies for the tourists who visit from Mexico and beyond. At the time of my fieldwork, only around two hundred tourists visited the butterfly center per year.

Mostly women participate in the program, although some men and children capture butterflies, primarily peleides blue morphos (*Morpho peleides*), a species also known as "The Emperor," whose wings (with a span of up to eight inches) are covered in millions of tiny scales that diffract the light and generate a dazzling, iridescent blue. A similar program in nearby Chajul, in Guatemala, also sells dead butterflies to international collectors, and both projects are considering exporting live butterflies to "Butterfly Worlds" across the globe. Pupae, chrysalides, and larvae can be frozen to slow their metabolism during transport, and then heated back up at the final destination—Canada, the United States, the United Kingdom—to be transformed into butterflies for display. When we enter one of the large cages, the brilliant blue butterflies are so huge I can hear their flapping wings whoosh through the air. One lands on the professor's back and it looks like he has radiant blue wings.

Powerful partnerships drive joint "conservation" ventures like Playon's butterfly ecotourism project, ventures that are increasingly common in Mexican forests and biosphere reserves. These are partnerships between the Mexican government and the likes of Playon's butterfly project sponsors— WWF, Carlos Slim, PEMEX—in addition to other key actors like Conservation International (CI) and Pulsar Internacional (PI), influential NGOs, and well-connected corporations that have financial interests in the region—in biological and genetic resources, agriculture (tobacco, bamboo, African palm, and ornamental plants), eucalyptus pulp (to meet the packaging needs of maquiladoras—export assembly plants [see N. Harvey 2001]), and oil. In response, resistant Indigenous and local groups protest repeatedly against what the environmental organization Maderas del Pueblo del Sureste calls a "global strategy of 'territorial clearing and control' disguised as a philanthropic 'conservationist spirit' [that] answers to multinational corporate interests of what's called green capitalism" (Bellinghausen 2012).

These fraught politics coalesce in conflicts over RIBMA, a reserve funded by CI, PI, PEMEX, and the World Bank. RIBMA is a "bank" of conservation capital, biological capital, and genetic capital; the location of dozens of human settlements the state deems "illegal"; a home to millions of animals (including many of Mexico's last surviving members of their species); and a major source of trafficked animals. The day after visiting the butterflies, I cross the Lacantún River from Playon into the reserve.

PLAYON DE LA GLORIA
October 29, 2011, 5:00 a.m.

Rueben and I get up before the sun and head down to the river to a slim, wooden, motorless rowboat lodged on the riverbank. By 6:00 a.m. Rueben has used a long pole to push us off the bank out into the Lacantún, a wide, fast-moving river brown with sediment (figure 1.1). We have set out several hundred meters up the river from our destination on the opposite bank, to account for the current, and our speed floating downstream far exceeds our speed paddling across the river. Howler monkeys' chilling shrieks echo out from the reserve as we slide through the water. Several flocks of birds fly by. Rueben paddles us to the place on the bank where we need to disembark. We

FIGURE 1.1 Paddling across the Lacantún River (photograph by the author).

head off on a trail to the camp of another ECOSUR professor who is leading a group of graduate students learning how to conduct wildlife population surveys in RIBMA.

The Mexican government established 331,200 hectares as RIBMA, its first biosphere reserve, by presidential decree in 1978 with the backing of the funders mentioned earlier. Conservation organizations like WWF and CI have drawn on Myers's (1988, 1990) influential "hot spot" approach (a term later renamed a "biodiversity hotspot" metric), which identifies what are thought to be the globe's most biodiverse and ecologically important regions, to argue for RIBMA's ecological significance and to justify their persistent urging of the Mexican government to forcibly remove local and Indigenous settlements from the reserve. These organizations argue that the "illegal" residents conduct destructive controlled burns. Some groups are permitted residency in and around the reserve, including the Lacandon, a small Indigenous group that in 1971 was issued communal forestland, part of which would later become RIBMA, even though they never before lived in the area (Enríquez 2011). A year later, a forest company was permitted ac-

Chapter One

cess to the communal land. Other Mexican Indigenous groups living in the forest—the Tseltal, Ch'ol, Tojolabal, and Tzotzil—were not granted rights, and violent evictions continue in RIBMA; Indigenous groups report government officials sometimes descend in helicopters to burn homes ("Dark Blue" 2010). Critics argue that the evictions merely pave the way for government, conservation and corporate interests, and global capital to privatize the region and commodify its resources. Several scholars have tracked these moves and the protests against them, protests that are prevalent throughout the "Maya Forest," a region so named by the very conservation organizations that have advocated and even insisted on these evictions and exclusions.[9]

This is the complicated sociopolitical terrain into which spider monkeys and other animals who live in these forests are born. These wider political contexts shape animals' birth as lively capital. For example, drug trafficking and wildlife trafficking do sometimes go hand in hand—drugs and animals are occasionally traded by the same individuals and networks and are linked through the popularity of so-called narco-pets for drug lords. Animals can also become key political actors in environmental and geopolitical struggles.[10] Politics thus play an important role for animals living in these places, and for the animals who become lively capital ensnared in trade circuits that take them far away from these forests.

Unlike inert capital, these living beings that become lively capital are born twice: first as sentient beings, then again as tradable, thinglike bits of property. The first birth, described in the next section, launches the animal's enmeshment in complex social, ecological, and familial networks. The second act, capture, which I describe later, extracts the animal from these networks. It all happens in the complicated space of RIBMA, home to Mexico's last free-flying macaws.

RIBMA
October 29, 2011, 7:00 a.m.

Along the narrow trail to the research camp in RIBMA, Rueben stops suddenly and points upward. Visible through a break in the canopy are two scarlet macaws flying side by side, their red, blue, and yellow plumage a bright splash of primary color against the blue sky. Their long tail feathers jut out behind them in a distinctive, graduated point. As they fly they call to each other through a series of varied, hoarse vocalizations. It is a rare sight:

only around two hundred wild scarlet macaws remain in Mexico, most of them in RIBMA (Estrada 2014).

The two macaws crossing the sky above the canopy are likely a breeding pair, and barring death or capture, they will stay that way for their entire lives, usually forty to fifty years. Scarlet macaws, or *Ara macao*, as christened by Linnaeus in 1758, are the largest species of parrot (order Psittaciformes): up to thirty-six inches from beak to tail. With their wide, strong wings macaws can reach speeds of more than fifty-five kilometers an hour above the canopy as they fly in search of foods such as forest nuts, berries, and seeds. Their complex and piercingly loud vocalizations can carry for several kilometers above the forest. The birds almost always journey in pairs, lone couples traversing the canopy, except at night, when they gather in flocks to sleep. Macaws breed approximately every one to two years, producing a clutch of two to four eggs, which are incubated primarily by the female for twenty-four to twenty-five days. Families nest from January to April in the holes of upper-canopy, deciduous trees, often preferring dead trees. After hatching, the young stay with their parents, both of whom provide care for one to two years. At first, the male regurgitates and liquefies food to feed the chicks. The parents will not raise another set of eggs until the previous young have become independent. Scarlet macaws reach sexual maturity at three or four years of age.

A macaw chick cracks out of its shell into a nest in a hole in a tall tree in the rain forest canopy. It experiences moments such as its first flight, being cleaned by its parents' beaks, receiving liquid food from them, and cracking down on a nutshell with its own sharp bill. For thirty, forty, fifty years this macaw might fly above the trees, building nests, sleeping in flocks, incubating eggs, and raising chicks. This free-flying life constitutes and is constituted by a network of relations: relations with nuts, trees, the air and the sky, a mate, offspring, rain and sun. This is the macaws' socio-ecological reproductive network: the constellation of beings, energies, knowledge, materials, and relations that enable and reproduce their collective life. This is an especially crucial network during macaws' early years. During an extended period of parental dependence, young macaws develop the complex behaviors and ability for communication that have led humans to bestow on scarlet macaws the distinction of being one of the world's smartest birds (figure 1.2).

FIGURE 1.2 Captive scarlet macaws keeping an eye out at ARCAS, Guatemala (photograph by the author).

Unfortunately, this intelligence and the ability to mimic human speech, coupled with the birds' beauty—their brilliant primary coloring—make scarlet macaws both one of the most expensive and popular pets and one of the most commonly trafficked animals. Due to the pet trade and habitat loss, scarlet macaw populations have been reduced to a fraction of their former numbers, and, while macaws are still a widely distributed species, their remaining populations tend to be confined to fragmented habitat and limited numbers. In 1985, the Convention on International Trade in Endangered Species of Flora and Fauna (CITES) listed scarlet macaws as an Appendix I species, meaning their commercial trade is prohibited. But illicit trade thrives, and even some legal trade in wild-caught birds continues. Since 1997, for example, under CITES, Surinam has been allotted an annual export quota of one hundred live, wild-caught scarlet macaws. Importing permits for these birds are only awarded for ostensibly noncommercial purposes—namely, scientific or educational. Import destinations include Singapore, the United States, the United Arab Emirates, Thailand, South Africa, Russia, the Netherlands, the Philippines, Mexico, Bahrain, and the Dominican Republic.

The path along the river takes Rueben and me to the researchers' camp: around ten tents, blue tarps, a picnic table, and a food tent, all of which look diminutive dispersed among the massive tree trunks. The forest on this side of the river is much thicker, denser, and cooler in temperature. In the camp, more than a dozen people are waking up to the dappled morning sun, making breakfast, getting dressed. They are all graduate students taking a field course with Eduardo Naranjo, a professor at ECOSUR. This week in RIBMA, the students learn things like how to make transects, track wildlife, and recognize edible forest foods such as jobo (*Spondias mombin*), a delicious, small tree fruit with a variety of medicinal uses, such as combating intestinal worms, leprosy, and inflammation.

A clean-shaven, tall man dressed head to toe in khaki walks over and introduces himself as Eduardo. He almost immediately notes my lack of proper attire—I am wearing thin jeans, short boots, and a light, long-sleeved shirt. Eduardo wears loose-flowing clothing that is made of thick, light-colored tracksuit material, his pants tucked into sturdy, knee-high rubber boots. He explains that the boots and long pants and shirt are to ward off ticks (although nothing can keep them all away), and as I later find out, his assessment of my inadequate footwear and clothes is spot on; for days to come I will be pinching blood-gorged ticks off my skin. Eduardo assures me that these ticks are quite harmless, and that it is the botflies that are really disgusting, laying their larvae on mosquitoes so that when mosquitoes feed on animals the warmth of the animal blood triggers the larvae to drop into the mosquito bite, where the eggs grow into maggots under a swelling, itchy red bump on the animal's skin. If you detect such a bump on your own skin and you wish to avoid hatching botflies out of your arm, you must place a piece of tape over the bump so that the larvae, which come up to breathe at night, are suffocated. They can then be squeezed out. The botfly is among the least pleasant animals in a forest area that is one of Mexico's most diverse, home to what brothers Javier and Roberto de la Maza (1985) estimate are fifteen thousand species of nocturnal butterflies alone.

Eduardo and I sit down amid the mosquitoes on a wooden bench at a table so he can tell me about his years of experience studying human-wildlife interactions in this region. He tells me immediately that Mexico is no longer the significant wildlife exporting region it was in the 1980s, when *pajaderos* (people selling parrots) commonly strolled town and city streets, tall stacks of birdcages piled on their backs. The reduction in exports is in part due to bans on wild-caught bird imports that were implemented in the United States and the European Union in 1992 and 2007, respectively. But Eduardo is quick to note that it is not concern for animals that has driven the disappearance of pajaderos and the decline of wildlife exports. Instead, he cites a constellation of other factors, namely, the increased military presence in the aftermath of the Zapatista movement and in response to US pressure on Mexico to crack down on drug and human trafficking across the Guatemala-Mexico border. There is also more demand in Mexico's urban centers for exotic species, like Australian songbirds. So, Eduardo concludes, "I wouldn't say there is no trade at all. There's still some trade, I'm sure of that" (Naranjo 2011). My search of the CITES database today, years after Eduardo's comment, corroborates his suspicion. Over the last ten years, Mexico has continued to legally export thousands of wild-caught CITES-listed animals per year, mostly to the United States: everything from pythons to scorpions, alligators to manatees, and, still, despite the United States' importation ban, parrots—albeit for reportedly scientific purposes.[11] And these are just the CITES-regulated legal trade flows. Furthermore, ongoing seizures of illegal shipments of animals at borders and in markets and airports make evident that the illicit trade still exists, even if possibly in diminished form.

Eduardo's students are ready for their first lesson of the day, so he grabs his machete and we set off into the trees on no discernible trail. He cuts at the bush with his machete in smooth, downward-arcing motions alternating on left and right. I walk behind him, and we continue our conversation. He says parrots, including macaws, are among those animals still trafficked out of Mexico, and he explains how people actually catch these elusive animals, his account later corroborated by multiple other interviewees.

The majority of wildlife trappers do not work full-time catching animals in the forest (Pires 2012). Trappers are predominantly male, a heterogeneous group: campesinos, *chatarreros* (scrap merchants), *chicleros* (locals who collect chicle, a gum from tropical evergreen trees), fishermen, Indigenous people, hunters, farmers, loggers—people who work or live in or near the forest. They do not specialize in trapping (it is not their exclusive income source), but neither are they purely opportunistic trappers. They have refined and extensive knowledge of the forest and know when, seasonally and daily, and how to find animals. To catch birds, like macaws or red-lored Amazon parrots (*Amazona autumnalis*), trappers must seek out the animals from May to August and navigate the dense forest through which I am currently following Eduardo.

Typically working alone or in pairs, with one person acting as a lookout, trappers locate nests and either climb trees with spikes and ropes to access the chicks, or cut trees down and harvest the chicks from the fallen nest. Trappers require only "climbing spikes and a little piece of rope; that's all it takes," an NGO official told later told me. "And the gumption to go up trees and get up there and bring these birds back" (McNab 2011). Depending on the species of bird, and its respective price, trappers will catch and trade as few as one bird (in the case of macaw chicks) or assemble dozens of birds to sell at once (for less lucrative species, such as red-lored Amazon parrots; figure 1.3).

As I follow Eduardo through the bush, I ask him if it is possible that fewer macaws are now traded in Mexico because of the simple reason that there are just far fewer available to be captured. He shrugs and tilts his head to the side, appearing to neither agree nor disagree. Previous decades of widespread parrot capture in the region certainly have had a severe effect, but whether this has affected trapping numbers is difficult to ascertain. Most animals do not survive the dispossession and series of forced disentanglements from their socio-ecological reproductive networks. Various

FIGURE 1.3 Red-lored Amazon parrot (photograph by the author).

studies estimate that between 30 and 70 percent of birds die before reaching their purchaser (Wright et al. 2001; Gonzales 2003; Guzmán et al. 2007; Martinez 2011; Pires 2012). The negative effects ramify beyond captured birds, however. As two interviewees noted (Cantu 2011; Martinez 2011), for every bird caught, a number of nests are destroyed (the process of raiding nests generally renders the nesting site useless for future nesting [Weston and Memon 2007]), trees are cut, and breeding adults are killed, delivering much more serious blows to the population than the mere number of trafficked birds might suggest. For example, a study in Peru found that 48 percent of all blue-and-gold macaws die when their trees are felled (Gonzales 2003). Researchers estimate that, to compensate for these mortalities, up to four times as many parrots are captured than make it to market (Michels 2002). The effects of trapping wild birds, then, are borne not only by indi-

vidual captured parrots but also by wider parrot populations. Legal and illegal pet trade is thus identified as one of the leading reasons that several
parrot species are on the brink of extinction (Weston and Memon 2007).
This leads multiple researchers to conclude that parrot pet trade has devastating affects both for wild populations and for the welfare of individual
wild-caught birds.[12]

If parrots survive the journey, it is unlikely that their new homes will
provide the life supports they require. Nutritional disorders like hypovita-
minosis A and diseases—particularly respiratory diseases—are prevalent in
captive birds (Weston and Memon 2007). As Weston and Memon (2007,
80) note, it is "difficult if not impossible" to replicate parrots' wild diets in
captivity. In technical terms, adult captive parrots also "often express affect dysregulation, hypersensitivity to environmental change, and an in-
ability to self-regulate that presents commonly as uncontrollable aggression,
general anxiety, and excessive screaming," resulting in many cases "from
the disruption or diminished quality of parent-young developmental interactions, what is referred to as relational trauma" (Bradshaw, Yenkosky, and
McCarthy 2009, 1). Some researchers even argue that these captive birds
suffer from a form of post-traumatic stress disorder (Yenkosky, Bradshaw,
and McCarthy 2010). Many of the birds I will meet later in the research process, birds being bought and sold at auctions in the United States, exhibited
these characteristics.

Spider monkeys, too, are still trapped from RIBMA, albeit on a smaller
scale, and researchers have identified similarly devastating impacts on populations and individuals. Because spider monkey babies spend most of their
time physically attached to their mothers, high in the trees, trappers most
commonly catch a baby by shooting its mother out of the trees. The baby,
if it survives, is plucked from its dead mother's body. It is common for the
father and dominant members of the troop to descend from the trees in an
attempt to ward off the threat. These monkeys are sometimes shot as well.
For both monkeys and parrots, one interviewee remarked, "there's a lot of
death in the animal group in order to get one" (Morales 2011).

Capturing an animal, usually an infant or chick, can be thought of
centrally as a process of *severing* the animal from its ecological, familial, and
societal context and supports. In this case, macaw chicks are captured from
nests; spider monkey babies are pulled off of their mothers' bodies. The captured bodies are then enclosed: they become the property of the capturer,

and they are placed in cages, on leashes—they become individuated, controlled. A system of replacement supports is subsequently implemented to ensure the baby animal stays alive: food, water, shelter. These supports can also be viewed as a means of controlling the animal in its new environment. The replacement supports are usually inadequate, and coupled with the stress of passing through three or four people's hands from capture, to transport, to sale, many if not most animals die en route or in the first few days of life in their new "home" in a cage in a living room, backyard, or porch.

This process establishes conditions necessary for commodification to occur—necessary for these animals to become tradable goods. In his theory of markets, Michel Callon (1998) uses an example of a human organ to describe his idea that commodities are formed through a process of selectively forging and severing ties, that "commodities are the outcome of a double process of entanglement and disentanglement" (Callon 2002, 292). To be transformed into a good for exchange, an organ must be freed of its prior attachments: vascular and fleshy and also imaginative. Or, as Margaret Lock (2002, 83) explains, in order for body parts to be tradable, "they must first be conceptualized as thing-like, as non-self and as detachable from the body." Once the organ is disentangled, it can be exchanged as a commodity, and new material and discursive ties multiply around the organ. This disentanglement is precisely what is accomplished through the abrupt and violent act of capture, which severs the animal from its previous ties and, perhaps most important, from its ability to provide for itself and its community. The act of capture is thus an act of dispossession.

Having been disentangled from its original network, the animal is entangled in a new network of human-provided supports. To survive in these new networks, animals must adjust to a radically different life: their life as lively capital. They do not have kin; they do not search for their own food; they do not fly, swim, or swing through the canopy; they do not reproduce, unless they are selectively bred in a controlled manner. Instead, they may be given iPads, stuffed animals, colorful plastic rings, and ice cream. They also have different bodies: clipped wings, surgically removed teeth, fur or feathers covered in decorations or clothing or diapers. The conceptualization of animals as thinglike becomes manifest and embodied in the figure of caged and leashed pet. Animals' survival now depends not only on the extent to which their new life is adequately enriching but also on the extent to which they can unlearn wild behaviors and acquire new habits and methods of communication. This added requirement speaks to the main difference between an exotic pet and most other forms of capital: the pet is *not* a mere thing. It is not only alive but also sentient, companionable. This, too, is part of its value, although it is not admitted to the extent that it would destabilize the animals' eligibility as property, as ownable thing, as commodity.

Forming lively capital in the exotic pet trade thus relies on two competing framings of animal life. An animal must, like any bit of capital, be perceived as an object, as nonhuman, in order to be commodifiable. And yet an exotic pet is also expected to actively demonstrate its liveliness and companionability, which depend on a degree of sentience. As we will see in the next chapter, often the more sentient and companionable the animal can demonstrate itself to be—the more words it knows, for example, or the more cuddly it is—the higher the price it will fetch. These two framings of the animal—as inert, mute object and as lively, sentient being—exist in tension not only in exotic pet trade circuits but also, in slight variations, at zoos and in scientific research and testing facilities, where the more "human-like" the animal, the more desirable or useful it is, even as captivity and testing rely absolutely on animals' relegation to the realm of the inferior, subordinate nonhuman.

After several hours following Eduardo through the dense brush with his students, we return to the camp. Later this afternoon I will cross back over the river with Rueben and leave the reserve. My mind is beginning to turn to the question of how captured animals make this same journey. How are the parrots whose wings are clipped and the monkeys whose necks are ringed with leashes first moved out of the forest? Once animals are captured and enclosed, and the path to commodification is paved, how and where does the commodification—the buying and selling—occur? To answer these questions, I later traveled to Mexico City, an international hub for wildlife trafficking. In the meantime, Eduardo, his students, and I gather back around the picnic table. Someone spots a tick on my pant leg. I pull it off, and Eduardo shows me how to crush it between my fingernails.

MEXICO CITY
December 15, 2011, 1:00 p.m.

In a library coffee shop in Mexico City's trendy Condessa district, Juan Carlos Cantu, director of the Mexican branch of Defenders of Wildlife, takes out a pen, pulls my notebook toward him, and starts sketching four permu-

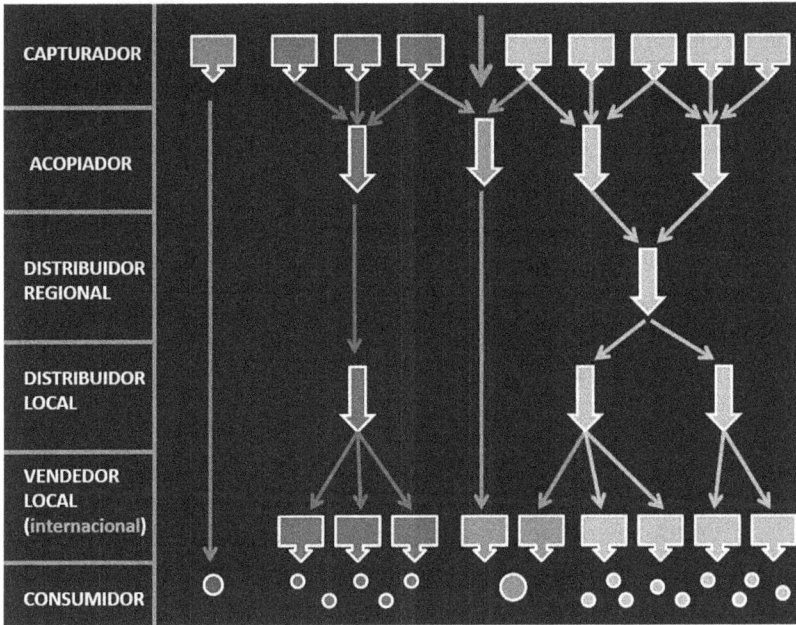

FIGURE 1.4 Schematic outline of different commodity chains (from left to right): (1) direct selling from trappers to buyers, (2) local chains (no regional distribuitor), (3) international chains, and (4) national chains (created by Juan Carlos Cantu, reproduced with permission).

tations of the now-illegal parrot pet trade commodity chain in and out of Mexico (figure 1.4). In 2008, Mexico banned all native parrot exports and internal trading, and ceased issuing parrot trapping authorizations. Since then, as mentioned earlier, parrot exports have declined significantly, but the country has become one of the world's largest bird importers. In spite of declines in exports, an illegal wild parrot trade continues to operate in and out of Mexico (Pires and Clark 2012). How are birds shuttled out of the forest and potentially across borders?

It happens in different ways, Juan Carlos tells me. "Always, first there are the trappers." He draws a clump of dots at the top of the page. "Most of them they sell directly to an *acopiador*, a hoarder." He draws the letter *H* a third of the way down the page and connects it with several vertical lines to the dots. In return, even at this early, local stage in the chain, trappers reportedly may receive as much as US$100 per macaw chick, which is easily several months' income for campesinos. Even so, the trappers usually make the least amount of money in the chain (Cantu 2011; Morales 2011).

The acopiadores are middlemen and middlewomen who are more likely to be specialists working full-time and year-round. Trafficking is usually their sole income. Some of these hoarders have experience working as past bird trappers, but most, according to Juan Carlos, are just salespeople. Hoarders tell trappers where to meet: in the trappers' own homes or at crossroads or other out-of-the-way places. Sometimes trappers are unaware of who the hoarders are, but trappers report that hoarders always seem to know where to find them (Guzmán et al. 2007). The hoarder is generally well known by community members; trade networks are not completely clandestine. As Bergman (2009) reports after an extended period of investigative journalism in Ecuador, which included following trappers to macaw nests, "capturing animals in the jungle is common. It's not the shadowy activity people might think; it's more like an open secret."

Moving from community to community, acopiadores gather captured animals, buying parrots from multiple trappers, often across several states, and stockpiling birds until they have enough to transport (or sell to a transporter) and deliver, in big trucks or trailers. Hoarders then have two primary options. First, they may sell directly to individuals who will move the animals across borders. Animals are transported not only by truck over the border but also by air and boat to ports around the world. Another interviewee reported knowledge of seizures of shipping containers "filled with animals—thousands of animals in a container being moved out by sea" (Morales 2011). Second, hoarders can funnel animals to a regional distribution center in more populous regions, like Mexico City. At this point animals are reallocated to local sellers in city markets. Distributors and sellers, like hoarders, are more likely to be working full-time in wildlife trade. If the macaw chick who was purchased from a trapper for a hundred dollars makes it to Mexico City, or to the United States or Europe, the chick could fetch thousands of dollars.

Juan Carlos subsequently draws a local chain, similar to the national chain but lacking the regional distributor, so hoarders sell directly to local distributors. Then he draws a chain with no distributors at all, where trappers sell directly to buyers. These chains are often between families and friends, and are especially "dark," he tells me: it "is impossible to know how many there are, where they are, who they are. You have to go all over the country, and it is impossible. Some people have estimated that there are around twenty thousand local trappers. They will trap, in the case of parrots, one parrot or two parrots a year. And not every year." Juan Carlos implies that the localized trade is largely insignificant compared with national trade. He looks up, shrugs, and shakes his head. "So it's very complicated and it's not one chain, one company. . . . It's very, very complicated."

Although there are few studies of exotic pet commodity chains, those that exist corroborate Juan Carlos's account (Beissinger 2001; Pires 2012; Pires and Clark 2012). As his sketch makes clear, the trade at this stage is diffuse and decentralized. Animals who are dispersed across forests are collected and moved into cities and markets, across borders, into homes. Money accrues unevenly by the generalized principle that the "further" along the chain (away from capture), the greater the profits—casting doubt on the touted potential of wildlife trade to benefit local communities.[13] Although the precise methods of capture and transport and the overall commodity chain vary from species to species and from region to region, generalizations can be made about the moment the animal is formed as lively capital.

Recall the spider monkeys I described looping through the canopy in Guatemala in the beginning of this chapter. Their lives depend on an intricate network of relations with each other and their environments. If they were to be captured, these relations would be severed in order to make the monkeys mobile and tradable. Upon capture, the monkeys are connected to a new network of relations: human-provided supports such as food and water. This amounts to the production of new natures: enclosed bodies and closely managed lives in which capital can accumulate. An essential part of the formation of animals as lively capital in global exotic pet trade is thus that their wild and social lives are "taken apart" in the sense that they are disentangled from their previous behaviors and ecological, familial, and social networks. The degree and form of disentanglement are unique to live animal capital, distinguishing them from, say, a commodity like a television set. To create the monkey on the leash—the thinglike object of living capital—the monkey must be severed from its home and family. Its former life must be nearly extinguished.

Forming lively capital can therefore be seen as a series of entanglements and disentanglements that represent a realignment or rearrangement of the relations and terrain of life for captured animals, *a shifting of the relations that constitute the animal.* I have suggested here that this amounts to an act of bodily enclosure that dispossesses animals of their capacity to provide for themselves, to be world-making subjects, contributing to their communities. This act of severing, or bodily enclosure, thus marks an important enactment of animal fetishism, where the animal is cut off from the complex histories of its own being, alienated from the relations of socio-ecological reproduction that produced the animal in the first place. The animal can then begin to appear as if it does not have a life of its own.

What life emerges instead? The animal life at the heart of lively capital in exotic pet trade has three dominant characteristics. First, exotic pets live individual lives; generally they are bought and sold as single units, severed—or severable—from their familial and social relations. Second, exotic pets are permanently encounterable. Although animals may be encounterable without being pets or capital—indeed, I have described several of my own encounters with wild animals in this chapter—exotic pets have no choice but to be encountered, to be touched and met face-to-face by their owners. Third, and stemming from this, their encounters are tightly controlled. So are their lives in general: their movements, their space, when and what they eat, whether or not they may breed, whether or not they can keep their offspring. Captivity thus refers to literal spatial confinement in a cage or by a leash, and it also refers more broadly to a state of forced dependency in which animals have few opportunities for choice, movement, or play—self-directed or otherwise. This chapter has tracked the process through which this life begins, focusing in particular on capture as a crucial onetime act of enclosure that forms lively capital and establishes the conditions necessary for commodification. In the next chapter I turn to the act of exchange, to consider how commodification intensifies animal fetishism and compounds the characteristics of lively capital as individual, controllable, and encounterable.

MEXICO-GUATEMALA BORDER
October 30, 2011

My time in the Mexican forest has come to an end. A burly taxi driver takes me east along the Carretera Fronteriza, around a sharp, ninety-degree left turn in the road where Mexico's southwestern border with Guatemala reaches its corner, then north through Benemérito de las Américas to Frontera Corozal (see map 1.1), where I spend the night. Early in the morning I take a *lancha* across the Usumacinta River, which serves as the border between Guatemala and Mexico, to La Técnica, a tiny border town on the Guatemalan side, where I wait for a bus to Flores (via customs at Bethel, a town several kilometers south). While I am waiting, a busload of young Honduran men rolls up. They intend to cross into Frontera Corozal the way I had just come, headed ultimately into the United States, with plans to live in Texas and California. In our brief encounter they seem intent on a sort of symbolic exchange of currency, pressing some Honduran dollar bills into my hand. I give them my remaining pesos and a Canadian toonie, just in case.

All manner of people and goods cross this swift river border daily, both legally and illegally. Spider monkeys; boxes of turtles, parrots, or baby crocodiles; cages of macaws are also going in the opposite direction that I am, destined north into the United States. They are unlikely to make it, not because they will be discovered at the border and confiscated but because they will not survive the journey. The animals who do survive might arrive at a pet shop or be sold online. Or they might, for example, be flown into the Fort Worth airport in Texas and be driven to a place like United States Global Exotics (USGE), in Arlington, Texas, which was one of the United States' largest sellers of exotic animals, supplying major pet stores like Petco and PetSmart, until it was shut down in 2009. While it functioned USGE shipped mammals, reptiles, amphibians, insects, and other animals to pet stores, breeders, and wholesale distributors, including suppliers to the major pet chains all over the United States. An undercover worker from People for the Ethical Treatment of Animals (PETA) discovered and reported that tens of thousands of exotic animals—snakes, lizards, turtles, sloths—were being confined in crowded and filthy enclosures in USGE's Texas facility. A subsequent Society for the Prevention of Cruelty to Animals (SPCA) raid seized twenty-six thousand animals (Ashley et al. 2014). Hundreds more animals were found frozen to death in a freezer. USGE was charged with animal cruelty under Texas criminal cruelty laws. During the subsequent court proceedings it came to light that USGE had an animal "turnover" or mortality rate of more than 70 percent every six weeks. In court, the defense argued that this was the industry standard.

Millions of animals passed through USGE's warehouse, and although few other warehouses of that scale exist in the United States, there is a vast network of smaller companies buying and selling exotic animals, places like Country Ark Exotics, Critter Country Animal Farm, or Vic's Exotics—all companies whose names I saw, over the course of fieldwork, advertised on people's jackets or vehicles. The next chapter describes one manner in which this exchange popularly occurs: at exotic animal auctions across the United States. While this chapter sought to explain how animals are first made lively capital, the next chapter examines auction exchange as a site and process in which animals' commodity status is performed and consolidated juridico-politically, socially, and materially.

Noah's Ark on
the Auction Block

Auctions serve as rites of passage for objects shrouded in ambiguity and uncertainty.
—Charles Smith, *Auctions*

These deviates are using our laws of freedom to attempt to enslave us. They are not trying to free animals. They are trying to ultimately force your surrender to socialism—total government control of every facet of your lives. While our sons and daughters and grandsons and granddaughters are fighting in the name of freedom throughout the world, there are those of evil, insidiously stealing our freedoms right from under us, more effectively than any army's bullets or terrorist bombs will ever do to our country.—Exotic animal owner's description of animal rights activists' protests against exotic pets, Pat Hoctor, "Editorial," *Animal Finder's Guide*

Like Abu Ghraib for tigers.—PETA writer's description of a tiger menagerie in Nevada, Jeff Mackey, "Victory: Authorities Pull License from Tiger Tormentor!," *The PETA Files: PETA's Official Blog*

MT. HOPE, OH
March 29, 2012, 9:00 a.m.

A series of country roads in Holmes County, Ohio, wind through mist, over and around rolling green hills dotted with leafless trees, plain two-story farmhouses, horses, and farm equipment, and finally deliver me to Mt. Hope's center: a four-way stop marked on opposing corners by Mrs. Yo-

FIGURE 2.1 Looking toward the Mt. Hope auction, Mt. Hope, Ohio (photograph by the author).

der's Kitchen and a small shop selling groceries, pizza, and ice cream. I drive straight through and immediately spot the auction on my left. A long gravel driveway ends in a football-field-sized parking lot, where I pull my dusty VW Golf alongside a row of trucks: F350s, one-ton Rams, full-sized Suburbans and Silverados. Some of the trucks' boxes are filled with cages stacked two or three high, and other trucks are pulling long horse trailers. There are license plates from Tennessee, Louisiana, Illinois, Indiana, and of course Ohio, and bumper stickers calling for "Palin for President" and variously supporting the Tea Party, Ron Paul, the National Rifle Association, American troops, Rick Santorum, and Operation Iraqi Freedom. It is early in the morning on the first day of the auction, which officially starts at noon. The parking lot is not even a quarter full, but there are already more than a hundred trucks parked, and dozens more idle in line to register and deliver their goods (figure 2.1).

They are not typical auction items like antique divans, works of art, or self-storage units. This event is officially known as the Mid Ohio Alternative Bird and Animal Sale. In Mt. Hope, for three days, three times per year, people from across the United States gather to buy and sell exotic animals

Chapter Two

to stock their petting zoos, private ranches, backyards, and living rooms. Trucks unload cage after cage, box after box, and trailer after trailer of exotic animals: insects, reptiles, snakes, parrots, monkeys, camels, and zebras— "We've got zebras from five states!" the auctioneer at Mt. Hope later crowed into his microphone. As one auction poster boasts: "If it was on Noah's ark, chances are we have it here." This was not the first or last reference I heard to Noah's ark.

Under the recently passed Senate Bill (SB) 310, Ohio auctions are no longer permitted to sell "dangerous wild animals" (Ohio State Legislature 2013), including large predators like wild cats (cougars, tigers, and lynxes) and bears (although auctions in a few other states can and do sell these species, as I witnessed). But anyone at this Ohio auction can sell anything else as long as the corresponding permits are secured, and in some cases, namely, when the animal is an endangered species, with the stipulation that the animal is not transported across state lines. These simple requirements are more than many other states require; Nevada, Alabama, and Idaho, among others, do not regulate exotic animal ownership at all (see map 2.1). The Mt. Hope auction I am about to enter is one of a handful of auctions that operate across the United States in those states where regulation permits such sale and ownership.

From January to May 2012, I crisscrossed the United States on interstates to attend five of these auctions: the Triple W Alternative Livestock and Exotic Bird Auction in Cookeville, Tennessee; the Kalona Exotic Animal Sale in Kalona, Iowa; the Mid Ohio Alternative Bird and Animal Sale in Mt. Hope, Ohio; the Lolli Brothers Livestock Market Exotic Sale in Macon, Missouri; and the Kifaru Exotic Animal Auction in Lampasas, Texas (map 2.1 and table 2.1). Although many of these auctions began operating as long ago as the 1940s, they all started selling exotic animals only around the 1980s and 1990s. The first dedicated exotic animal auctions can only be traced back to the 1970s, although it is likely the odd exotic animal—a parrot or a lizard—turned up at regular auctions far earlier than that. Many of the auctions are family run. All are located in or on the outskirts of small towns. Most of them are dedicated to livestock or horse sales year-round and only transform themselves into exotic animal auctions periodically.

At each auction I conducted what geographer Jan Penrose (2003) calls in her research on rodeos "spectator observation." This meant attending the auctions as an audience member from open to close and observing con-

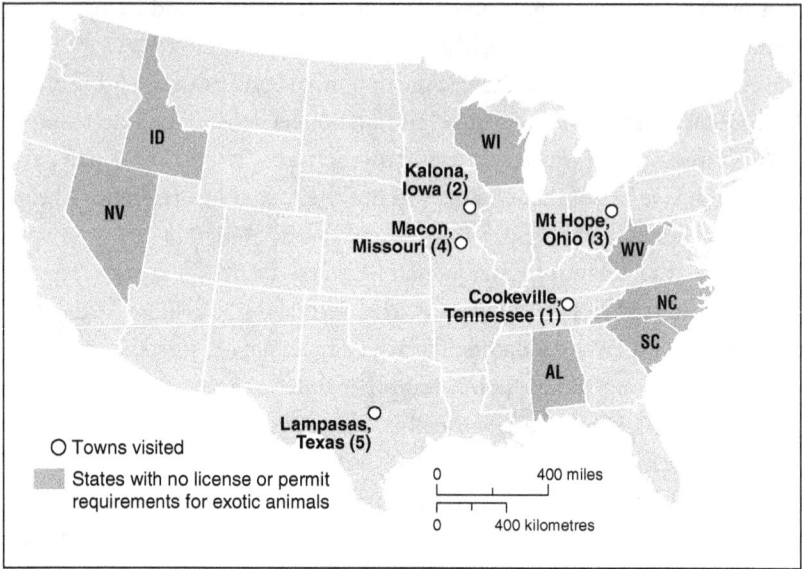

MAP 2.1 US exotic animal auction research sites. State permit requirements shown are at the time of research (map by Eric Leinberger).

versations, gestures, and flows of animals in and out of the ring, as well as investigating the buildings and grounds around the auction ring, including areas of loading and unloading and storage. I also carried out multiple casual conversations and a handful of informational interviews with auction goers, buyers, sellers, auction owners, and "ring men," who mill about the auction ring with the animals and register and drum up bids from the audience. At each auction I paid particular attention to the process of auctioning—how the auction was laid out spatially; how the bidding operated; who was buying, selling, and auctioneering—as well as sociopolitical activities and, finally, what animals were being exchanged, at what prices, and what features of the animals were emphasized in attempts to achieve the highest price possible. With this research, my aim was in part to investigate the function of auctions within the exotic pet trade. But I was also interested in what the auction process and performance suggest about what mode of life is central to the lively capital of the global exotic pet trade. How do animals appear in the auction ring as they are bought and sold? What does this reveal about the relationship between animal fetishism and commodity fetishism?

Table 2.1 Auctions attended in 2012

	Auction	Location	Times per Year	Date Attended
1	Triple W Alternative Livestock and Exotic Bird Auction	Cookeville, TN	4	February 29–March 3
2	Kalona Exotic Animal Sale	Kalona, IA	4	March 23–24
3	Mid Ohio Alternative Bird and Animal Sale	Mt. Hope, OH	3	March 29–31
4	Lolli Bros Livestock Market Exotic Sale	Macon, MO	5–6	April 11–14
5	Kifaru Exotic Animal Auction	Lampasas, TX	About 1 per month	May 5–6

Note: Numbers at left correspond to map 2.1.

Lively capital and the relations that sustain it are precisely what is performed in the auction ring again and again, and so the research was fruitful. Open to the public, the microcosmic auction offers a peek into embodied, intimate relations that are often closeted from view (Geismar 2008). These auctions offered unparalleled access to an otherwise dispersed and even furtive economy and to the spaces and spectacles of exotic animal exchange. Primarily, this research uncovered a critical site for the legitimation and reproduction of exotic pet commodities. Auctions are key institutions for conferring legitimacy on what have been variously called "contested" or "liminal" commodities—commodities whose status as such is in flux.[1] Auctions do so through two main mechanisms that I will elaborate shortly. First, they are collective centers of calculation, drawing together goods, people, and information and facilitating exchange of commodities as well as political information, petitions, and lobbying efforts. Second, in front of this gathered collective, the auction process is a spectacle in which repeated interactions between bodies, gestures, and words actually perform that in which they are trafficking: in this case, the pet—an encounterable, controllable, and individual animal. When this particular commodity is under threat, as is currently the case in many jurisdictions across North America, the auction is a means of reasserting its commodity form.

In Mt. Hope, after I have gathered my things from the car—audio recorder, notebook, snacks (no camera as they are prohibited at all auctions for reasons I will discuss shortly)—I walk toward the entrance: a small wooden booth where auction goers are paying entrance fees (five dollars per day) in exchange for attendee stickers before entering through a gap in the high chain-link gate. Near the entrance a tall man with a long white ponytail and wearing a black baseball cap, denim jeans, and a denim jacket is attaching a five-by-three-foot sign to the chain link fence surrounding the auction area. In bold red capital letters at the top it reads: "THIS IS STILL AMERICA!!" Following, in slightly smaller red capitals:

> STOP GOVERNOR KASICH AND JACK HANNA'S ANIMAL ERADICA-TION PLAN. TELL THE HUMANE SOCIETY OF THE US TO GO HOME AND TAKE THEIR SENATE BILL 310 WITH THEM. OHIO DOESN'T NEED THEIR ANIMAL "RIGHTS" LEGISLATION.

The rest is in black capitals:

> SUPPORT OHIO'S ANIMAL INDUSTRY. JOIN THE OHIO ASSOCIATION OF ANIMAL OWNERS. PROTECTING ANIMAL OWNERS' RIGHTS IN OHIO FOR OVER 22 YEARS. MEMBERSHIP APPLICATIONS AND ADDI-TIONAL INFORMATION HERE.

The sponsoring association—the Ohio Association of Animal Owners—is setting up a booth area beneath the sign, with a table of papers, brochures, donation jars, and T-shirts and long-sleeved sweatshirts in black, green, orange and gray, emblazoned with the group's logo and the slogan "Protecting PEOPLE'S Rights." This pro–animal ownership paraphernalia is part of an effort to rebrand the industry, or counteract the idea that exotic pets are dangerous or inappropriate. With a dollar I buy a red bumper sticker with white writing: "SAVE A SKUNK. ROAD KILL AN ACTIVIST." Great, I think. Just the place to be strolling around looking like you do not belong.

By this point—my third auction—I am aware that my Canadian accent, my appearance (plain clothes, sneakers), and my constant scribbling of notes in a book mark me not only as an outsider but also as "activisty," and much more worthy of suspicion in this context. While adults at the auctions regularly eyed me with distrust, children would directly ask, in tones of wonder or puzzlement, "Where are you from?" or "Whatcha writin'?" I felt and looked as out of place at the auctions as I did at rural markets in southern Mexico. The degree to which I was labeled as an outsider may have been similar, but the form that "not belonging" took was quite different. At the auctions, I experienced outright hostility at times. Many people would not speak to me at all, or if they did, they avoided eye contact and my questions. I had to be delicate in my conversation and inquiry because auction goers are alert to undercover "animal rights people" who "try and say the animals are being abused," a woman later complained to me as she held "Mia Marie," a one-year-old pet spider monkey wearing a pink dress over her dark, baby-soft fur. Photographs and film are banned at all auctions, but people were reluctant to tell me why until finally an auction owner confirmed that photos are banned because of the suspicion of undercover agents, of "animal activists waiting until something bad happens or goes wrong and then snapping a picture and putting it up all over the internet and newspapers." I never attempted to contravene this rule.

In Mt. Hope, after purchasing my three-day entrance pass, I walk toward the cluster of buildings. There is an almost soccer-field-sized open-air barn-style warehouse into which dozens of cages of birds (the ones who can tolerate cool temperatures) are being unloaded from trailer beds and stacked several cages high in row after row. A permanent auction building about the size of a high school gymnasium, complete with an auction ring surrounded by bleacher-style seating climbing up to the high roof, is attached to another barn full of stalls that empty into corridors leading in and out of the barn and toward the entrance to the auction ring. Larger animals like camels, zebras, and exotic cattle (often called "African hoofstock") are being unloaded into the stalls. Finally, several impermanent trailers are set up as "warm rooms" in which animals requiring warmer temperatures are kept in small cages and Tupperware containers: snakes, tortoises, birds, sugar gliders. A section of one trailer is roped off with a "DO NOT ENTER" sign, reserved for animals deemed more dangerous, primarily kinkajous and some snakes.

Even outside the auction, the noise and smells are overwhelming. There are so many different animal sounds that not one is distinguishable; they all meld into a complete and constant racket. Already dozens of people are milling around, setting up random items for sale (not auction) around the auction yard: welcome mats, belts, pet products, rusty car parts, art, and more. In the open yard, a couple walks toward me, both the man and the woman in matching black hooded sweatshirts that say in white capital letters on the front: PETA. I watch, intrigued and shocked by their bold display of animal rights in such a hostile environment, and then understanding dawns as they approach close enough that the fine print underneath becomes readable: not

"People for the Ethical Treatment of Animals," but "People Eating Tasty Animals." Michael Doughney registered the domain name peta.org in 1995 to host the website People Eating Tasty Animals, which proclaims itself "a resource for those who enjoy eating meat, wearing fur and leather, hunting and the fruits of scientific research." The "official" PETA (People for the Ethical Treatment of Animals; hereafter PETA) sued Doughney for trademark infringement, trademark dilution, and cybersquatting. This court battle over and between the PETAs was initially heard in 2001 in the US District Court for the Eastern District of Virginia, which granted summary judgment to PETA but did not require People Eating Tasty Animals to cover PETA's legal fees. Both PETAs cross-appealed, and so the case moved to the US Court of Appeals Fourth Circuit, which affirmed the districts court's ruling because it held that Doughney's action was not malicious (US Court of Appeals 2001).

It is challenging to write about these groups involved in animal politics—that is, the two PETAs, or both animal rights activists and animal owners—without caricaturing them. Both groups are obviously heterogeneous. The category "exotic animal owners" includes Siberian tiger owners and owners of millions of exotic birds kept as pets in the United States (American Veterinary Medical Association [AVMA] 2018), and individual pet owners often exert a curious mix of what Yi Fu Tuan (1984) called "affection and dominance" toward their pets. Equally, under the banner "animal rights activist" might fall people ranging from direct action protesters to SPCA animal adopters and many pet owners who also exhibit both dominance and affection toward their pets. Despite this heterogeneity and even some degree of shared love of animals, there is often heated conflict between exotic animal owners and animal rights activists, particularly in debate about exotic pets. Dividing lines tend to be black and white, and few people seem willing to inhabit a middle ground. Extremes mark the debate, and, as this chapter's second and third epigraphs demonstrate, each group uses hyperbolic rhetoric to advance its position. Each group claims to "know" animals and animals' well-being, and with no way to ask animals themselves, debates often feel at an impasse.

It was due in part to the bitterness of such disputes that I was unable in my auction research to carry out official, formal interviews. I did have dozens of conversations in which a high degree of informality was necessary to retain the participation of the person with whom I was speaking. These casual conversations were at times informative, although people were cagey about the details of where and how they purchased various pets. This was especially true at the Mt. Hope auction. A few months before I attended it, an event had occurred a mere hundred kilometers away that changed the tone of exotic pet ownership in Ohio and beyond, perhaps permanently.

For decades Terry Thompson—a sixty-two-year-old former Harley bike shop owner, drag boat racer, aspiring blues guitarist, gun aficionado, pilot, and Vietnam vet—operated a private animal farm on his seventy-three-acre property near Zanesville, in east-central Ohio, a local legend called T's Wild Kingdom. In animal pens scattered on the patio and driveway resided all manner of large animals: monkeys, cougars, wolves, grizzly bears. A black leopard lived in Thompson's basement, and two tigers and two lion cubs in the garage. While his was a private collection, Thompson did on occasion use his animals for commercial and public purposes: he rented Heidi Klum tiger cubs to pose with; did a photo shoot with Newt Gingrich; and appeared on Rachel Ray's television show as an animal trainer. Thompson was questioned several times about the conditions in which he kept the animals, but he held permits for all of them and was operating entirely under the law (at the time Ohio had among the weakest state exotic animal regulation in the United States), so when Thompson's home was raided in 2008, it was not for his "wild kingdom" but for 133 seized guns, a few of which were illegally possessed (Heath 2012). After serving a year and a day in federal prison, Thompson was released, but his wife had left him, and he was in significant debt. On October 18, 2011, Thompson cut open several cages, freed fifty-six of his animals, and then shot himself.

Sheriff Matt Lutz's office started receiving phone calls at around 5:30 p.m. that day: wild animals were loose on a road that runs under Interstate 70. Neighbors spotted a black bear and then a lion wandering around Thompson's property. The county sheriff's deputies and other law enforcement officials came to the property first with handguns and later with assault rifles, and over two days they shot forty-nine of the fifty-six released animals. One other animal has never been found—a macaque, which is presumed to have died at the hands of a big cat—and six animals were tranquilized and brought to a quarantine area of the Columbus Zoo. Various species of monkeys found alive in cages inside the Thompson house were similarly quarantined. In a rare common voice, animal rights groups and exotic animal owners both criticized the mass killing. But Sheriff Lutz (in Bishop and

Williams 2011) maintained, "We could not have animals running loose in the county." He went on: "We are not talking about your normal everyday house cat or dog. These are 300-pound Bengal tigers that we have had to put down." A thirty-foot-deep hole was dug on the farm, and on a wet Wednesday afternoon, the animals were lifted by the backhoe load and dropped into the hole, where dirt was dragged over them in the mass grave. Jack Hanna (in Nir 2012), former director of the Columbus Zoo and former exotic animal owner who now advocates stricter laws for animal ownership, arousing the animosity of many animal owners, helped at the scene and described the slaughter as "beyond any horror." "It was like Noah's ark crashed," he said.

In the year after the event, SB 310, which was already in the works to tighten restrictions on animal ownership, was pushed through in Ohio. But even with new legislation, no one has any idea how many wild kingdoms like Thompson's exist, and many animal owners are refusing to apply for permits. It is also difficult to answer the question of where and how Thompson acquired his animals. In a manner typical of the exotic pet trade, the animals came from multiple sources: Thompson was given some people's unwanted animals as "rescues"; he reportedly sometimes traded for them with guns; and he purchased many of them at exotic animal auctions, including the Mid Ohio Alternative Bird and Animal Sale.

It is worth diverting to this tale for two reasons. First, the ending of T's Wild Kingdom provides a vivid demonstration of animals' disposability, especially when their lives become uncontrollable. Lively capital must be controllable or it becomes untenable. Second, whether or not this event actually was instrumental in pushing through the already pending legislation to ban some exotic animals from ownership, many exotic animal owners perceive it as the nail in the coffin of "free" animal ownership in Ohio, and even in the United States more broadly. Some animal owners are so convinced of this event's significance, and of the extent to which "animal rightists" (the term some animal owners use for animal rights activists) will go to ban exotic animals, that they publicly claim that animal rightists murdered Terry Thompson, staged it as a suicide, and released his animals, all in an attempt to further the animal rightist agenda and, ultimately, turn everyone in the United States into a vegan socialist or "veganarchist" (see Heath 2012; Hoctor 2013a, 2013b). The degree of hostility between animal owners and animal rightists is at a fever pitch. During fieldwork I heard multiple

Chapter Two

stories of property damage, death threats, and violence on both sides of the conflict.

Several US states—Nevada, Missouri, Indiana, and Tennessee, among others—are indeed either considering banning ownership of certain exotic pets or have already set these bans in motion. Across Canada, a similar story is playing out. In 2009, British Columbia banned more than one thousand species of exotic animals from ownership and sale after a man's Siberian tiger killed his girlfriend in the town of 100 Mile House, British Columbia; Ontario has begun considering strengthening its minimal exotic animal regulation in the aftermath of a tiger killing his owner, who was at the time, in the worst kind of irony, the president of the Canadian Exotic Animal Owners Association. The tragic deaths of two young boys, asphyxiated by an escaped python while sleeping above an exotic pet shop in New Brunswick, sparked similar debates in that province in mid-2013.

Exotic pets in Canada and the United States are thus what legal theorist Margaret Radin (1996) calls "contested commodities": things whose ability to be legitimately bought and sold is the subject of controversy and moral and political debate. In a similar vein, geographer Bronwyn Parry (2012), writing about the uneven acceptability of commodified human body parts and derivatives, observes that "unstable" commodities like body parts, or in this case exotic pets, engender "curious markets" (214). This is certainly the case for exotic pets. Curious is where it starts for the markets I observed, and across North America, people's ability to buy, sell, and own exotic pets is increasingly indefinite. However, unlike human lives, bodies, or parts, the default, and even unspoken, status for exotic animals is that they *are* commodifiable. Exotic pet bans do not replace laws that explicitly authorized exotic animal ownership. Rather, the bans typically fill what was previously a legal void. In the absence of these bans, the prevailing assumption is that animals are legitimately and perpetually commodifiable, similar to Jesse Goldstein's (2013) formulation of *terra economica*: land that is always potentially ready to be owned or capitalized. Live native wild animals may not be owned and traded because they are already the state's property (although they are subject to "harvest," and their dead bodies may be owned and, in some cases, bought and sold). Exotic animals, in contrast, are assumed ownable and tradable, although their ownability and tradability are increasingly contentious.

In such an unstable political and legal context, auctions play a critical role—one that exceeds their function as a site of simple exchange between buyers and sellers—within the larger economy of the global exotic pet trade and its production of a particular kind of lively capital. At the exotic animal auction, control over animals is deployed in multiple ways—bodily, spatial, behavioral—to facilitate exchange and to reconsolidate the relations that support lively capital.[2] In this sense, the auction space itself is generative of the kind of market exchanges that take place, and the auction process is a means of reenacting and affirming the very mode of lively capital that is first produced through capture—animal life that is individual, controllable, and encounterable. For contested commodities, auctions play an especially crucial role as a collective and even exuberant performance of sociopolitical-economic legitimation of particular commodities. Especially in the space-time before potential illegalization (when markets are potentially in the process of being *unmade*), the auction event becomes a critical space for negotiating price and enacting sociopolitical alliances intended to resist illegalization. Among the sparse scholarship on auctions, this is nowhere better recognized than in Charles Smith's (1989) account of auctions, which he argues are an ideal mode of exchange for objects whose commodity status and value are uncertain.

According to Smith, commodities can be communally sanctioned and legitimized through the auction process. Echoing Baudrillard's (1981) claim that the auction is a legitimizing force, Smith (1989, 79) writes: "Objects are reborn in auctions. They acquire new values, new owners, and often new definitions. . . . For these new identities to be accepted as legitimate, they must be seen as having a communal sanction. It is this search for legitimacy that underlies the communal character of auctions." Throughout history, therefore, auctions have often been a means of establishing the value of commodities that are ambiguously valued or even not otherwise deemed salable (DeLyser, Sheehan, and Curtis 2004). For an object whose commodity status may soon end, whether due to lack of economic value or to illegalization and/or other forms of regulation, the auction event can be a reassertion of not only the object's life as capital but also its commodifiability—its ability to be bought and sold.

This legitimation of the exotic pet's commodifiability occurs in two primary ways at the auction. First, exotic animal auctions are collective, both in the sense of being constituted by multiple entities and social groups, and, relatedly, in the material sense of actively collecting objects and people into one place. As "centres of calculation" (Latour 1987), auctions depend on things from afar being rendered mobile enough that they can be transported to the center (the context for Latour's writing was a scientific lab in a colonial center, for example); kept stable so that they can be moved around with no disruption, distortion, or decay; and made combinable so that they can be aggregated and cumulated. Auctions' role as centers of calculation is not scientific but economic: to facilitate calculations that enable the exchange of commodities. This involves disentangling entities, drawing them together in a central space, and undertaking an assessment or calculation before redispersing them again. This is precisely what geographer Trevor Barnes (2008, 1435) has described as the function of markets, which "are produced on the ground by an enormous effort bringing together, and aligning multiple agents in order that market calculation occurs." Auctions are in this way collective calculative devices par excellence. Auctions have a strong spatial momentum, as markets do. In the case of the exotic pet trade, they bring together otherwise sparsely distributed and far-flung animals and people, enable assessments of animal bodies and behaviors, and calculate a price, before hurling the animals back out in new directions. In addition, auctions serve as a space for forging social collectivity and exchanging political information and animal care resources, such as discussing how to deal with a sick reptile, or handing out flyers protesting an exotic pet ban bill.

The second main way that auctions reaffirm and consolidate the lively capital form is through an embodied spectacle in the auction ring, in which animals are performed as exotic pet commodities, enacted as individual, encounterable, and controllable. To "perform" here, building from feminist and socioeconomic scholarship, means, at its most basic, to bring forth and shape the world. For socioeconomic theorists, markets, like gender, are performative effects, meaning that they are continually enacted through different arrangements of ideas, actions, devices, objects, technologies, experts, and so on. At the auction, these socio-material arrangements include the series of gestures and calls between auctioneer, ring men, and bidders; the interactions between ring men and the animals in the ring; as well as the whole constellation of technologies—electronic auction boards, microphones, and so on—information, and histories that are mashed together at the auction. Auction space itself is part of this performance: the layout of the bleacher seating, the ring, the cages, the means by which the animal is forced through auction space, delivered from one owner to another. The action plays out in front of an audience that includes not necessarily only buyers and sellers but likely also members of the public for whom auctions are a source of entertainment, especially if the "objects" being exchanged are themselves a spectacle, like giraffes or baboons or cougars.

The performative function of auctions is strengthened through the spatially and temporally repetitious nature of their spectacle. Repetition is a key way that performances work, or have an effect, the point being not just that a performance's effect is strengthened through repetition but that reiteration is how that effect is established, anew, over and over again (Butler 2010). The auction performance itself is almost mind-numbingly repetitive—an animal dragged out, ridden on, pushed out the door, one after another, at auction after auction. There is also repetition for individual animals, who may be sold upwards of a dozen times over their lives. I watched several of the same individual animals be auctioned at more than one auction in the space of a few months. In this sense the repetitive nature of the auction performance can be seen as an integral aspect of reiterating human-animal relations and political-economic relations, namely, the status of the animal as a commodity, the supremacy of human use values, and the erasure of animals' histories—as commodities and as complex social beings.

MACON, MO
April 12, 2012, morning

"You don't have any cowboy boots!" a young boy says to me when I sit down at the back of the bleachers for the second day of the Lolli Brothers Livestock Market Exotic Sale in Macon (pronounced like "bacon"), Missouri. He's looking down, shocked, at my sneakers. "Where's your cowboy boots?" He is about five years old. He repeats everything the auctioneer says, but shouts it. His daddy's buying a buffalo, he tells me. The walls around us are plastered in beef ads—"It's what's for dinner." Below, a baby capuchin monkey, leashed and diapered and wearing a pink, sparkly floral dress, is perched on an older woman's shoulder. Someone asks her, "Is that the same one you got down here last year?" She nods. The monkey chitters, high-pitched. The boy is telling me how fast buffalo can run. We are having a hard time understanding each other, due to our different accents—his strongly southern. He yells "Hurry up!" at the auctioneer. He is impatient for the buffalo. Finally, one comes out. The boy leans back and crosses his small cowboy boots, satisfied. "I love him," he says.

The auction ring has been filled with sand to make it less slippery for hooves. There are a lot of ranchers in the audience today, unsurprising given that this morning is dedicated to exotic cattle. But the buffalo are not working animals; they are for petting zoos. The auctioneer continues to pepper the audience with evidence of good disposition: "Used in displays!" he booms. "This one's from a pettin' zoo!" "She'll come across the pasture for a nugget!" The boy shouts enthusiastically along with the auctioneer. "Sold to buyer 667," the auctioneer reports. "667!" the boy cries jubilantly. The agitated buffalo slip and skitter in the bare patches of the ring. In an unsettling coincidence, the book I have brought along is *The Last Report on the Miracles at Little No Horse*, a fictional work by Louise Erdrich. I am reading a section about the US government's slaughter of the buffalo in the late 1800s, about how, Erdrich writes, the buffalo mourned each other and eventually committed suicide because "they saw the end of things . . . and did not care to live." Later, I search the internet for any references to buffalo suicide, to no avail. But in the moment, her words speak hauntingly to the scene before me at the auction.

Lolli Brothers had one of the widest collections of animals I observed (see examples in table 2.2), and auctioneers frequently guaranteed "you won't see another one like this again" for some species of boas and pythons. Many of these animals will be familiar to anyone who follows popular media because they have been in the news over recent years as "celebrity pets," a status that enhances the animals' appeal among these celebrities' fans. Baby Luv, Paris Hilton's pet kinkajou (illegally smuggled into LA), bit her; Justin Bieber's pet capuchin monkey, Mally, was recently confiscated in Germany; and two Mikes—Tyson and Jackson—owned Bengal tigers, among other animals.

Later in the afternoon that day, the Lolli Brothers barn has become hot and crowded. Several people in the stands hold baby monkeys and baboons in overalls and dresses drinking pop out of straws. One baboon is having its diaper changed. Hundreds of auction goers lean forward in their seats each time another round of cages are wheeled out into the auction ring for sale. Now, out comes a lineup of beige plastic cages, like medium-sized dog kennels, stacked two on two, and spectators strain to glimpse the cages' occupants. A murmur of excitement ripples through the audience when long, thin fingers slip out through some cages' cracks. Half a dozen adult spider monkeys are on the auction block, in cages they cannot stand up in.

Table 2.2 Examples of species and sale prices from Lolli Brothers Exotic Sale, September 2011

General Category	Species	Price Range (US$)
"Pet shop birds"	African grey parrot	300–500
	Rose-breasted cockatoo	450–675
	Umbrella cockatoo	925
	Blue-and-gold macaw	300–675
	Harlequin macaw	550
	Scarlet macaw	350–1,450
"Nursery animals"	Arctic fox	400–550
	Coatimundi	50–400
	Fennec fox	1,600–1,700
	Kinkajou	500–1,400
	Sulcatta tortoise	70–575
	Two-toed sloth	3,000
Monkeys	Capuchin	2,100–6,500
	Celebes macaque	1,000
	Olive baboon	1,000
	Spider	7,500
	Vervet	3,600
Cats	Bobcat	100–1,000
	Bengal tiger	50–550
	Caracal	1,700
	Cougar	585–675
	Lion cub	700
Camels	Adult male dromedary	3,450–3,800
	Adult female dromedary	3,000–8,500
Zebras	Adult male	2,500–3,700
	Adult female	3,300–5,500

Source: Lolli Brothers, September 2011 Exotic Sales Report, 2011, accessed April 12, 2012, www.lollibros.com/LinkClick.aspx?fileticket=KmoYNoJXQ5Q%3d&tabid=68.

They are brought forth as "breeding pairs," and none of them have "been on display," meaning that they are not monkeys for interaction or performance. One particular nineteen-year-old female, the auctioneer reports, lost her right eye eight years ago, and had two middle fingers half amputated. "But all her lady parts work," he assures the crowd. She sells for $2,500, a far cry from the baby monkeys' prices. These older monkeys are all "proven breeders," no longer small and docile enough for display, or to be cuddled, diapered, and clothed in pink dresses and denim overalls. Their value is as breed-stock, producing babies to be sold for $10,000 at next year's auction, or maybe the one in Texas or Ohio.

These breeding monkeys have reproductive value, offering the promise of future lively capital. They are the exception, however. Most exotic pets are forbidden from reproducing. Their value is found, rather, in the three specific features of "life itself" that are the target of and produced by commodification, three features that consistently brought a higher price for auctioned animals, as I detail in the next section following an explanation of the auction process. First, unlike some other more standardized commodities, exotic pet life is worth more if it is essentially nonreplicable: individualized and rare. Second, commodity life should be docile and controllable. For example, moments of animals behaving "out of turn," such as a zebra braying loudly, or a monkey pulling hair, were always met by raucous audience laughter and delight, but the deployment of a technique of control quickly followed, such as swatting the zebra with a stick to move it out of the ring, or placing the monkey on a leash. Finally, an exotic pet's life must be encounterable. The animal must be available for intimate and embodied encounters with its owner. This is perhaps the most central quality of lively capital, in that it relies on controllability and liveliness. Controllable, individual, and encounterable—this is the nature of lively capital in the global exotic pet trade. And auction space is constructed to facilitate its enactment.

TRIPLE W ALTERNATIVE LIVESTOCK AND EXOTIC BIRD AUCTION, COOKEVILLE, TN
February 29, 2012, 9:00 a.m.

The auction is poised to begin in a huge, barnlike structure that is dark and cavernous (figure 2.2). The smell immediately upon entering is a mix of manure, sawdust, and hay. Faint sounds of various animals can be heard,

FIGURE 2.2 The morning of opening day at the Triple W auction in Cookeville, Tennessee (photograph by the author).

but many of them come from outside the barn, where people crowd around owners with their chittering monkeys and talking parrots. Inside, it is, at least for now, pretty quiet. There is open seating in bleachers, off to each side of the reserved seating, which costs more money for its front-and-center vantage point, facing the auction ring. The air is thick with sawdust that is being layered down in the ring, despite water being sprayed on it to keep it from spreading. High horizontal orange safety bars frame off the ring, which is shaped like a horseshoe with sides bent outward into a wide U.

Before taking a seat for the auction, I wander the barn's labyrinth of stalls. You can do so along the ground, where you can look a skittish camel or zebra in the eye, or from the catwalk, where you can gaze down at the maze of animals below. The stalls are fairly small—maybe six feet by six feet—and some of them house families of animals that will likely soon be separated through an auction bidding process known as "choice," where the bidder with the highest bid is authorized to choose his or her preferred animal among the bunch in the auction ring. The family may be sold one by one all to the same bidder, but it is more likely that it will be split up. Animals are also sometimes auctioned off as a group, where the auctioneer will announce, for example, "ten times the money," which means that all ten animals are for sale as a group, and so whatever bid is settled on will be multiplied by ten for the final price. I observed this technique used mainly for small caged birds and exotic poultry. Animals are for the most part auctioned off individually.

The zebra family I am looking at now—a mother and two colts—might very well be the one that later today I will see enter the auction ring as a family and leave, separated, with different owners. This zebra family has been transported from its previous home—likely a private ranch or petting zoo somewhere in the United States—to this auction, where it is further severed from its family in order to be reattached to a new location, owner, and other entities. In other words, first, living animals are materially and discursively detached from their contexts to become mobile before, second, new linkages can be established, and new connections made.[3] We have seen this two-part process before in this book, with the initial capture of wild animals and their enrollment in exotic pet trade circuits—although this first alienation is by far the most wrenching and crucial to lively capital, necessary before any later alienations can occur through exchange. For many of these auction animals, too, such disconnecting and reconnecting occurs multiple times within their lives, as they change owners and roles. For example, the same animal might labor at a petting zoo, then work in the film industry, then become a private pet, then work almost exclusively as a "breeder." Each shift in role is usually accompanied by a remaking of the animals' set of relations— new owners, new homes, new environments.

I find a seat off to the side in the public section, and the lights come on around the ring, illuminating the sawdust so it almost glows. Men with goatees and long moustaches dressed in cowboy hats and jeans, much of their clothing fabric camouflage print, enter the ring, move casually around the sawdust-covered ring floor, and lean against the safety rails. The auctioneer, a middle-aged man in a black cowboy hat who sits in a raised booth at the center of the ring, introduces them as the ring men—those registering bids from the audience and "handling" the animal(s) in the ring. Two women flank the auctioneer. They will record all of the sales by hand, taking notes. There is no computer system at this auction, although there are at most other auctions I attend. The audience begins as whistles and a few "Yeehaws!" ring out over the crowd.

The beginning of the auction is a bit anticlimactic, as the auctioneer starts with an eclectic mix of homemade birdhouses, taxidermied animals, and skulls. He moves quickly through the bids, and the audience continues to pour in and fill the seats. In the meantime, animals are being shuffled in stages from their stalls down the hallways of the barn toward the door that enters into the auction ring. Often the workers in charge of shepherding and prodding the animals around the stalls are younger men or boys, some of whom are possibly working their way up the auction labor ladder (see R. Wilkie 2010). The animals then wait in a holding stall before entering the ring, where the ring men interact with the animals, encouraging them to trot around and occasionally picking up chairs and play fighting with the horned animals. When an agitated bull enters the ring, the ring men climb the safety bars in a mock display of terror. They also attempt to ride many of the animals, and in some cases succeed, which drives up the price, especially for camels, which garner higher prices if they demonstrate a placid nature and the ability to take children and adults on their backs. ("At five dollars a ride, you'll get your money back quick!" one auctioneer remarks.) The ring men use a variety of implements—whips, swatters, chairs, leads, harnesses, their own bodies, prodders, and so on—to exercise control over the animals in the ring. For zebras, exotic cattle, and camels—animals that are not caged but run loose in the ring, although they likely have a halter or leash—I only ever observe male ring men. When the auction shifts to smaller caged animals—which can include large monkeys and wild cats—women occasionally participate in the ring, holding up small animals as they stroll back and forth across the ring, cuddling the animals and kissing them in front of the audience.

There are eleven men in the ring now. A clump of young exotic calves run out from behind the entrance door to the left of the auctioneer booth, and the door slams shut behind them. "Anybody with a backyard can have one," the auctioneer declares. "Your choice on anything in the ring!" These remarks are known as "fillers" in the auctioneer's chant: comments with which auctioneers "fill in time," inserting pieces of information to help potential buyers make up their minds. The auctioneer starts with a high bid and works his way down until someone in the audience waves a hand or jerks a head to register interest. The man in front of me is bidding, and he just gives a slight nod to indicate he wants in.

The bidding begins, and the bid climbs higher and higher. This is an "ascending-bid" auction, the most common kind of auction.[4] In it, the auctioneer raises the price successively until there is one bidder left, the winning bidder, who buys the object at the final bidding price. The ring men scan the audience for bids and shout "Ho!" and sometimes raise a fist when they see one. The ring men develop a relationship with specific bidders, and when there are only two or three bidders left, the ring men urge them on to continue bidding: "She's a real pretty one!" or "You won't regret this, Bob." When the calves are all auctioned off, they are herded out the exit door to the left of the auctioneer booth. The women on either side of the auctioneer register all the bids and the "lot numbers"—the label that is given to each animal, usually as a tag on the ear or a piece of paper attached to the animal's cage. The door shuts behind the animals, and it is the last the audience sees of them, unless you are one of their new owners. One of the calves is bought by someone in Florida, seven hundred miles away, but only forty miles away from the Floridian who is selling the calves.

The entire process from the time the animal enters the ring to when it leaves can run as long as several minutes, but this is only a blip in the longer process of loading, transporting, unloading, registering, and then, with a new owner, reloading, transporting, and unloading, perhaps halfway across the country. Within and beyond the ring, the auction house works quickly, but there are so many animals, and often time is taken to describe their special characteristics. This identification of specialness is expressed in backroom conversations between owners and prospective bidders, or in informational papers taped to cages that explain features of the animals, for example, what words a parrot knows ("No swear words" is a common refrain). The auctioneer further elaborates on these qualities while taking bids, all in an attempt to drive up the price. "The '05 model [born in 2005] loves pettin'!" the Triple W auctioneer exclaims about a camel that has a little blonde girl riding its back. A zebra that does not want to enter the ring, which is a bad sign, follows shortly after the camel. The auctioneer attempts to recover the zebra's value: "She's used to everything!" he says. But she does not sell: the owner wants $5,000 and bidding is stalled at $3,500. "If she ain't worth five thousand, there ain't a cow in Texas," the auctioneer quips.

At each auction I observe a similar process, logic, and spatial layout. The embodied performances staged between human and animal enroll devices such as whips, chairs, and prods. They occur in enclosed spaces such as cages, Tupperware containers, stalls, and the auction ring itself. From riding camels to placing parrots on shoulders, these performances are intended to emphasize and perform one or a combination of rarity or individuality, docility and controllability, and encounterability.

First, the rarity and individuality of the animal are highlighted through emphasis on its unique abilities, like speech and tricks. Auctioneers would also frequently make comments such as "You'd have the only ones like 'em!"; "We haven't sold one of those since . . . you tell me"; "You don't see these very often"; "The only one here like it!"; "You'd probably be the only person in ten counties to have one"; or "Probably only a thousand of them in the US." The animals that fetched the highest prices at the auction were endangered species, like two hyacinth macaws I will later see at the Kifaru auction in Texas, which sold for $6,000 each (and I was told that only a few years ago the going price was $20,000 for a breeding pair, or $15,000 for a chick). Or the critically endangered cotton-top tamarin pair I saw in a small cage, awaiting auction in Tennessee. They are one of the world's rarest primates, and their owner expected $5,000 for them. Rarity is not produced through the auction process but rather is emphasized repeatedly.

The most expensive animal I watched being sold was also the only one of its kind I saw auctioned: an adult giraffe, who could not be brought into the Ohio auction ring because it was too tall. The owner, a short older man wearing a black cowboy hat, a red plaid shirt, blue jeans, and leather boots, entered the ring instead. He spoke into a microphone about his object for sale: "He's very gentle. Has been down the city streets. Been in New York City walking down the city streets in Rockefeller place. Been in lots of movies, lots and lots of commercials. Very tall, very handsome. Nice park animal. Real gentle." The auctioneer chimed in: "And that's what it's all about—with the kids." He reminded the audience: "He'll haul 'im wherever you want to go. Anywhere in the country." The bidding stalled at $30,000, and the auctioneer paused, then interjected: "You'll never see another one like 'im!" A final flurry of bidding followed, and the winning bid stood at $32,000. The audience cheered. The giraffe was heading to West Virginia.

A second quality auctioneers and owners frequently mentioned, and which consistently appeared to drive up the price, concerns animals' docility, or tameness, and their controllability. This quality was emphasized by both auctioneers and sellers and was performed by the animals themselves. At the Lolli Brothers auction in Macon, for example, a woman from an exotic animal agency sold two identical male monitor lizards. She spoke into the mic from the audience as a woman in the ring held them up one after the other. Of the first, the owner claimed, "He's dog tame. He'll wear a harness. We use him for programs." This lizard sold for $235. The second lizard, she confessed, was less tame. He "gets nerved up," she said, but could be handled without gloves. This lizard sold for $175. In addition to direct claims of tameness, there were indirect means of conveying controllability, tameness, and docility. I learned that "bottle-fed" animals, like monkeys, camels, zebras, and so on, are considered much tamer and more docile than "mother-raised" animals, which are believed to have bonded less with humans and therefore retain a degree of "wildness" that makes them less controllable. This is also why bird chicks are much more valuable than adult birds. As a "bird expert" told me at Kifaru, "If you want a tame bird, you can't buy an adult; have to buy a baby and hand rear it, form a bond with it."

Animals were also directly enrolled in embodied performances of docility and controllability. These performances occurred in concert with the human owners, or with the ring men, and with technologies of control such as leashes, harnesses, prods, and crops (horse whips). Camels were forced to display tricks such as lying down on the ground, being ridden, or taking a bottle from young children to demonstrate their ability to interact gently with kids, a necessary feature for petting zoo animals. Servals, or medium-sized African wild cats, were paraded in front of the audience on leashes, pacing back and forth slowly across the ring under the close hand of their owners. In one especially crowd-pleasing performance in Mt. Hope, the owner of a massive buffalo from Tennessee rode him into the ring with a saddle. These are all examples of a spectacle of human domination, of a performance of animals' controllability in encounters.

Finally, and related to animals' controllability and docility, is animals' encounterability—that is, their ability to enter into tactile encounters with human beings—both owners and potentially paying customers. At auctions, many encounters were advertised, including the ability of an animal to be fed from a person's palm; an animal's willingness to be petted and touched by anyone (e.g., a monkey who "loves everyone!" or a parrot who will "go on anybody!" or a serval who will sleep on a bed with its owner) or "handled" (for snakes and spiders); and the willingness to be ridden (if a large animal) or to be carried on one's shoulder (if a bird), or to be played with without fear of aggressive behavior, for monkeys. These qualities were demonstrated over and over both in the auction ring and in the audience, where auction goers sat with their exotic pets, especially monkeys. In the ring, dinner-plate-sized tarantulas were removed from their Tupperware containers and placed into a ring man's palm. Boa constrictors and pythons were draped over ring men's shoulders, more than one at a time. Juvenile monkeys gave high fives. At one auction, two similar male African grey parrots sold back-to-back: the first, whose sign proclaimed he "wants to be petted," is "really friendly," and "has a vocabulary," sold for $750; the second, whose sign noted he "doesn't like to be petted," sold for $550. But the difference in price between "breeder" monkeys and "pet" monkeys provided one of the starkest contrasts of animals' price if they were or were not encounterable, as illustrated by my earlier recounting of the spider monkeys' sale in Macon.

The auction space and process enact and consolidate lively capital—individual, controllable, and encounterable—through repetitive performance. In the auction, human use values dominate. All the information, quips, and selling points that the auctioneers' rattle off to drive up exchange value are either about the animals' future potential exchange value, or their use value, often specifically their encounter value, for humans. It goes without saying, but nevertheless bears stressing, that nowhere mentioned, let alone emphasized, are animals' use values to each other, or for themselves—how they are siblings, kin, parents, children, workers, good at obtaining food for the community. Animals' use values for each other are rather suppressed and severed through the auction process. The auction performance is entirely about demonstrating the animals' companionability to humans, encounterability to humans—their softness to the touch, their amenability to their owners or to paying visitors at a petting zoo. The auction, then, is another site of active erasure of animals' histories of arrival, of the denial of animals' own needs. At the auction, animal fetishism is reenacted along with lively capital.

KIFARU EXOTIC ANIMAL AUCTION, TX
May 5, 2012, 9:00 a.m.

Another round of thunder and lightning storms had cracked open around me as I drove into Texas the previous night, compounding my feeling of dread about today and tomorrow, when I will attend my last auction, thirteen miles south of Lampasas on Highway 138. Now, driving to the auction on a cooler morning than yesterday, thanks to the previous night's storms, I scan the highway for the Kifaru Exotic Animal Auction. There are no more of the windmills and oil well pumpjacks that together incongruously

FIGURE 2.3 Roadside view of Kifaru Exotic Animal and Bird Auction, Lampasas, Texas (photograph by the author).

littered the landscape on the drive into central Texas, only the scrubby dry land of large private ranches with huge gates periodically marking their entrances. Suddenly Kifaru's sign flashes past me on my left (figure 2.3), and I have to turn around at the next crossroad to backtrack.

This auction is the only one I attend that exclusively sells exotic animals. Its owner, Jurgen Shulz, comes from an ancestral line of exotic animal traders: his grandfather worked as a collector and trader of exotic animals—chimps, monkeys, parrots—from West African ports to Germany in the late 1800s, and eventually worked capturing and shipping animals worldwide. Jurgen Shulz was born in South Africa in 1937, after his parents left Germany after World War I. He was trained early in capturing and training exotic animals, including giraffes, zebras, antelope, rhinos, and carnivores from all over Africa. In 1975, he formed the Shulz Company, which became well known for shipping animals to zoos and private individuals across the globe. He also worked for years with Hollywood film crews making movies in Africa. In 1992, he moved to Texas and purchased what became the Kifaru Exotic Animal Auction in Lampasas. Later today, during the auction, we will sit together for a time in conversation, interrupted occasionally by a passing auction goer, to whom Jurgen will tip his cowboy hat and direct a polite inquiry about a mother or other relative. For now, I once again pull my even dustier Golf next to a long line of pickups and prepare for my last auction.

There is no need for a warm room at Kifaru because the air temperature is already adequate for the tropical creatures. The animals awaiting sale—mostly birds—are lined up in rows in a covered but open-air area beside the barn stalls. Despite the heat, many of the birds shiver. I walk up and down the aisles of birds, who are in varying states of health. Some have picked at their feathers or those of another bird in their cage so that goose-pimpled flesh is exposed around their necks or backs. There are two stunning purple-blue macaws with yellow-rimmed eyes in a large cage. I later find out they are named Barbara and Bandit. They are incredibly rare hyacinth macaws, endangered birds that CITES lists in Appendix I, its highest level of international trade regulation. It is not surprising that Barbara and Bandit are being sold here; Kifaru specializes in birds. Its proximity to Mexico, where birds are popular pets, means that people may purchase parrots here and transport them into Mexico. This demand drives up bird prices in Texas. In addition to the hyacinths there are dozens of scarlet macaws as well as African greys, one of the most popular pet birds. One bird sits with a towel over its cage, and a sign requests the towel not be disturbed. Later, when I am watching the bidding, this cage comes out, and when the towel is removed, the African grey inside goes berserk, throwing himself at his cage walls and beating his wings furiously. It is a rare moment when the individuality of an animal is asserted amid the mass commotion of the auction space, and it recalls studies on African greys and how intelligent and emotional they are.

An American named Irene Pepperberg conducted prolonged research on African greys, including the now famous bird Alex, with whom she conducted research for thirty years before his death in 2007, at which point he was given an obituary in the *New York Times* (Carey 2007) and the *Economist* ("Alex the African Grey" 2007). Pepperberg bought Alex at a pet shop when he was around one year old, one bird with clipped wings among eight in a cage, and named him Alex, an acronym for "avian language experiment."

He lived out his days in a ten-foot-by-six-foot room with no windows, shared with other parrots. When Alex died he could speak more than 150 words, and Pepperberg (2008) claims her tests illustrated he had the cognitive intelligence of a five-year-old human and the emotional intelligence of a two-year-old. (Another African grey, N'kisi, has a vocabulary of more than 950 words. Upon meeting Jane Goodall after having seen a photo of her with chimpanzees, he famously asked her: "Got a chimp?") Their ability to speak and what is considered a "gentle nature" have made African greys one of the most popular pets in the United States.[5]

The capture from the wild to serve the pet trade has decimated African grey populations.[6] The International Union for Conservation of Nature lists them as endangered, and they became a CITES Appendix I species in 2017 (after having been listed as an Appendix II species since 1981, during which time, as an Appendix II species, they could be traded internationally for commercial purposes but their export required a permit). According to BirdLife International (2020), data suggest that up to 21 percent of the global population are being taken from the wild annually, primarily for the pet trade, with the total number of birds extracted from the wild from 1982 to 2001 potentially more than one million.

The costs of this trade go beyond defaunation. Once captured, parrots experience a host of negative effects. Their cognitive and emotional capabilities, which make them desirable pets in the first place, may also make them especially susceptible to developing stereotypies: abnormal, repetitive, unvarying, and functionless behaviors that are often performed by captive animals and are considered an indication of poor welfare. For parrots, stereotypies include spot picking, in which a bird will repeatedly touch the tip or side of the bill to a particular spot, either an object or a body part, or route tracing, in which a bird will follow a precise and invariable route within its cage (Engebretson 2006). I observed many such behaviors at the auctions.

Seated on the hard bleachers at Kifaru as the agitated African grey is wheeled off-stage, I remember how a month earlier, at the Lolli Brothers auction, after eleven hours of watching hundreds of birds—African greys, macaws, parakeets, cockatiels, and on and on—auctioned off, many plucked down to goose-pimpled skin, wings clipped, pacing in their tiny cages layered with excrement-covered newspaper, I left the auction in a daze. I was exhausted, totally overwhelmed, and on the verge of tears. I drove the ten minutes back to the state park where I was camping. At the time, April, it

FIGURE 2.4 Flying geese at sunset, Long Branch State Park, Missouri (photograph by the author).

was empty, but I imagined it would be popular in the summertime, surrounded by tall, grassy fields that slope toward a lake. As I sat down at the picnic table in the last of the day's light, I heard a rush of beating wings. A long, wavery V of geese flew into view and out over the silvery lake, quickly fading to flecks against the pale pink sky (figure 2.4).

As I watched the flock of birds disappear, the contrast with my day at the auction could not have been more striking. Exotic animal owners assert that they should have the "freedom" to own these animals, and they exert this at auctions. But their freedom to buy and sell and own animals depends on animals' lack of freedom. The auction, like the exotic pet form more broadly, has as its condition and product the subordination of the animal body to human control. The animal body that generates the highest price is a docile, controllable one, and the performance of lively capital in the auction ring is a performance of human dominance—a human riding a camel, forcing it into particular spaces, to act in particular ways. The moment of sale reifies the power relation in which the human owner is dominant and the animal subordinate. This relation exists before the auctions, of course, but the auctions are a critical site within which it is reinstituted, both aggregately and abstractly, and in a concrete, fleshy way for the individual animals who are commodified in the auction space, alienated from their previous relations and entered into new relations with new owners, new homes. On the auction block, animals appear thinglike, divested of these previous contexts, divorced from their histories of human production, as in the classical conception of commodity fetishism, but also, maybe more profoundly, divested of their histories of socio-ecological reproduction, of the complex networks that first gave them life and sustained them. Commodity fetishism and animal fetishism combine in the moment of auction exchange to produce the thinglike bit of lively capital—an object treated as if it has a life of its own, and an animal treated as if it has no life of its own.

There is a feeling of relentlessness at the exotic animal auctions. The seemingly endless chain of animals onto and off the auction stage, the breathless auctioneer chatter, the background racket of dozens of animal calls—lively capital here begins to seem like an impenetrable, unstoppable force. And yet there are attempts to undo animals' commodity status and rebuild their lives outside the cage. Around the world, sanctuaries, like the one where Darwin lives, take in former exotic pets and guarantee they will not be sold again. These animals remain captive, though, and do not regain the full expression of lives of their own. Currently, the possibility of a life of their own for former exotic pets is reserved for animals whose commodification is interrupted before they leave their countries of origin, and who are brought to rehabilitation facilities. As we will see in the next chapter, however, even at these facilities, animal fetishism is not easily undone.

Crafting the Unencounterable Animal

Stevie squats hunched between his knees on the cement floor and glares up at me with enormous black eyes that have no whites. His blond fur sticks up in wet spikes, and the sunlight catches the tufts from behind so that each ends in a golden point of light. Stevie seems to hate being wet. His long, bone-thin arms whip around his body, rubbing crossly at the fur around his ribs, his skull, and the long white whiskers around his chin. He chitters softly, rapidly, high-pitched. *Cheat-cheat-cheat*, it sounds like. Stevie is only a juvenile spider monkey, but he has already been cheated. As I explained in chapter 1, wild spider monkeys live their lives high in the trees. Stevie's mother was likely shot dead out of the canopy when he was a baby, and he was removed from her fallen body. A leash went around Stevie's neck, and it did not come off until he arrived at ARCAS, a wildlife rehabilitation center in northern Guatemala (maps 1.1 and 3.1) where animals are brought when they are caught being trafficked as pets. This is where I am now, scrubbing the floor of Stevie's cage—his home shared with four other juvenile spider monkeys. Thirty seconds earlier he had tapped me on the shoulder, so I sprayed him (figure 3.1) because, along with cleaning cages and preparing and delivering food, my job is to instill in Stevie a deep fear of humans, to make him unencounterable to humans. According to ARCAS's directors, staff, and veterinarians, aversion to human contact is a prerequisite for Stevie's release. It is, I'm told, his best chance at survival beyond the walls of his cage.

FIGURE 3.1 Stevie just after being sprayed (photograph by the author).

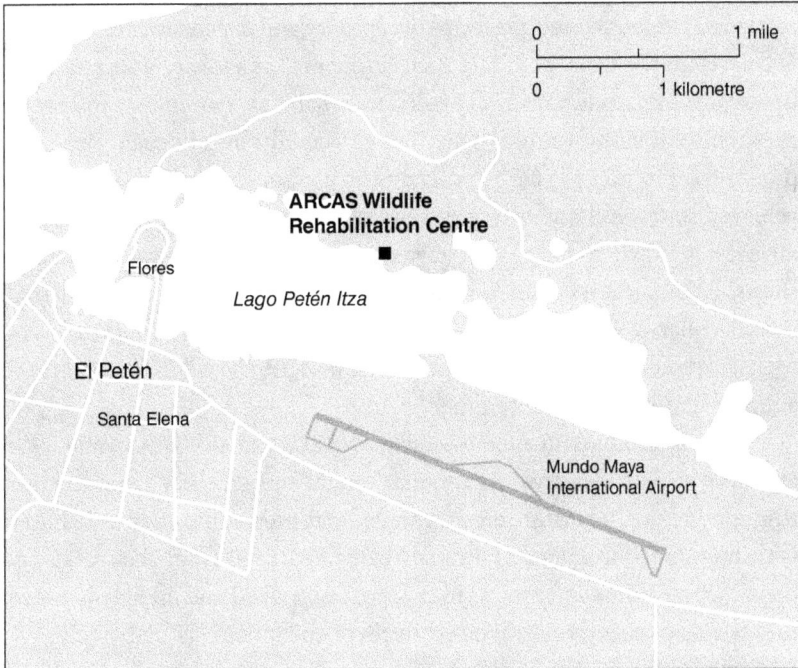

MAP 3.1 ARCAS, El Petén, Guatemala (map by Eric Leinberger).

Two general assumptions underpin this goal of making unencounterable. First, rehabilitators assume that if animals have contact with humans after their release, they are at high risk of being killed or recaptured and recommodified (Martinez 2011; Megan 2011; Morales 2011). Second, rehabilitation's general goal is to instill "natural" behaviors in animals, which is taken to mean undoing the anthropomorphisms they acquired while moving through exotic pet trade circuits. Fear of humans is considered an element of animals' natural disposition. The spatial expression of this vision of what is natural is a terrain in which humans and wild animals are segregated and do not meet. Rehabilitation's "naturalizing" approach—complete with its separation of humans and animals and its misanthropic distrust of humans—is at the heart of ARCAS's practices. But its efficacy is unproven. Few studies follow released animals to determine their survival rates (Martinez 2011), and what studies do exist have found generally low rates of release success.[1]

The approach is also paradoxical. As the anthropologist Juno Salazar Parreñas (2018) shows in her ethnographic research on orangutan rehabilitation in Borneo, in practice, the goal of instilling autonomy in animals is carried out through multiple forms of captivity and dependence on humans. She develops the concept of "arrested autonomy" as a way of understanding how wildlife rehabilitators try to cultivate rehabilitant animals' capacity for autonomy while these animals are living in conditions of dependence. The promise of autonomy is perpetually on the horizon as a potential but never achieved state. And not only is this promised autonomous condition unrealized, but efforts to promote it have their own violent effects, as Parreñas shows. Rehabilitators adopt a hands-off approach to injurious, even lethal, meetings between orangutans—meetings that occur more frequently and with less protection than in the open forest because the wildlife centers have a higher density of orangutans per hectare.

Making animals unencounterable at ARCAS is similarly paradoxical and even violent. Cultivating animals' unencounterability is undertaken through various forms of forced, tactile, and even intensified encounters with humans—for example, animals being captured from their cage and bound with various constraints in order to be weighed and medically tested. I myself ambivalently participated in these encounters as I labored at ARCAS for thirty straight days inside the center's spider monkey cages, as well as with scarlet macaws, owls, hawks, falcons, tortoises, turtles, crocodiles,

Chapter Three

green parrots, guans, and military macaws. I experienced the clear tension within the project of crafting an unencounterable animal through prolonged, tactile encounters. On the one hand, the type of encounter between human and rehabilitant animal at ARCAS is strictly policed—the emphasis being on enacting unpleasant and sometimes even punishing encounters between humans and juvenile and adult animals, especially the monkeys. On the other hand, there is no avoiding the role of human caregivers at ARCAS: to provide animals with the replacement supports for what they would themselves work to secure in the wild through socio-ecological reproductive networks, such as food, water, shelter, entertainment, love, affection, and so on. The demand for these supports is never-ending, and staff and volunteers spend long days feeding and caring for animals and cleaning cages.

Alongside conducting participant-observation work in this capacity, to get a sense of ARCAS's methods and rationale, I carried out semistructured interviews with ARCAS employees, including the director and head veterinarian, the assistant director/vet, the volunteer coordinators, and primatologists, as well as dozens of conversations with volunteers. But my day-to-day work with ARCAS's animals figures most prominently in this chapter. The purpose of my labor and ARCAS's main mission are twofold. First, ARCAS seeks to build an animal's capacity for a wild life—to equip the animal physically and mentally for a life outside the cage. (To be sure, achieving this first project depends on other conservation practices—to ensure, for example, that there is adequate habitat outside the cage to which animals can return.) Second, rehabilitation aims to undo an animal's status as lively capital—dismantle the individual, encounterable, controllable life this book has shown to be produced through capture, bodily enclosure, and commodification.

This means wildlife rehabilitators working with former exotic pets attempt to divest animals of their dependence on human inputs and of their pet-like behaviors. Recall how lively capital is formed: animals are severed from their familial, societal, and ecological networks and are entangled with human-provided supports so that they are dependent (unable to reproduce themselves in daily ways) and encounterable. Rehabilitation's goal is the opposite: to destroy these ties to humans, reentangle animals with their former networks, and make them unencounterable—rebuild their lives of their own. Producing an unencounterable animal is attempted through the deployment of what I call "misanthropic practices," signaling less the goal of making animals misanthropic, and more the misanthropic stance of rehabilitators, who by and large have little to no faith in humans' aggregate ability to live well with wild animals. Misanthropic practices are actions and routines designed to instill in animals fear of humans, underpinned by rehabilitators' certainty that contact with human beings puts animals at high risk of death, suffering, and recapture or recommodification. This potentially recommodified future looms over rehabilitation practice, motivating efforts to craft an unencounterable animal.

A starting point for this chapter, then, is that wildlife rehabilitation in this case is a type of decommodification, an attempt to unmake lively capital. Decommodification is a process that destroys the commodity form (i.e., its ability to be exchanged), even if only temporarily, and "reduces the scope and influence of the market in everyday life" (Vail 2010, 310), in this case, the everyday life of the animal. Decommodification, then, involves the removal of an entity from circuits of exchange, which is precisely what rehabilitation aims to do. This is not to say that if formerly traded animals are rehabilitated and released from a wildlife center, they are not and will never again be commodities. There are markets in which wild animals may be commodified, like ecosystem services, or form the conditions for market exchanges, as in ecotourism. Nor is rehabilitation itself isolated from the market. Although wildlife rehab centers are usually nonprofit institutions, they are also often part of an industry referred to as "voluntourism" or commercial volunteer tourism, an industry with distinct neocolonial contours (Vrasti 2013; Parreñas 2016), as I will explain shortly. Finally, taking commodities apart, as I will show in this chapter, is perhaps more easily accomplished than taking animal fetishism apart. It is one thing to destroy the commodity form, to remove animals—at least temporarily—from commodity circuits. It is another matter entirely to rebuild animals' lives of their own, to reconnect them to their socio-ecological reproductive networks, particularly within an institution and process in which animals remain captive, or subject to bodily enclosure, even if this is with the best intentions.

Consistent with the rest of the book, my effort to understand rehabilitation's techniques and practices occurs in a specific "multispecies contact zone"—in this case, at ARCAS—and is directed toward developing a fuller picture of lively capital and its politics. So far this book has been about the creation and maintenance of lively capital embodied by dispossessed animals who are fetishized as commodities but also, more crucially for this book, as objects divested from their socio-ecological reproduction and the lives of their own, lives in which they craft and shape their own worlds. This chapter is about a process that attempts to undo lively capital and animal fetishism. Yet the practices this chapter traces are not divested of relations of power, and the fetishized animal does not disappear during and after decommodification. If, following Neil Smith (2008) and Haraway (1997), commodification is not denaturing but a production of nature, then it follows that decommodification, too, is a production of nature rather than a renaturing. So, what nature does rehabilitation produce, and what animal and human subjects? To answer this question and tune into the political forces in play in wildlife rehabilitation, the main body of this chapter unfolds through the narration of one day's work at ARCAS—a mundane day like any other.

ARCAS
A Day in Early November 2011, 6:30 a.m.

With a dull knife I chop long, julienned carrots and toss them by the handful into a cracked plastic bin full of pineapple cut like french fries, chunks of cantaloupe, unpeeled banana pieces, and slices of beets. It is the first day I will work in cage two, with a group of juvenile spider monkeys, and this is the first morning I spend preparing their breakfast. The beets bleed pink juice over the produce, and it leaks out through the cracks in the bin into a thin stream along the cement counter, dripping onto the floor. Yesterday millions of red ants moved in, and they now migrate through the kitchen in a pulsing river. It is important to keep an eye on these ants as you chop, should a tributary develop up your boot, your leg, and into your loose cotton pants. Even hours later you might be pricked as if with a burning match on your torso and find an ant pinned under your shirt.

Carefully, you can follow the surging ant river out of the kitchen, under locked chain-link doors, into a long, dark hallway lined with thick, black, dead-bolted metal doors, each leading to its own anteroom, and beyond each anteroom a cage (figure 3.2). But the industrious ants do not detour into any of the cages; they blow past the spider monkeys, the green parrots, the howler monkeys, the ocelots, the margays, the scarlet macaws, the turtles, the boa constrictor, the hawks, the owls, and the crocodiles. They especially do not stop for the tamanduas, genetic cousins to anteaters. You can follow

FIGURE 3.2 *Cuarantena* hallway (photograph by the author).

the ants past all of these caged animals, past the wildlife center, but you lose them in the thick forest.

In the mid-1990s ARCAS reportedly received up to 1,000 animals per year—monkeys, margays, crocodiles, kinkajous, and hundreds and hundreds of parrots—but that number has since decreased to an average of approximately 250 animals per year from 2014 to 2017. These animals, who technically are supposed to be native to Guatemala and not have left the country, can arrive at wildlife rehabilitation centers by two primary means. First, they can become unwanted pets—they grow too large or are too much work, or people move and can no longer care for them. Second, if they are illegally traded commodities, they may be confiscated. Most of the animals delivered to ARCAS are birds, but each year several monkeys arrive as well. There are often also large intercepted shipments of iguanas, among other animals (table 3.1).

Later in the month, I will interview ARCAS's director, who will explain to me the horrifying math involved in the 2008 shipment ARCAS received of 470 live iguanas being traded for food. The iguanas arrived in one container at ARCAS's Guatemala City office. More than 200 of them died getting there, due to asphyxiation. *Consejo Nacional de Areas Protegidas*, a Guatemalan government agency responsible for biodiversity and protected areas, decided to send the remaining live iguanas to ARCAS in Petén; 211 arrived alive. Many of the females who arrived were pregnant with anywhere between 40 and 60 eggs. ARCAS staff wanted to release the animals immediately before any more of them died, but because of an ongoing court case involving the man who had initially illegally transported the iguanas, the center could not release them right away. Instead, the iguanas were moved into the large parrot rehabilitation cage. But "they didn't eat. . . . They lost all their eggs. . . . And most of them died" (Martinez 2011). In the end, staff released 28 iguanas in total. But, as Martinez will remind me in the interview, "We're talking not just about the 450 iguanas." Tens of thousands of iguanas were potentially lost as eggs.

As the iguana case illustrates, when some animals arrive at ARCAS, the faster they are released the better. In the event that there are legal proceedings involved in the animals' confiscation, though, animals must remain at ARCAS until the court case is resolved, much to ARCAS staff's frustration. But most animals who arrive at ARCAS, if they are still alive, are kept on the

Table 3.1 Number of animals for selected species (not including species less commonly traded as pets) received by ARCAS in Petén and Guatemala City, 2008–2017

Common Name	2008	2009	2010	2011	2012	2013	2014	2015	2016	2017	Total
Howler monkeys	11	8	11	12	8	9	7	7	11	14	98
Spider monkeys	21	14	7	6	19	15	7	15	11	10	125
Coatimundi	12	8	4	5	6	8	5	3	7	7	65
Kinkajou	4	5	3	3	3	2	3	2	1	4	30
Tamandua	0	1	0	3	5	3	7	3	3	9	34
Margay	3	2	4	0	1	2	6	4	1	3	26
Ocelot	4	0	0	0	0	2	1	0	1	0	8
Red-fronted parrot/red-lored Amazon	59	101	43	32	49	44	98	27	26	11	490
White-fronted parrot	50	34	30	22	33	16	37	27	21	17	287
Scarlet macaw	14	10	21	16	6	11	9	13	5	7	112
White-crowned parrot	12	10	15	6	16	4	30	4	6	3	106
Aztec parakeet	7	12	10	6	2	0	0	1	0	0	38
Orange-fronted parakeet	0	4	4	6	1	0	0	0	0	1	16
Mealy parrot	9	8	13	3	9	9	8	6	5	1	71
Green macaw	0	0	0	3	0	0	0	0	0	0	3
Military macaw	0	0	5	0	0	3	2	1	1	1	13
Blue-and-gold macaw	0	0	2	0	0	0	0	0	0	1	3
Yellow-lored Amazon	0	0	0	2	0	0	0	0	0	0	2
Yellow-naped Amazon	2	0	7	0	3	5	1	0	2	6	26
Orange-chinned parakeet	0	0	0	0	0	0	4	2	0	0	6
Green parakeet	0	0	0	0	2	5	0	0	2	7	16
Olive-throated parakeet	0	0	0	0	0	3	7	12	2	8	32
Yellow-headed Amazon	0	0	0	0	0	0	1	2	0	1	4
Keel-billed toucan	1	1	0	2	0	3	1	4	3	2	17
Mesoamerican/red-eared/pond slider (turtle)	3	9	3	101	20	23	7	29	3	15	213
Morelet's crocodile	6	11	15	11	1	8	17	6	5	8	88
Boa	2	4	3	8	1	5	1	1	0	2	27
Furrowed wood turtle	2	6	8	3	0	4	0	3	7	1	34
(Green) iguana	13	470	646	2	5	3	10	4	3	3	1,159
(Spectacled) Caiman	4	1	2	0	0	0	0	0	0	1	8

Source: Compiled from ARCAS's annual reports, https://arcasguatemala.org/who-we-are/arcas-publications/.

premises and undergo a prolonged rehabilitation process. The length of time depends on the animal. For example, while reptiles can be released almost immediately, monkeys can take up to six years. If the animals are young and not too "humanized," their chances at rehabilitation are higher. But for animals who have already been living as pets for some time, the outlook is bleak. ARCAS (2010, 3) and other wildlife rehabilitators believe that these humanized "animals, once they are removed from their natural home, are biologically 'dead' and can never return to fulfill their rightful place in the ecosystem." Many of these animals are also psychologically and physically injured from years of abuse sustained from previous owners. These animals—as well as ones who do not begin to properly exhibit "wild" behaviors in the rehab process—are not released. Instead, they are kept as educational "ambassadors" at ARCAS. This means that they live out their days as permanent residents in cages in a separate section of ARCAS that is publicly accessible. In this area, close to the lake, visitors can wander cages of monkeys, alligators, birds, and wild cats—animals who will die in their cages—and read signs about their habitat and the risks the pet trade poses to their uncaptive kin (figure 3.3).

The rehabilitant animals, in contrast, are off-limits to visitors, meant to be isolated from too much human influence. These animals are unmade commodities and are no longer encounterable within exotic pet trade circuits, although they are encounterable to paying volunteers and paid workers. Their decommodification thus paradoxically involves a great deal of intense encounter with humans, most of whom come from wealthy countries to pay to work at ARCAS.

Several of these volunteers, myself included, are in the kitchen now, as I fill this leaky bin with sliced produce for Stevie and the other four juvenile spider monkeys in cage two. The monkeys receive ten pounds of juicy, ripe fruits and vegetables every morning and an armful of green leaves in the afternoon. They also receive dry dog biscuits every other day, for protein. The produce arrives on fruit-run days: Wednesdays and Saturdays. When word comes that the fruit has arrived, scrub brushes, trash bags, rakes, shovels, or whatever implements are being used are dropped. If the delivery is by boat, the group of volunteers and workers unfurls itself in an evenly spaced chain up the steep dirt stairs that are littered with roots down to the dock on Lago Petén Itza. Off the boat come crate after crate of bananas; bags of watermelons, carrots, cantaloupe, and beets with long, thick greens; and

FIGURE 3.3 An ARCAS sign warning people not to purchase exotic pets. It reads: "We are products of illegal trafficking. When we were transported illegally, we were hurt and suffered bone fractures and amputations. Some of us were pets for several years and believe we are humans, we became aggressive and we are no longer loved. They taught us how to talk, whistle and they cut our wings. Due to that we will never be free again" (translation by Natalia Perez, photograph by the author).

sacks of pineapples with heads spiky enough to draw blood. Up the chain go the sacks, bags, and crates, all the way up to the cages, where hundreds of animals are waiting for their next meal. If the delivery comes by truck, the workers and volunteers carry each crate, sack, and bag from the kitchen to the cages down a winding gravel path through the trees. The amount of food required is enormous—in less than a week more than sixty empty banana boxes accumulate outside of the kitchen (figure 3.4)—and it is only one aspect of the inputs required to sustain the animals, to replace what it is that they themselves would be working to receive from their socio-ecological reproductive networks in the wild. It is an incredible amount of work—hours and hours, day in and day out—to provide a bare-bones, often inadequate, replacement for these seemingly effortless wild networks.

FIGURE 3.4 A week's worth of banana crates (photograph by the author).

The most dangerous and unpleasant work, including working with the adult spider monkeys who are incredibly strong and can be aggressive, is assigned to the adult Guatemalan men who work at the center. But a willingness to undertake certain demanding, dangerous, and gross tasks around ARCAS—cleaning up bamboo roofing infested with scorpions and wasps, inching out on your belly onto chain-link roofing thirty feet in the air between metal poles to sweep debris off tarps, leveling out months' worth of "compost" (steamy, maggoty piles of animal feces, the solids removed from drains around the cages and center, food scraps, berry branches)—brings a degree of legitimacy and respect to volunteers who are willing to take them on. Like Parreñas (2016, 2018), through my research I became aware of how wildlife rehabilitation operates within a postcolonial and in some places postindustrial political economy in which manual labor may be celebrated and romanticized. This works alongside racial and class hierarchies at ARCAS. In general, those who could afford to pay to work at the center were predominantly white women from developed countries, while those who were paid to work were Guatemalans.

Crafting the Unencounterable Animal

It is important to situate ARCAS in a broader political-economic and postcolonial context in which the volunteer industry is ascendant. Guatemala in particular has a strong program for international commercial volunteers (see Brown 2009; Vrasti 2013). These programs cannot be separated from their "imperial undertones" (Brown 2009, 14)—for example, the manner in which they mimic the missionary work that was instrumental in colonial expansion—and Guatemala's colonial history and contemporary positioning (see Galeano 1997; Nelson 1999). In the past few decades, conservationist and environmental politics in the region have been especially loaded with imperial weight. ARCAS was born into this context. A group of Guatemalans established ARCAS in 1989 as a Guatemalan NGO, catalyzed by the lack of an adequate wildlife rescue center to receive confiscated animals as stipulated in CITES, to which the Guatemalan government has been a signatory since 1980. The Columbus Zoo and an individual US citizen's fund-raising drive provided the funding for the rescue center in Petén. International volunteers' fees—which they pay to "help" and to have interactions with animals they would not otherwise be able to encounter—provide most of ARCAS's financial maintenance.

The volunteers predominantly come to Guatemala from the United Kingdom, the United States, and Germany, although another of the center's largest volunteer groups in terms of number of volunteers (as opposed to number of volunteer days) is from within Guatemala itself, usually Guatemala City, where the country's wealth is concentrated.[2] The volunteers pay around US$140 per week (which covers their food and basic lodging) and work upward of seven hours per day, seven days a week. Markers of volunteers' raced and classed privilege are evident at ARCAS, with volunteers frequently complaining about the food ("The animals eat better than we do!" one young Swiss woman complained to me), undertaking less dangerous tasks than the Guatemalan workers, and taking days off for excursions to Tikal and other tourist attractions. At ARCAS, being "tough" with the animals—not being there to just "pet a baby monkey"—generates a lot of social capital among volunteers and between volunteers and staff. Many wildlife rehabilitation volunteers confess to wanting to take a monkey home, even though they know this is way off limits. Volunteers quickly learn to separate themselves from those "other" volunteers who seek merely to "hold a baby monkey," thereby attempting to legitimate their objectives and their relationship to animals.

At the center I was confronted with my own implication in these networks, forces, and desires, having flown to Guatemala, paid the fees, gazed in awe at the baby monkeys, and slept poorly for fear of snakes and scorpions. I could shake the latter, but not my privilege to come and go, and to choose to pay to labor and conduct research there. At the same time, the organization is committed to improving the lives of hundreds of animals. Alongside my ambivalence about my own embodied labor with ARCAS animals, I was and remain ambivalent about the wider context within which my labor was embedded.

7:30 a.m.

Putting aside the monkey's bin of fruit and vegetables for later, I grab a sparsely bristled scrub brush and enter the deafening racket of the parrot cage. The floor of the cage is coated in a continually regenerating thin layer of green mold whose dampness can sneak into the lungs of birds. Millennia of high-flying lifestyles have not prepared them for such moisture. As ARCAS's head veterinarian (Morales 2011) says to me: "Parrots don't live at this height. They live up there. And that's fifty meters of difference; there's a difference in humidity, speed of air, density, amount of light. So we need to . . . avoid everything that's down here that affects them, because they're meant to be up there."

As part of this effort, parrot cage floors are only sprayed sparingly once per day. On hands and knees we scrub the mold every morning. I kneel until I cannot feel my legs. All of the muscles in my wrists, forearms, upper arms, shoulders, and back burn from the exertion of scrubbing. The birds still get sick. Later that day, I will hold one feather-light green parakeet from another cage in my hands, my thumb and pointer finger around its throbbing neck, as a veterinarian forces a long tube down its beak. It has not eaten in days and does not move, one leg dangling awkwardly through the bottom of the cage. The bird will go back in the cage and be found dead the next morning.

The parrots' change in altitude upon capture exemplifies a wider shift in the relations that support their lives. Prior to capture, parrots' lives are constituted by kinship, ecological, and social ties. As I described in chapter 1, capture severs these ties to make the parrot mobile and to form lively capital, a new life in which a parrot most often lives alone in a cage, is dependent on its owner for food, water, and stimulus, and is perpetually encounterable. The parrot's former life, the wild life, is diminished through this shift in relations—the parrot becomes thinglike, enclosed. At ARCAS, where rehabilitators are seeking to rebuild wild lives for the rehabilitant parrots, parrots exist in a liminal state between lively capital and a wild life. They begin to socialize with other parrots again, but they remain down at the forest floor, enclosed, and dependent on humans as opposed to engaging in the work of their own reproduction. Their liminal lives at ARCAS demonstrate the extent to which the relations in captivity are barely adequate—if not inadequate—for their survival, let alone any full expression of their social lives.

In the parrot cage I turn back to the moldy floor and am greeted by a fat splat of bird poop on my shoulder and hand. I am working in a cage that contains about a dozen smaller cages, each housing two to five young parrots. Their breakfasts alternate each day between servings of cut-up bananas and cut-up oranges, and they receive wild berries and a water change in the afternoon. If they mature, remain healthy (which is challenging because the cramped and damp conditions mean disease spreads quickly, and their immune systems are weak), and become strong enough to fly, they will eventually transition to a cage with no smaller cages, where all the parrots zip around the enclosure together. In these cages, volunteers string up the berries on the cage walls so that the birds can approximate the sensation of eating while clinging to branches. Eventually, the birds will be moved to an even larger enclosure, the size of a small barn, in which they will gain more strength flying. They are expected to fly away from humans, and if they fly toward them they will not be released.

At all of these stages, the volunteers working with the parrots are strictly prohibited from speaking in their presence. Parrots readily adopt sounds, including human speech. ARCAS staff members believe that parrots' human speech inhibits their ability to make mating sounds and communicate with each other in the wild. If a bird learns any human words, even *hola*, it will not be released (see figure 3.5; "If they can speak, they cannot be free!!!"). "Good morning, preciouses!" I would say in my head each morning on entering the parrot cage.

The tension and misanthropic assumptions in rehabilitation thought and practice are evident here. The goal at ARCAS, and among wildlife rehabilitators more broadly (see Guy, Curnoe, and Banks 2014), is to craft rehabilitant animals who demonstrably avoid humans before they are released,

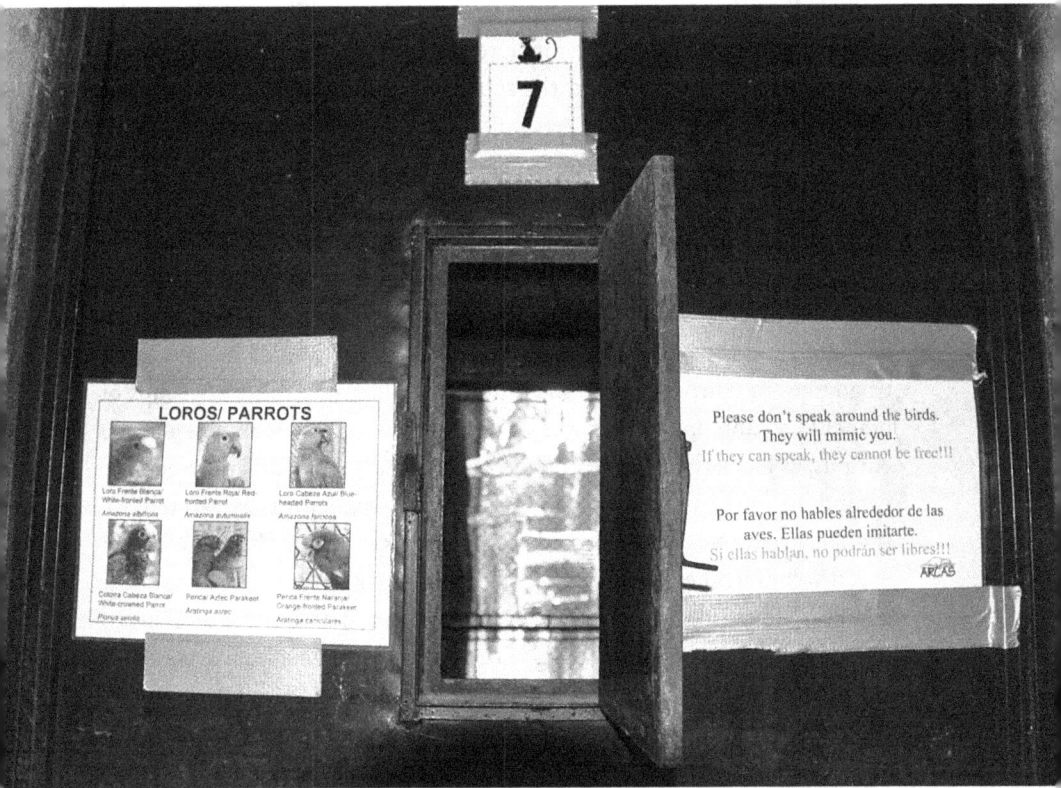

FIGURE 3.5 Sign on parrot cage door (photograph by the author).

animals who are not, in the language of rehabilitators, "habituated." This is based on the assumption that released animals will fare better if they do not encounter humans, who would put them at risk of death or recapture. A study of vervet monkeys' release in South Africa following their rehabilitation indicated that indeed, some former pet monkeys did seek out humans once released (Guy, Stone, and Curnoe 2011). Of the ten radio-collared monkeys (out of a total of thirty-one members of the troop), one was euthanized after it raided a house for food, and it was speculated that one other monkey died at the hands of humans (after his radio collar was found in a pit toilet). The authors conclude, based on this evidence, that humans pose a "serious threat to the released monkeys" (Guy, Stone, and Curnoe 2011, 313). The veracity of the misanthropic assumption aside, though, more profound are its consequences. The misanthropic practices that are deployed as a result embody lingering power relations at work within rehabilitation. In seeking to craft an unencounterable animal, rehabilitation actually reperforms the dominant human subject and the subordinate animal object. Nowhere is this more evident than in the rehabilitation process for monkeys.

8:30 a.m.

After leaving the parrot cage, I have my first meeting with Stevie and the four other juvenile spider monkeys in cage two—about ten feet wide, twenty feet long, and fifteen feet high to a tarped chain-link roof. They are squatting knees to chins, huddled shoulder to shoulder in two tight groups on branches strung up between the chain-link walls. They look down at me, curious, as I lock the door behind me, leaving the bin of fruit and vegetables behind me in the anteroom. I am nervous and wonder if they can tell. My trainer, Brian,[3] has accompanied me in the cage, and as the more experienced volunteer, he is in charge of the hose. The hose wielder should be in charge—the master of the proceedings—not timid and awed, as I am today, on my first occasion working with monkeys. Instead, I am armed with cleaning supplies—a broom, a scrub brush, and a bottle of diluted chlorine disinfectant that I will shortly put to use on the concrete half walls and feces-littered floor that slopes down to a trench and drain grate, all the while trying to avoid being bombed with more poop from the monkeys whizzing around overhead.

Entering the cage, Brian holds up the hose and jabs the nozzle toward the monkeys, whom he deems to be sitting too close to us. They shrink away automatically, chittering, and leap high onto the walls. The blond one, Stevie (although he is no longer supposed to have a name), I have already heard about. He does not flee with the others but scowls back at us with what looks like defiance or even belligerence. Brian sprays Stevie directly with water, and he retreats with the others to the wall, glaring down at us. With a free hand he wipes water droplets off his body with furious gestures. Brian tells me how important it is to make sure the monkeys stay far away from us while we spend the next hour cleaning their cage. This is one of many rules that attempt to establish and maintain our distance and dominance. We must always be two volunteers, and it is preferable that one of us be male. We should stand tall. We should shout at the monkeys and spray them if they come near us, especially if they touch us or steal any piece of our equipment as we clean the cage, the food boards, and the water tub and then, finally, feed them and refill their water, twice each day. The monkeys eat everything with a focused relish (figures 3.6 and 3.7), and only when they are eating can I relax and turn my back without risk of hair pulling, cage escapes, hose theft, tank top strap yanking, or even once, to my total surprise, getting a wedgie. All those things really happened in the following weeks, and Stevie was the perpetrator nearly every time.

These monkeys in cage two arrived at ARCAS as babies and as such proceeded through a period of being nurtured by surrogate "parents": long-term human workers and volunteers at ARCAS who provide affection, snuggling, care, and food to the babies (figure 3.8). But as they grew, the baby monkeys began to be separated from their human caretakers. They were placed into a small cage with the other young monkeys with whom they will be expected to form a troop. At this stage the young monkeys were still cared for by a surrogate parent, but the surrogate did not spend as much time with the monkeys and was less proximate. In my last three days at ARCAS, I was given this (much sought after) position of taking care of another generation of baby spider monkeys, the beginnings of a new aspirational troop. Three of them had recently been moved into a concrete cage: a five-by-five-by-five-foot box with two chain-link walls. Previously, each spider monkey had been the "child" of a human surrogate parent, so these monkeys, while timid, lacked the fear of humans that had already been instilled in the juvenile monkeys in cage two.

The monkeys were not much bigger than a newborn human baby, with large dark eyes set in small faces; when they brushed up against my bare arm, I was surprised by how soft their fur was. They buried their heads in the food I gave them—sweet powdered Nestle infant cereal called Nestum, mixed with water—then looked up at me with faces white with paste. One time as I pulled the bowl of Nestum away before it was completely licked clean, one monkey reached out quickly and grabbed my arm. For a few seconds I gazed down, transfixed by the sight of its long, skinny fingers wrapped around my forearm. When I looked up at its face, it looked back at me assertively, even fiercely. How confusing it would be for these young monkeys, I thought, raised lovingly by a human surrogate, then having all contact cut off, and, finally, being subject to a program of harsh treatment, sometimes bordering on violent interactions—now in the name of "tough love"—meant to induce fear and flight, like that in which I was involved

FIGURE 3.6 Juvenile spider monkeys eating breakfast
(photograph by the author).

with the juvenile monkeys. All the while, humans continue to provide food
and water and to regularly encounter the monkeys in cages, even as the
monkeys are supposed to be developing into autonomous and unencounterable entities. One of ARCAS's primatologists, Megan[4] (2011), explained to me
that it amounts to an imperfect art of trying to balance the "right level of
human maternal care to give to orphan primates so that they are still wild
and can still successfully reproduce in the wild, but also if you don't give
them enough they won't survive as babies."

Eventually this young troop will outgrow its cage, as Stevie did. The
young monkeys will lose their names, as Stevie was supposed to do. At this

Chapter Three

FIGURE 3.7 Five juvenile spider monkeys in cage two
(photograph by the author).

FIGURE 3.8 ARCAS primatologist with a baby howler monkey
(photograph by the author).

point, the point at which I meet Stevie, all human contact is meant to cease,
as the monkeys are encouraged to bond with each other. As the monkeys
move from smaller cages to larger and larger ones, they are expected to begin
exhibiting more wild behaviors, such as remaining high on the cage walls,
grooming each other, and avoiding their human caretakers. The same AR-
CAS primatologist (Megan 2011) will later explain to me these criteria for the
monkeys' release:

> Are they able to cope with a really large cage with a lot of trees, or are
> they sitting on the floor? Spider monkeys live their entire life in the
> trees. They don't ever go to the ground. And going to the ground can
> kill them, easily, because all their predators are on the ground. So if they
> go down to the ground a lot, there's no point in releasing them, because
> they're going to be eaten straight away, or caught by a human! . . . Are
> they more inclined to stay in the trees or are they trying to go to the
> fence, trying to touch ropes, because those are the makings of traps and

hunter snares and things like that. If they're going for things like that there's no point in releasing them because they're just going to end up back in the situation we tried to save them from.

Eventually, like the parrots, the monkeys will graduate into a large, thickly vegetated enclosure that most closely resembles their natural habitat. At this point they will be exposed to flares and firecrackers, blanks will be shot at them, and fences will be electrified to ensure that they are fearful of both people and fencing. These monkeys will have spent the first stages of their lives—the formative bonding time of childhood—being cuddled by a human surrogate parent and fed by humans. Now they will be expected to shrink away from humans, to paradoxically prove their readiness for autonomy by demonstrating total submission to years of dehumanization, and adequate fear of and subjection to human subjects. In my month in cage two, I brandished the hose with discomfort. I was hesitant to punish animals for "acting out" and asserting their independence, but also did not want to cultivate behaviors in the monkeys that would one day prevent them from being released.

It is, of course, a real risk that released animals will be recommodified, recaptured, and caged or leashed anew ("the situations we tried to save them from"). Exotic pets' decommodification is impermanent. This point is consistent with socioeconomic scholarship on many commodities. Decommodified objects can be recuperated as a whole back into exchange—an antique chair is found in an attic and restored to be sold at an auction. Or former commodities like ships or cell phones are taken apart, and any potentially valuable components are repurposed. Either way, the decommodified object enters into a new commodity phase.[5] But the lingering commodifiability of animal life—the never completely extinguished commodity life of former exotic pets—is somewhat different in two ways. First, lively capital lives on in material-semiotic ways in the bodies and behaviors of decommodified animals: leash scars, learned behaviors, trauma etched into bodies and memories. An exotic pet cannot be tidily dismantled as a commodity, unlike a computer that can be disassembled into hundreds of parts.

Second, animal life in general remains perpetually commodifiable. The broader and dominant discursive framing of animal-as-resource, animal-as-subordinate, creates a condition of possibility for animals' enclosure, their enrollment into circuits of capital. Animals' status as lively capital is arguably unextinguishable under these circumstances. So for animal commodities, or what Rhoda Wilkie (2005) calls "sentient commodities," the potential for recommodification is ever-present. In her research on cattle ranching and the relationships that farmers form with their farm animals, Wilkie finds that often, especially on smaller farms like hobby farms, farmers begin to view particular cows as individuals, even giving them names. For Wilkie (2005, 218) this more "humanised and individualised style of human-animal interaction" represents a degree of decommodification, whose most pronounced expression is in the pet cow. She writes, however, that even these individualized and, according to her, decommodified animals may be sold again. Wilkie's assertion that the commodity status of livestock is not fixed (decommodified cows may at any point be recommodified) is an important one. It points to how in capitalism animals are, in the absence of laws specifying otherwise, always commodifiable: always "commodities-in-waiting" (Parry 2008).

Further, unlike Wilkie's cows, which she argues are decommodified through a *strengthening* of affective ties with humans, of the "concerned attachments" that are expressed in practices of companionship and naming, the sentient commodities of the exotic pet trade are decommodified through a *divestment* of their ties to humans. This process, like the process of initially cultivating the encounterable animal—lively capital—can be broadly conceived as one of entanglement and disentanglement. This is also consistent with recent thinking about commodification and decommodification of things like ships and e-waste. But again, the kinds of relations being severed and formed in ship making and ship breaking are different than those under construction and destruction in the exotic pet trade. As sentient, social, and alive, wild animals always exist within supporting networks: ecological, social, familial. It is these networks from which the animal is severed in order to create the encounterable, controllable, and individual exotic pet commodity life. Rehabilitation is an attempt to rebuild the relationships and skills animals will require after release. Workers and volunteers feed the animals foods they would eat in the wild; encourage them to form troops, mating pairs, and flocks; and attempt to instill in them the capacities necessary for survival beyond their cage walls. These include skills of movement (flight, acrobatics), food acquisition, and sociality. After release, the animals are expected to reentangle themselves in the networks from which they were originally extracted. At the same time, rehabilitation attempts

Chapter Three

to sever the animal from the relations that sustained lively capital, including the almost total dependence on captors that characterizes any captive life. Animals who were dependent on human beings are trained to fear and avoid them. The challenge as a rehabilitator is to do so while acting in no uncertain terms as a captor, crafting the unencounterable animal through intimate and prolonged encounters with the rehabilitant.

The rest of my own day wrestling with this paradox is spent doing chores like cleaning drain grates, scrubbing more cages, assisting the veterinarians, then after lunch returning to the cages for the second round of feeding and cleaning before dinner. The volunteers and workers eat fresh tortillas and beans in the same covered open-air dining room but at separate tables, as the sky around us darkens and the shrieks and calls of hundreds of animals trail off with the sun.

8:00 p.m.

There is a last task before bed, and it is done in the dark. A few days into my month at ARCAS, I began working with two white owls who had arrived at ARCAS as chicks. They live together in a concrete cage between two large parrot cages. Their enclosure is about six feet deep, four feet wide, and five feet high, with two tree branches jammed across the cage as perches, and a food board at the back. Earlier that day, another volunteer and I took a small frozen chicken out of the freezer to defrost in the kitchen, as we did every other day. Every other night we deliver part of the defrosted chicken to the owls. Tonight is one such night, and so by flashlight we make our way down the root-laden path to the cages. It is not raining and there is no wind. The air is still and thick with moisture. We slip into our rubber boots, dip them in the trough of chlorinated water, and enter the *cuarantena*, the quarantined animal enclosure area. I lean against the counter while the other volunteer cuts up the chicken and sets aside half to feed the hawks during the day tomorrow. A bowl of two cold chicken parts in hand, we creep through the eerily quiet cuarantena, passing the spider monkeys cages where all the monkeys sleep knees tucked to chins, huddled together in what one volunteer calls a "monkey ball." Besides our squelching boots, the only sounds are the flapping wings of nocturnal birds.

The owls are easy to spook. I enter their cage in a low crouch, moving slowly and steadily. Still, especially at night, the owls become agitated. They begin swooping toward and over me, back and forth across their cage like phantoms. I put the bowl down, glance around the cage to make sure everything looks in order, and then retreat a little more quickly than I entered. The next day I will gather the leftover chicken bones and clean the owls' cage. For now, I head back to the dorm room feeling a bit spooked.

In a couple weeks, not long before finishing at ARCAS, the head veterinarian will ask another volunteer (my former trainer, Brian) and me to move these two owls into a massive enclosure, the last stage before their release. They will each have already been caught and placed in an individual carrier when we arrive to pick them up. Brian and I will each take a cage and try not to jostle it on the ten-minute walk to their new cage. It is at least fifty feet by fifty feet, and twenty feet tall, thick with vegetation, and surrounded by similarly vegetated forest. When we enter the cage and open the carriers, the two owls sit seemingly stunned for a moment before flying straight out, all the way to the back of the cage, out of sight. This will be the first time they have flown more than six feet, and their ability to do so will bode well for their future release. One of my jobs for my last few days at ARCAS will be to periodically hike up to their cage and make sure they are both still there and eating their chicken. It will be an infinitely more pleasant task than feeding them in the dark while they whoosh over me in tight, low swoops. In this big cage it will always take several minutes—sometimes ten or twenty— before I can spot them somewhere in among the greenery. Sometimes I will not see them at all. They will no longer be permanently visible. While still "significantly unfree," to borrow Haraway's term, the owls will be almost unencounterable.

———————

ARCAS has an intertwined two-pronged approach to rehabilitation: first, keeping animals alive, and second, preparing them for return to the wild. Megan (2011) expresses this dual goal when she tells me: "We've had lots of animals come in really rough conditions. We've had . . . baboons that have been set on fire, just horribly tortured. And some of our animals come in such horrible conditions, covered in ticks and really lost to the world, in a way. And trying to bring them back, it's just a constant effort of trying to get these animals healthy again. And once they're healthy, that's just the first part. Then it's teaching them to be wild again, which is even more difficult." Far from neutral or apolitical, the practices that constitute this approach—getting the animals healthy and then teaching them to be wild again, bringing back animals who are "lost to the world"—involve the exertion of power at an intimate and embodied level. ARCAS is a multispecies contact zone in which differently positioned beings encounter each other in ways that are always saturated with the operation of power and the consolidation of difference into hierarchy. The preceding narration of a "day-in-the-life" of a volunteer wildlife rehabilitator affords the observation of two particularly key modes of power's operation in wildlife rehabilitation that I would like to draw out further in the remainder of this chapter. These are two sets of practices that correspond to the two prongs of the rehabilitation approach outlined earlier. And they are two sets of practices that are about performing certain figures of the human and the animal. The first power mode and set of practices is biopolitical, involving a continual prioritizing of (certain) biological lives and an even forced state of life, or living. The second dominant way that power operates at ARCAS is through a distinctly misanthropic humanism, whereby a distrust of humans is nonetheless bound to a conception and performance of humans' distinctiveness, control, and dominance. Both the biopolitical and the misanthropic practices play out in embodied encounters between the rehabilitators and the rehabilitant.

The first part of ARCAS's work—making and keeping animals healthy—is accomplished through multiple biopolitical practices documented earlier in this chapter: feeding (even by force), medicating, cleaning and disinfecting, and veterinary care, including necropsies. These practices are all about monitoring, managing, and intervening at the level of individual and aggregate animal life at ARCAS. When the animals are young, these practices also entail providing the affection and nurturing that their mothers would have provided, especially the primates.

These practices, as well as ARCAS's rigid release criteria for its animals, point to how in wildlife rehabilitation the animal's life is more important than anything else. Keeping the animal alive is a goal that subsumes and may even subvert any directives regarding quality of life, except to the extent that quality of life is necessary to keep the animal alive. This is exemplified in ARCAS's implicit policy that a captive life is preferred to a death outside the cage, which explains why workers and volunteers shout at monkeys and spray them, why I only spoke to the parrots in my head instead of out loud, and why any animal who is deemed unlikely to survive upon release is kept at ARCAS to live out the rest of its life in captivity. Wildlife centers such as ARCAS are sites of biopolitical work, in which volunteers and workers labor to "foster life." As in any biopolitical mode, fostering one life often entails putting others to death. One experience at ARCAS especially crystallized this biopolitical calculus.

Harold, a blind, half-dead heron, was delivered to ARCAS midway through my month there. He was listless, refused to eat, and would stand motionless in his cage, his cloudy eyes unseeing. He seemed shut down to the world and did not express any registerable interest in living, avoiding food and water. Two volunteers had to force-feed him. One of us would hold his delicate bony body with a towel in two hands, and the other would pry open his large beak and drop small fish (caught by another volunteer each morning from the lake) into his throat, tilting his head back to ensure he would swallow. Harold's fish intake was meticulously recorded each morning and evening. A minimum of twelve free-swimming fish were force-fed to a heron that to all appearances did not wish to be of this world. Contrary to what ARCAS's assistant director told a room full of volunteers one evening, that "in the end, it's all about freedom," in fact *life* (and "saving" it) is prioritized at ARCAS, and some individual animals' lives over the lives of others. This is biopolitical in the sense that the target of intervention is biological life—its maintenance, management, and fostering.

Alongside these biopolitical efforts like force-feeding and medicating, ARCAS deploys misanthropic practices to produce the unencounterable animal, to teach the animal to "be wild again," as mentioned by the primatologist. This chapter, like my own labor at ARCAS, has been littered with such misanthropic strategies: spraying animals if they exhibit "unnatural" behaviors (such as approaching the floor too often, for monkeys; or coming too close to humans), not speaking in front of parrots, being stern to and distant from animals and avoiding touch, and finally exploding firecrackers and shooting blanks at animals in enclosures with electric fences in order to drive home the point that humans are to be feared and avoided. These practices—or performances—are all part of ARCAS's efforts to dismantle animals' entanglements with humans and circuits of capital. Yet rehabilitant animals are forced into a relationship of dependence with their human caretakers. During the rehabilitation process they remain captive even as they are promised independence and autonomy. This points to a central paradox in the rehabilitation process: the goal of making animals unencounterable is pursued *through encounter*; cultivating animals' "freedom" and independence occurs through forcible human dominance and dependence.

These encounters are performative. Rehabilitation produces particular human and animal subjects. At ARCAS, the belief in a cruel, violent human enrolls volunteers and workers to perform this very role in an attempt to generate fear in the animal. The human/animal dualism is played out again and again in the cages, with the master human subject subordinating and segregating the animal. ARCAS's pronounced lack of faith in an abstract and homogeneous humanity, then, retains the notion that humans are in control, are dominant, are exceptional—not only in their capacity for violence but also in their capacity to "save," for at ARCAS it is the humans that liberate the animals, when they decide to. Instead of acknowledging "humans are not the only ones caring for the Earth and its beings—we are in relations of mutual care" (Puig de la Bellascasa 2010, 164), ARCAS embraces the narrative of the human savior. ARCAS's misanthropy, then, does nothing to trouble "the human" or "the animal" as subject categories, with all their attendant power inequalities. Rather, this misanthropy retains and reperforms a bounded and dominant human subject. While railing against "humanity," rehabilitation remains attached to human exceptionalism. In seeking to produce autonomous animal subjects, rehabilitation continues to be attached to a particular understanding of "nature" and wildness as "out there," distinct and separate from humans and humanity. This view of nature and wilderness is problematic not only for its colonial legacies but also for its treatment of animals as never belonging where "we" are, and as the passive objects to our own active subjectivity. ARCAS's practices, then, leave the exceptional and distinct human subject both materially and discursively undisturbed.

Yet at the same time, ARCAS has a profound function in the lives of some individual trafficked animals. ARCAS reportedly releases dozens to hundreds of animals per year, but releases are rare. In my month at ARCAS, only one occurred, and it was not a rehabilitated animal but a nocturnal bird of prey a local person had captured and brought to ARCAS. A vet checked it out and deemed it healthy, and so one night in mid-November all of the volunteers gathered outside the kitchen in a line in front of a cardboard box. Two volunteers opened the box, and nothing happened for a few seconds. Then a blurred black shape burst of the box and flapped up and away, a fast retreating shadow against the starry sky. Aspirationally, this bird would reconnect with a socio-ecological network that supports its wild life.

A series of entanglements and disentanglements thus constitutes wildlife rehabilitation. Indeed, it is possible to characterize the wildlife rehabilitation process, in the case of wildlife rehab after capture for the pet trade, as in many ways the reverse of the process that made the animals into lively capital in the first place. While lively capital was formed by severing the animal from its ecological, social, and familial networks, and then entangling it with human-provided supports, rehabilitating the animal for return to the wild is accomplished by slowly severing the human supports and entanglements in order to reattach the animal to its former socio-ecological networks. While making lively capital is a rapid process, unmaking it can take years. The rehabilitation process reveals the sophisticated, busy socio-ecological worlds of animals and how disrupted they are by capture and exchange—it is no easy matter to simply reintroduce animals to the forest.

Animals are also often traumatized—psychologically, physically, and mentally—from their time as capital among humans. In captivity at AR-CAS, they often barely fare better, and frequently do not survive. Almost as often, they fail to be divested of their ties to humans and human-like behavior—monkeys continue to approach their caretakers or remain on the floor too often, parrots learn to speak—and so are condemned to live out the rest of their lives at ARCAS. This speaks to the difficulty of undoing animal fetishism, of rebuilding animal lives of their own, particularly in conditions of enclosure.

The rehabilitation process can therefore be critiqued on many levels. Practically, the option of rehabilitation is open to only a small pool of animals, and as this chapter shows, even these animals are easily rendered ineligible for release according to rehab's rigid and misanthropic criteria (i.e., the requirement that animals fear and distrust humans). The success of wildlife rehabilitation is also largely unproven. More abstractly, rehabilitation can be critiqued for its restoration of an idealized "first nature" that is "out there," cleaved apart spatially and subjectively from human beings, and for casting the human subject as the dominant agent in this restoration, "saving" wild animals from an otherwise tainted and polluting homogeneous humanity.

Given these critiques of wildlife rehabilitation, how is possible to stay ambivalent about it? Is there anything we can recuperate from the complex and contradictory space and practices of rehabilitation? No matter what, rehabilitation involves, to some extent, making life-and-death decisions for another being who cannot speak, placing an arguably impossible dilemma at the heart of wildlife rehabilitation. The main goal ought to be to avoid ending up in the place where that choice needs to be made on another's behalf. This means rehabilitation cannot achieve much on its own without also transforming broader structures around it—structures that lead to animal capture in the first place and create the likelihood of recapture on release. Prime among these is the global exotic pet trade itself, and the demand for exotic pets largely emanating from countries elsewhere.

But in the interim, as the work of dismantling these broader structures occurs, rehabilitation will remain a crucial last resort for captured animals. So it is important for the wildlife rehabilitation community of practitioners and scholars to have some reflexive conversations. What would rehabilitation look like if it held less tightly to a biopolitical imperative? How would the day-to-day practice of rehabilitation shift if the primary goal was less life at all costs, and more an open-ended, no-guarantee-of-life move outside the cage? How might the rehabilitation process introduce more choice for animals—even choice over where and how they die? I ask these questions knowing that rehabilitators grapple more than anyone with the tensions and paradoxes of their practice, and to urge a reconsideration of some of the assumptions that might be exacerbating these tensions.

Releasing the hawk from the box, catching sight of former ARCAS monkeys who had been released and are now living and having offspring in the forests around the center, and losing sight of the owls in their thickly vegetated large enclosure—these were moments that lead me to hold on to the possibilities of rehabilitation as a decommodification practice. The project to restore animals' autonomy should not be abandoned. I elaborate on this ethical and political task in the following and final chapter.

ARCAS
November 29, 2011

In the monkey cage anteroom, Stevie stares through the chain-link door (figure 3.9). Because he's tawnier than the others, his eyes look bigger and blacker, each framed by a diamond-shaped hole in the chain link. His gaze is fixed on mine, but his four slender fingers don't stop testing the lock. A few minutes ago he pulled my hair, then sat on the cement floor gnawing a stick, like an old man chewing on a toothpick. Tomorrow is my last day here. I'll think of the animals often in coming years—I still do. Later this afternoon

FIGURE 3.9 Stevie looking through the chain-link cage (photograph by the author).

I stop to watch the monkeys, to remember. They make faces at me, sticking out their tongues, pursing their lips, looking skyward and then back at me. Two sit side by side, so close they looked conjoined.

In chapter 1, I described seeing two spider monkeys flit through the canopy as I sat high above the trees on the ridge of a Tikal temple in Guatemala. It was mesmerizing. In chapter 2, I wrote about watching spider monkeys in cages too small for them to stand auctioned for a couple thousand dollars in Missouri. I hid my tears in the crowded bleachers. At ARCAS I worked daily with spider monkeys in their concrete enclosure, and they pulled my hair and yanked my tank top straps, and Stevie gave me a wedgie. To navigate the day-to-day work with captive animals, I have to shut part of myself off to registering their sentience. But at ARCAS at least, spider monkeys have a chance to regain the life I observed fleetingly above the canopy, an uncaptive life. This book, then, comes full circle—but not smoothly. Although commodification may be temporary and even reversible, the animals are never unchanged from their experience of moving in and out of lively capital status. Their bodies bear the modifications and marks of their captivity:

leash scars, clipped wings, pulled teeth, removed claws. And just as there was no pure state at which the animals began, there is no pure state to which they are returned. In evaluating the modes of relational life that these animals pass through, however, it is my task, to paraphrase Haraway, to identify those relations that have a chance for life.

On this, my second-to-last day at ARCAS, a troop of wild howler monkeys appear at the center for the second time that month, swinging into the lofty canopy that calms the sun's glare into patchy shadows down at ground level, on the cages' concrete floors. The captive howler monkeys cling to the walls, their heads touching the chain-link ceiling of their cages, as high above the shady floors as they can get, and they start to communicate with the wild howler monkeys squatting a hundred feet above, peering down. The monkeys' small bodies shake with the exertion of their screams; their finely detailed, wrinkled faces contort to allow their jaws to gape. They shriek on the exhale and draw a ragged deep gasping breath on the inhale, a dozen of them raging in unison so that there is never a moment of still, silent peace. This is the only work that they can do: grip the cage walls and howl at their kin high in the free treetops. The wild monkeys howl back. It is ear-splitting, but from the ground all we can see are black shapes flickering through the leaves.

4

Wild Life Politics

After following the exotic pet trade around several countries, into biosphere reserves, exotic animal auctions, convention halls, and rehabilitation centers and sanctuaries, I never expected my research would follow me to the small town where I grew up on the southwest coast of Vancouver Island, in the province of British Columbia. In 2009, the province banned more than a thousand species of exotic pets from private ownership, as discussed in chapter 2. Even before the ban, the most exotic pet I saw growing up was a guinea pig. But a few winters ago, while my sister and I were home visiting our parents for the holidays, a surprising event happened on one of the almost daily walks we take to the ocean.

On these walks it is not unusual to be surprised on the rocky beach. Often, there are carcasses: once, a skate skeleton; another time, bald eagles feasting on an enormous rotting sea lion whose body lasted for weeks lodged at the tideline. The dried-out bones of a giant gray whale who washed up on shore in 1989 are now strung together with invisible wire and hang in my former high school's foyer like a ghost. From the beach, seals, sea lions, and river otters peer at you across the waves; minks scamper over the rocks. Every year hundreds of turkey vultures amass to form their airborne bodies into a swirling vortex, flying in circles up and up in a towering cyclone with enough momentum to take them altogether across the Salish Sea to Washington State.

On this walk, though, it was on our way home from the beach that the surprising event happened. A passing neighbor told us a cougar was in the

FIGURE 4.1 Escaped serval on Otter Point Place.

area; another neighbor had snapped a photo the day before and posted it on the neighborhood bulletin board next to the community mailboxes. This was not the surprising part; cougars are more densely populated on Vancouver Island than anywhere in North America. But I was surprised when I saw the photo. Cougars are large, tawny wild cats with thick bodies and long tails. The animal in the photo was smaller, more delicate, and black-spotted all over. I recognized it as a serval, a species of medium-sized African wild cat with the morphological distinction of having the longest legs of any cat relative to their body size. Servals have become popular pets in the last few years, and I had seen a number of them sold at the US exotic animal auctions I describe in chapter 2.

Like any good, snoopy neighbor/researcher, I asked around about this serval and found out that several weeks earlier a local woman's pet serval had slipped its cage. The escape felt triumphant. The photo of the serval shows an animal trotting along briskly and with what looks like purpose (figure 4.1). Servals' long legs allow them to reach speeds of up to eighty kilometers per hour, and they are known to cover as much as three or four kilometers

FIGURE 4.2 Serval hit and killed by a pickup truck (source: Facebook post by Peter Henry).

as they search for prey at night. Some neighbors were concerned about their domestic and farmed animals, but I undeniably rejoiced in the serval's new-found uncaptive life as a fugitive exotic pet, scrabbling around my parents' house, ranging along the narrow country roads, and making its own way among the Douglas firs and cedars.

My elation was cut off a couple of days later when news came through that a man driving a truck had hit and killed the serval on Otter Point Road (figure 4.2). The serval's death is the least surprising part of the story. When exotic pets escape or are illegally released into nonnative environments, it does not typically end well for anyone, including, in some circumstances, local wildlife who are killed or outcompeted, but more commonly the former exotic pet itself.[1]

This story is, then, a sharp reminder of the constraints around the kind of life available for exotic pets. Removed from the socio-ecological reproductive networks that produced them—networks that are reproductive not only

Chapter Four

in a biological sense, reproducing the population, but also in a daily sense, as in the "life's work" of reproducing oneself and one's community (Mitchell, Marston, and Katz 2004)—these animals are enclosed and made dependent on human-provided supports, as I have argued over the course of the book. Even if they escape or are released, they face new socio-ecologies to which they likely will not be able to adapt.[2] There are few if any options for a life outside the cage once animals are captured. But this story also signals two other things, to me. First, it encourages me to loosen my tightly held allegiance to life above all else. As I suggested in chapter 3, the biopolitical emphasis on life can license unfreedom for animals deemed less likely to survive in the wild. Second, and maybe most crucially, this is a story of an animal pursuing a life of its own: a life that encounters limits, risks, and vulnerabilities, but a life outside the cage, with freedom of movement and a degree of openness and choice; a life in which the animal not only can achieve a fuller expression of its being but also, to some extent, makes its own world. This is the kind of life that is stripped from animals to create lively capital: alienated, controlled, individuated.

Marx famously tried to see capitalism in the commodity, the "elemental form" of capitalism, in order to understand what social relations capitalism engenders, what the source of capitalist value is, how labor is exploited. In this book I consider what we can add to the picture by seeing capitalism in the exotic pet. What does the exotic pet tell us, especially, about capitalism's socio-ecological relationships, or the relationship between capitalism and animal life? I show how commodity fetishism—where commodity exchange creates the illusion of a world of objects that have lives of their own, masking the world of exploitative social relations that is actually producing commodities and value—compounds another kind of fetishism: the fetishism of the animal.

In animal fetishism, enclosure and the dominance of anthropocentric use values create the illusion of animals having no lives of their own, masking the complex histories of socio-ecological reproduction that actually produce individual animals and their species and enable their creative, relational world-making practices. Both fetishisms sever the object/subject of the fetishism from the conditions of its production: commodity fetishism severs exchanged objects from the uneven labor relations that produced them; animal fetishism severs animal subjects from the socio-ecological relations that produced them and that support their ability to pursue their own use values, to exert agency in crafting their own and others' worlds. Both fetishisms thus have concealing effects; they are both a forgetting, a naturalization that hides complex social relations. But they hide different relations. Commodity fetishism hides social relations that constitute commodity production. Animal fetishism hides the socio-ecological relations that constitute animals' individual and collective reproduction and facilitate their world-making practices and the enactments of their own desires. And while commodification compounds animal fetishism, it is not single-handedly responsible for it, as is evidenced by the persistence of animal fetishism after exotic pets are decommodified, for example, at rehabilitation centers or sanctuaries where they are no longer exchangeable. The persistence of animal fetishism after decommodification results from the material conditions that shape animal fetishism but are not confined to the commodity form: namely, enclosure. An enclosed animal is spatially and materially limited in its ability to engage in world-making practices, to craft its and others' futures.

Analyses of fetishism highlight the social relations that, when fetishized, are mistaken for objects. Such analyses have a political destination. When we are able to understand underlying social relations and processes and consider their often exploitative dynamics, we can build a political response. For Marx, commodity fetishism involves mistaking the exploitative social relations of labor, which produce commodities and their value, for objects in exchange, which appear as if they have "lives of their own," and whose value falsely appears to inhere in their physical form. An analysis of commodity fetishism urges workers to acknowledge their collective value—that their labor is the source of value—and their shared exploitation by capitalists, the owners of the means of production who do not pay workers what their labor is worth. An examination of commodity fetishism thus brings forth a political response that revolves around collective worker demands.

Ahmed's development of stranger fetishism in *Strange Encounters* (2000) has equally pronounced political implications. She identifies how the figure of the stranger "is an effect of processes of inclusion and exclusion" (6)—but a fetishism of the stranger implies the stranger preexists those processes. Building from Marx's notion of commodity fetishism, Ahmed suggests that the stranger is a fetishized figure, one that can appear as such when we assume it has a life of its own, by being cut off from the history of its determination. Ahmed digs into and highlights uneven relationships of production that determine the stranger—not only how the stranger is represented but also the stranger's "histories of arrival"—the global divisions of labor, power, economic flows, and so on—that allow the stranger to appear, in the present. Rather than turning toward a multicultural politics of inclusivity—in other words, a push to "include" those who appear as "strangers"—Ahmed urges a political response to the stranger that targets the processes that produce the figure of the stranger in the first place.

My attention to animal fetishism is similarly intended to contribute to a political response—in this case, to the global exotic pet trade, and also to the wider crisis-ridden socio-ecological context for this book: a global reordering of animal life in which domesticated animal life is proliferating and wild animal life is diminishing. And although there are fewer wild animals today than in human history, more wild animals than ever before live in captivity. More animals live enclosed lives, lives fashioned to serve humans, to fulfill human use or exchange values, not use values of animals' own.

Another way of thinking about this global reordering of life on earth is that more and more animals are fetishized in a manner that I have discussed in this book: animals' lives of their own are obscured; animals and their complex socio-ecological networks are mistaken as purely objects of human use. This is true of enclosed wild animals and of the vast majority of bird and mammalian life now on earth: industrially farmed domesticated animals. What, then, are some conceptual tools for the development of a political response that supports and advances animals' lives of their own? What might it mean for animals to live in an autonomous way? And how can we work toward this, politically? These are the questions I take up in this concluding chapter. My focus is on the global exotic pet trade, although I hope the concepts of animal fetishism and defetishizing the animal have bearing beyond this context to other animal capital, such as industrially farmed animals, for whom struggles to defetishize would have their own political shape.[3] For exotic pets, though, I suggest that an analysis of animal fetishism, and an attempt to defetishize the animal, can deliver us in part to a politics of wild life. My starting point is the understanding that a wild life is one lived in conditions of relational autonomy, which I explain shortly, drawing on a selection of critical theory, including feminist, Indigenous, and autonomous Marxist. I highlight one epistemological condition and one spatial condition that facilitate animals' relational autonomy: recognizing and prioritizing animals' own use values; and dismantling and resisting animal enclosure. As an interim step toward these goals, reducing demand for exotic pets should be a priority of all scales of government—including international intergovernmental initiatives.

Orienting toward Animals' Relational Autonomy

Autonomy is admittedly a concept with baggage. For a long time, for many thinkers, autonomy has been associated with rugged individualism, "self-made men," libertarians, and the ideal Enlightenment figure of what Sylvia Wynter (1995) refers to as "Rational Self" or "Man." Historically, Western thought framed autonomy as a state that could only be reached by subjects who had attained "rational self-mastery."[4] This view is consistent with systems of subordination and domination in which multiple Others to Rational Man (women, Black and Indigenous people, people of color) were considered incapable of such rational self-mastery; within these oppressive systems of thought, these Others could not escape their bodies, their "instincts"; they could not separate themselves from the animal *within* the human.[5] Autonomy was therefore the purview of white men.

These traditional, Western criteria for rationality—the ability to transcend instinct, the ability to reason, to be rational—are also famously denied to animals. This might all seem to make the concept of autonomy an awkward fit for animals. But different articulations of autonomy are central to other intellectual traditions and political movements—from feminist to autonomous Marxist to Indigenous. These alternative conceptions of autonomy are particularly relevant and useful for the kind of political response I want to work toward here.

While not all these movements conceive of autonomy in precisely the same way, there are commonalities. At base, autonomy is understood as the condition of having a degree of control over one's life and conditions of work. Accordingly, there is a sense that autonomy involves a distancing from oppressive power relations—for example, patriarchal power, or the power of capitalists, or colonial state power. But rather than seeking freedom for an atomistic self, the liberation that comes from autonomy is about the "ability to create new communities and ties of mutual dependence" (Graeber 2009, 266). Collectivity is not something to be escaped to achieve autonomy, but rather is central to autonomy as both a means and an end: autonomy is achieved through collectives, and autonomy makes collective life possible;

autonomy is, as anthropologist Kathleen Millar (2018, 91) says, "that which makes possible a continued, shared existence in delicate times." Autonomy and collectivity require each other. Autonomy is a way of building collective life, and this collective life has the quality of autonomous living—a life in which people have a degree of control of their lives and conditions of work.[6]

These insights together point toward what some scholars call "relational autonomy."[7] Here, autonomy is not a static state possessed by an individual but a dynamic capacity exercised and enacted in conjunction with others.[8] This reformatted conception of autonomy stems from a different understanding of the self, which is not understood as a discrete, self-mastered, rational subject, not a self that preexists its relations with others, but instead is a self that is from the beginning constituted through its relations.[9] It follows that autonomy is not a solo pursuit. Autonomy is instead also deeply relational; it can only be exercised with the right set of wider *conditions*—social relationships, practices, and institutions; it is made possible by and through relationships with infinite others. So autonomy does not mean being free of relations of connection and dependence, or not needing care, or withdrawing from social ties; rather, autonomy is enacted through care and through enmeshment in social structures.

Inspired by these interventions and compelled by the centrality of autonomy to emancipatory thought and practice, I want to consider how animals might be relationally autonomous, and how beings—human and not—are situated in socio-*ecological* conditions that enable their autonomy. But before I do, I would like to pause for a caveat and clarify what I do not mean by animal autonomy, or what I do not intend to suggest by approaching autonomy ecologically. To the extent that autonomy has been considered in the nonhuman realm, it has arguably expressed itself in wilderness movements and narratives that were long about banishing humans from wild spaces to preserve a pure and "pristine" *terra nullius*—"empty lands" that are both illusory and colonial. At times, these movements have been framed in the name of protecting the space nonhumans need to facilitate their autonomy. But this version of autonomy is based on separation—cleaving off human spaces from nonhuman ones, separating culture from nature. These wilderness movements often, in other words, exhibit dualistic thinking and practice. And they have been squarely critiqued from multiple angles for decades, not least of all because all around the world, these wilderness movements and ideals led to dispossession of local—often racialized—and

Indigenous people, who were and in many cases still are prohibited from entering the lands they managed and lived on.[10]

Today, as a corrective, critical scholars across disciplines tend to emphasize the inescapable entanglement of nature and culture, of humans and animals, thereby coming late to modes of thought long prominent within many Indigenous nations. I am cautious about how advocating animals' autonomy might prompt a return to dualistic thinking, where to be autonomous animals must live in a purified, human-free animal space. In bending autonomy toward ecologies and animals, we cannot abandon or separate out human politics, particularly given the way that wildlife management has historically operated by dispossessing already marginalized people of their access to wildlife.[11] On the contrary, I am partly attracted to autonomy as a concept for the ties it might help identify between animal politics and feminist, Indigenous, and Marxist politics. So, is there a way to acknowledge fundamental entanglement and advocate autonomy—perhaps even consider entanglement as a condition of possibility for autonomy? If so, what entanglements or networks of humans and nonhumans enable animals' relational autonomy?

When it comes to animals, I suggest that relational autonomy means, at its base, the condition of having "a life of one's own" while acknowledging how that life of one's own is indelibly relational. The "one" is constituted by many, especially by a socio-ecological reproductive network: a network of kin, minerals, foods, plants, elements, energies; a network that is always *working* to reproduce itself, to secure what is needed, not necessarily in harmony, but with creativity and agency. Again, by socio-ecological reproduction I do not mean to invoke reproduction as it is employed in biology, to refer to the reproduction of species. Instead, I invoke an ecologically inflected notion of social reproduction, a term feminist political economists have long used to describe the daily and largely unpaid work of reproducing individual people and communities—work like cooking food, cleaning, child-rearing, caring for those in need of care, and maintaining social bonds.[12]

So to be relationally autonomous is to make one's own way, to live a life of one's own, to have choice, to make decisions, to have openness, to work for oneself, to play—none of which is done alone. The point of relational autonomy, to borrow from an interviewee in Juno Parreñas's (2018, 154, my emphasis) ethnography of orangutan rehabilitation, is "not to achieve isolated independence, but rather to *become responsible*," where we might think of responsibility in terms of being able to care and provide for oneself and the collectives of which one is a part, being able to respond to one's own needs and the needs of others. This is not about projecting a "pull yourself up by your bootstraps," ruggedly individualistic, rational self-maximizing figure of autonomy into the animal world. It is instead about recognizing and promoting animals' capacities to live lives of their own—lives that belong to them and their communities and not to someone else, not to an "owner."

Living in a relationally autonomous manner also means, following the Zapatistas (2013), having what a community needs—having access to the land, air, food, kinship, shelter, play, and wider socio-ecological conditions to meet their needs. And it means being be able to decide what those needs are. Relationally autonomous animals should be able to produce and use what they need, for themselves, to work and care for themselves and their communities. They should have the ability to care for and educate their kin and be educated by their kin; to grow their own knowledge about socio-ecological reproductive work and pass that knowledge on to others in their communities. In other words, relational autonomy here is about socio-ecological reproductive work, everyday "life's work," the work that is, as described in the introduction, devalued but necessary within capitalism.[13] Relational autonomy is therefore not just about freedom from commodification (what we might think of as the equivalent of being in a wage labor relation for humans) but about *freedom in one's socio-ecological reproduction*. The work of caring for kin; maintaining social bonds; gathering, making, and eating food—animals should have the capacity to engage in this work, to set their own work rhythms and the patterns and intensities of their labor, to establish the parameters of their working and nonworking lives. All of this to feed and sustain their socio-ecological worlds—to be world-making subjects.

If we begin from an analysis of how something like the exotic pet trade involves a cutting off of animals from the complex histories of their own being, then any political response needs to revolve around resisting this severing. What this amounts to, to me, is fighting for the capacity of animals to lead wild lives, lives characterized by openness, possibility, a degree of choice, and self-determination, in which beings are understood to have their own familial, social, and ecological networks, their own lookouts, agendas, and needs. These wild lives are lived, as Val Plumwood (1993) says, by "uncolonized others," by *unenclosed* others. This cannot be achieved by separating out a wilderness, a purely animal space. The commonplace equation in which a wild life is de- or unhumanized (e.g., Palmer 2010) no longer holds. Instead, a wild life is made possible by collectives (which may or may not include humans) that facilitate freedom of movement, play, social life, and the ability of animals to work for themselves and their communities. Instead, again learning from the Zapatistas (2013), autonomy is about building connections while respecting difference, "building a world in which all worlds have a place"—including the worlds of animals. Animals access relational autonomy not by being placed in a pristine wilderness devoid of humans but instead by experiencing a degree of control over their socio-ecological work, time, and space, by being allowed "to sustain relationships, fulfill social obligations, and pursue life projects in an uncertain everyday," borrowing from Millar (2018, 71), and in changing environments.

To expand on a politics of wild life, in what follows I outline two main conditions for animals' relational autonomy. These conditions are less about concrete political strategies and more about political destinations—conditions to which wild life politics can orient itself and work toward: first, a proposal for recognition and protection of animals' own use values, where animals have what they need and want and decide for themselves what that is, and second, a refusal of enclosure.[14] I then highlight demand reduction as a more concrete and intermediary step in the direction of wild life.

Recognizing Animals' Own Use Values
(for Their Socio-ecological Reproduction)

Throughout this book, I have suggested that animal fetishism—the erasure of the complex socio-ecological relations that gave birth to and supported the animal (i.e., family, social ties, habitat, etc.) so that the animal appears as an object, or "thinglike"—is not only enacted through exchange, as commodity fetishism is. Exchange can compound animal fetishism, as I have suggested, but it is not its founding moment. Instead, I suggest animal fetishism is first enacted earlier, through the designation of being "useful" or having "use value." Use value, the usefulness of a thing, is the less-remarked-upon sibling of exchange value, which refers to the value of a thing in relation to another thing, or how much (money, usually) an object can be traded for. Exchange value is for Marx the activating force behind commodity fetishism. It is in exchange that the world of commodities appears as a world of objects with "lives of their own" as opposed to a world of social relations that produced those objects, and their value. Use value, in contrast, is for Marx rooted in the physical qualities of a thing. It is generally of much less interest to Marxists; as Marx (1976, 163) remarked, "So far as it is a use-value, there is nothing mysterious about it." Yet the usefulness of a thing is an intensely political matter. Useful *to whom*? To whose benefit? Under what conditions?

As valuable as Marxist critiques of exchange value and all the exploitative relations it hides are, they tend to leave untroubled an anthropocentric framing of use value. In political economic practice as well as critical scholarship, use value—the usefulness of a "thing"—is automatically framed in relation to human use and benefit. Use value is the usefulness of a thing *to humans*. This rather obvious anthropocentrism goes largely unremarked upon by critical scholars. Sara Ahmed (2006) and Jacques Derrida (2006) are exceptions. Both question Marx's implication of a pure, uncomplicated, and neutral originary stage of use value that precedes exchange. As I explained in the introduction, Derrida points out the very human, appropriative nature of use value, while Ahmed builds from Derrida to argue that objects are fetishized even if they are not exchanged. Objects are reduced to their physical qualities, but they are always products of their relations and histories. I have repurposed Ahmed's argument in this book to suggest that the animal "object" is fetishized in a particular way. Stripped of the complex history of its own being, the animal object—say, an exotic pet—appears as if it does not have a life of its own, severed from the socio-ecological relations of reproduction that produced it.

The assigning of anthropocentric use values to these animals is part of what propels this severing. Animals have multiple use values for their socio-ecological reproductive networks: as laborers, caregivers, kin. Animals have use values for themselves, providing themselves with what they need to survive and exercising their desires, including to live in the world. Yet think of the animals I have discussed in this book: from Darwin the Ikea Monkey to auctioned-off African grey parrots to the pet serval in Otter Point. For these animals, their use values—as companions, say, or as entertainment—mask, or at least trump, their own social world of use values: how they might be useful to themselves and their communities.

In her book about the teachings of plants, *Braiding Sweetgrass* (2015), Robin Wall Kimmerer, an ecologist, poet, and member of the Citizen Potawatomi nation, often returns to the differences between modes of political-economic thought and practice in which plants are thought to belong to someone, as an object, as property, and modes in which plants are considered subjects, in relation. Borrowing from Kimmerer's insights, animals, like the strawberries and sweetgrass about which Kimmerer writes, "belong only to themselves" (2015, 31). Billy-Ray Belcourt (2015), too, shares his Driftpile Cree community's nonspeciesist orientation to animals who "occupy sacred ceremonial roles from which the Earth and its occupants are created and are thus not subject to human domination" (8). The agency of animals evident in Belcourt's statement is echoed in Vanessa Watts's (2013, 23) description of Haudenosaunee and Anishnaabe thought as based on the premise that land is animate, meaning "full of thought, desire, contemplation and will ... [and] non-human beings choose how they reside, interact and develop relationships with other nonhumans . . . [in] ethical structures, inter-species treaties and agreements." Humans, Watts says, organize themselves into these societies; as the last species to arrive on earth, "humans arrived in a state of dependence on an already-functioning society with particular values, ethics, etc." (25). Here, humans need nonhumans, and nonhumans have their *own* needs and viewpoints.

These framings of and orientations toward animals are a far cry from the notion of animals as passive "resources," or the acquisitive posture of seeking out animal life to own it, to claim it as one's own. The problem is not that animals are useful to humans, or that animals have use value to humans. Watts makes clear that humans are dependent on animals; humans need to use animals to survive; and animals have their own agendas, desires—what I have been referring to as use values. Recognizing these use values that belong to animals ought not imply that human use of animals should end. Animal advocacy that revolves around a politics of nonuse has a terrible track record, marshaling and feeding elitist and culturally imperial energies and projects. In the Americas, for example, state-led wildlife management regimes have historically vilified and even prohibited subsistence use of wildlife, disrupting local and Indigenous hunting and eroding those people's own relational autonomy, or collective capacity to provide for themselves and their communities.[15] Advocating for nonuse of animals would fall into this same trap. Plus *use* is not the problem. Rather, the problem is the assumption that animals' value appears *only* in relation to human use values, as if animals have no interests of their own, no value to themselves and their socio-ecological communities, of which humans may or may not be a part. A wild life politics, a politics oriented toward animals' relational autonomy, must foreground animals' own use values. It must see animals as first and foremost existing for their own purposes and ends, not only for satisfying human uses, and not as pawns in a fantasy of human domination.

A Refusal of Enclosure: Lives outside the Cage

The story of this book and the story of the reordering of life on earth are partly a story of the ascent of animals' bodily enclosure, their confinement in cages, pens, and yards. I have argued that bodily enclosure is a key spatial mechanism that enacts animal fetishism, physically severing the animal from its socio-ecological reproductive networks and allowing the animal to appear as if it does not have a life of its own, outside the cage. It follows that recovering animals' wild lives, the lives of their own, and supporting animals' relational autonomy involves a spatial politics, specifically of resisting enclosure and its material expression in "the cage," which we can take to stand in for various modes of bodily enclosure. I would like to suggest that the cage is a key terrain of struggle in a wild life politics, akin to what the body is for feminists and what the factory was for Marx.

In developing an antienclosure animal politics, inspiration can be drawn from opposition to the enclosure of land commons—an opposition that is central to many critical intellectual traditions and movements, especially Marxism and feminism. As Marx and Marxists have argued for a century and a half, the creation of absolute private property rights over land in England that had formerly been subject to common usage rights was a fundamental step in the formation of capitalism, "freeing up" a population of landless people who could no longer provide for themselves by accessing this land for grazing animals or collecting turf or wood for fuel. Geographers and other scholars have shown how this "original" moment of enclosure has not been the end of the story—land enclosures have continued to be a key mechanism of capital accumulation.[16] And in many cases historically and today, land grabs or privatization creates a pool of landless peasants for whom there is no wage waiting after dispossession (Li 2010).

These historical and ongoing land enclosures have been challenged in thought and practice since their inception. Peasant and Indigenous movements have engaged in sustained legal and political struggle to deny the state's ability to turn over land to private companies, to privatize previously common-access land or materials (see Levien 2013). Often, these movements attempt to physically intercede in and block the act of enclosure, since this is a onetime act that is difficult to undo.[17] At the heart of the resistance to enclosure is the desire to retain or recover autonomy, to not lose access to the basis—land, materials, energies—from which one can, to an extent, reproduce oneself and one's community.

What can animal politics learn from these movements that resist dispossession and enclosure, promote the commons, and reclaim the ability to provide for oneself, reclaiming access to socio-ecological reproductive networks? There are important connections between land enclosure and animals' bodily enclosure—connections that suggest an animal-oriented, wild life politics might learn from strategies of land enclosure resistance. The geographer Michael Watts (2000) has already suggested some common roots between animal enclosure and land enclosure. He connects the "demise of the peasantry" through historic land enclosures in England to a simultaneous enclosure of animals who were themselves made property in the zoos and on the industrial feedlots that arose concurrently with the land enclosures.[18] There are also parallel effects engendered by each kind of enclosure. In chapter 1, I explained how animal enclosure, like land enclosure, rearranges social, political, economic, and ecological relationships so that enclosed animals can no longer provide for themselves, can no longer engage in their collective work of socio-ecological reproduction. Enclosed animals are made dependent on their owners, who provide life supports that had previously been provided by animals themselves, in conjunction with their communities.

Wild life is arguably impossible under these conditions of spatial constraint and forced dependence. A wild life has distinct spatial conditions— living a wild life depends on access to the space one needs, space for freedom of movement and work, for engaging in all of the activities that reproduce the multispecies commons and facilitate relational autonomy. Restoring connection to multispecies commons, or better, avoiding the severing of the animal from the commons in the first place, is in large part about resisting bodily enclosure of the animal—its enclosure in a cage or captive space that cuts it off from its socio-ecological reproductive networks. In a concrete sense, how can this severing of the animal from the commons be interrupted?

Shrinking Markets through Demand Reduction:
An Intermediate Response

Promoting animals' relational autonomy—recognizing their own use values, resisting enclosure—is a pretty abstract, far-reaching project. Often I am asked: What about in the interim—what is the best strategy for responding to the exotic pet trade in the short term? Trade bans? Education campaigns? The most concrete answer I can give is demand reduction. The global exotic pet trade is a demand-driven economy. Spikes in demand for clown fish and Spix's macaws following the popular animated films *Finding Nemo* and *Rio* engendered inflated trade numbers for both species. A study of wildlife trappers and collectors in Madagascar shows that they collect species type and numbers according to orders from exporters (Robinson et al. 2018), who in turn are responding to international demand. Calls for demand reduction as a strategy to combat negative effects of the exotic pet trade and wildlife trade more broadly have emerged in response.[19] So too have some campaigns along these lines.[20]

But these campaigns are still relatively scarce; they receive a fraction of the total funding and resources allotted to address wildlife trade (World Bank 2016); and they overwhelmingly target Asian demand, even though the United States and the European Union are top importers of legally and illegally traded live wild animals.[21] CITES (2016b) recently adopted a decision to encourage its parties to "provide the financial and technical support necessary to promote and facilitate the implementation of demand-reduction strategies." More than a year after the decision was adopted, parties reported back to CITES on activities they had implemented in response. While China and Vietnam undertook several campaigns and workshops, especially attempting to curb demand for ivory and rhino horn, respectively, the United States' reported activities include training law enforcement for seizures of products at its borders; providing funding for demand reduction in *other* countries; and raising awareness among American consumers traveling abroad (CITES 2017). This is a woefully inadequate response from the world's biggest consumer of wildlife when it comes to managing its own domestic imports.

Trade bans are arguably among the more effective demand-reduction strategies. The United States and other major trading blocs like the European Union have made strides in the past in this manner, implementing bans on wild bird imports that drastically reduced trade volumes, albeit in some cases pushing trade to other parts of the world.[22] Global trade bans would prevent this "hot potato" effect. In North America over the last two decades, though, we see neither national-level bans nor pushes for global ones. Instead, a patchwork of municipal and state/provincial bans to the ownership of exotic animals is sprouting up in the absence of meaningful national-level demand reduction. These bans are an effective way to decrease demand and therefore decrease the number of animals trapped from the wild. But like the US and EU bans on wild bird imports, these bans have generally been motivated by concerns about human safety. Expanding the list of animals banned—to include servals in British Columbia, for example—would require taking animal welfare more seriously as a consideration, something that many organizations, from the SPCA to Zoocheck, advocate.

Once animals are captured, severed from their socio-ecological reproductive networks, the outlook for those animals becomes quite dismal. Even for the few animals who are intercepted early enough to be directed to a rehabilitation facility, release back to the wild, without high risk of recapture, is rare. Rehabilitators face a difficult if not impossible situation, trying to cultivate animals' autonomy and unencounterability through relations of dependence and intimate encounters. The only real solution is to ensure animals are not captured in the first place. Doing so with supply management, by policing trappers, not only criminalizes and endangers those who profit the least from the trade and bear the consequences of ecological depletion, but also ignores the demand-driven nature of the global exotic pet trade. Working to erode demand and shrink markets for exotic pets must begin in top importing countries like the United States and trading blocs like the European Union. This is one crucial interim step in cultivating the conditions for animals' relational autonomy.

Lives of Their Own

The reordering of life underway worldwide is not just one in which there are diminishing numbers of living wild animals; it is one in which fewer and fewer animals live outside cages, unenclosed, able to pursue their own agendas, needs, and use values. Alongside a loss of life and species there is a widespread loss of wild life, of what I have described as relational autonomy. The global exotic pet trade is an engine within this global reordering, this loss of wild life, this advance of confinement. Confronting the global exotic pet trade and this escalating diminishment and confinement requires resisting capitalism and commodification, but more than that too. As I have argued throughout this book, the global exotic pet trade both relies on and perpetuates the reduction of animals to thinglike objects, lively capital that exists for human use alone, cut off from their socio-ecological reproductive networks, appearing as if they have no life of their own.

Amid this grim context it is crucial that we not stop asking, What world should we work toward? What world do we want to live in? Responding politically to the global exotic pet trade and a wider loss of wild life requires raising the possibility of recovering animals' wild lives, of promoting abundant and relationally autonomous animal life. A wild life is one in which animals engage in their own life-making practices, until they die. There is no guarantee of flourishing, only the conditions of possibility for a degree of creative self-determination and community. The animal is not only able to look back; it is able to disappear from sight. It is not a mere animal mirror polished, as Haraway says (1991), "so we can look for ourselves." But enclosed life, like the life of an exotic pet, cannot but disappoint, as John Berger (1980) has famously said of the zoo. Captive, dominated, controlled worlds leave little room for open endings. To counter a world of enclosure, of deadening and growing sameness, a wild world is one into which many worlds fit, a world with multiple, lively, and open ends, a world where animals live lives of their own.

NOTES

Introduction

1 The difference between absolute and qualified property for animals lies in the degree of power and control considered to exist over domesticated versus wild animals. Domesticated animals are classified absolute property because they are considered sufficiently under their owner's thumb whether or not their owner is in possession of them, whereas there is not adequate control in live wild animals to be absolute property as they may escape, or "regain their natural liberty" (Brantly 1891, 124). Property in live wild animals can only be "qualified": as in Darwin's case, the qualification is possession (*per industrium*), which is an indication of sufficient power over the animal for the animal to be property. See Brantly (1891).

2 Biologists Dirzo et al. (2014) coined the term "defaunation," seeking to capture more than extinction of species and to offer a term akin to "deforestation" around which scientists and the general public could mobilize (see Weis 2018 for a discussion of the significance of the term from the perspective of a social scientist). "Biological annihilation" is Ceballos, Ehrlich, and Dirzo's (2017) phrase to describe the severe losses of animal life that come into view when looking beyond species extinction to account for localized extinction—called "extirpation"—and loss of abundance. The WWF's *Living Planet Report* (2018) has documented such losses for vertebrates in reports published every two years since 1998.

3 The team of systems biologists (Bar-On, Phillips, and Milo 2018) who recently led this assessment of life on Earth determined that humans constitute only 0.01 percent of all life but have destroyed 83 percent of wild animals. Importantly, the study measures proportions of animal life

by biomass (in gigatons of carbon), not by numbers of individuals, and does not differentiate between captive and uncaptive wild animals in its assessment.

4 The modern numbers of domesticated animals are all the more stunning when we consider their artificially quickened and curtailed life courses. Biological interventions over the twentieth century transformed industrially farmed animals' bodies and life courses. For example, the average time to market for an industrial broiler chicken declined by 60 percent between 1935 and 1995 (Boyd 2001; also see M. Watts 2000; Weis 2018). The rapid turnover these animals experience from birth to slaughter means that the total annual number of domesticated animal individuals is many times more than their population at any given moment.

5 In this book, I use "thing" and "object" interchangeably to refer to something cast as inert, passive, nonagential, nonsentient, and lacking subjectivity. Many scholars from various fields have contested the idea that objects or things are passive in this way. I appreciate their arguments and do not contest the idea that "things" or objects are indeed agential. Yet, objects or things are still largely treated as passive, as lacking sentience. And it is their *treatment* more than their inherent capacities or potentialities that interests me. There is also, to me, an important difference to hold on to between living and nonliving "things"—in part because, in the exotic pet trade, this difference is crucial to whether or not a pet has value. But I also hold on to this distinction between living and nonliving because for me it is politically and ethically important. Living animals have sentience and can suffer (this being, in animal studies and beyond, a long-standing albeit intensely debated criterion for animals' ethical consideration). Living animals make different political and ethical demands (e.g., to alleviate or end their suffering), and they perform different roles in their communities (e.g., working to gather food, to creatively problem-solve in ways that can reproduce themselves and their communities). These roles do not end in death—animals' bodies decompose, feed socio-ecological communities—but the roles change here, and so do the ethical and political demands the animal makes. I thank Sainath Suryanarayanan for pushing me on these questions.

6 Nicole Shukin offers the first and most sustained investigation of animal capital in her book of the same name. She attends to traffic in both semiotic and material animal substance, showing how "animal memes and animal matter are mutually overdetermined as capital" (Shukin 2009, 7). The "tangling" of economic and symbolic animal capital is vivid in the exotic pet trade. In this book, though, I use "*lively* capital" instead of Shukin's "animal capital" because my focus is more on the performances and effects of being capital for animals. In the exotic pet trade, animal

capital must be more than animal; it must actively demonstrate its liveliness, within bounds. I also use "lively capital" as opposed to "lively commodity" (my previous go-to term to describe commodities whose central source of value is their active demonstrations of liveliness; see Collard and Dempsey 2013; Collard 2014) because, as I have indicated, many animals who circulate as exotic pets are not commodities. The term "lively capital" is helpfully more expansive. Recently, scholars in various fields have written about lively capital (see Haraway 2008; Sunder Rajan 2012; Barua 2019), although few offer definitions. I take a broad approach to lively capital, defining it as a "stock" of living objects that generate, or have the potential to generate, value of some kind. Often, this value is what Haraway calls "encounter value": value generated by transspecies relationships, value generated in meetings between subjects of different species. Haraway suggests that if a modern Marx equivalent were writing a book about biocapital today, the analyst would need to consider a "tripartite structure of value" that includes encounter value along with Marx's original concepts of use value and exchange value. Unlike Haraway, I see encounter value as a specific kind of use value rather than a third value alongside use and exchange. But her attention to the way that encounters lubricate commodification, and yet also how encounters are about more than profit or economic value, is crucial. Encounters are the exotic pet trade's bread and butter—they propel animals through commodity circuits. Encounters between people and their pets also cannot only be understood economically.

7 Environmental benefits (clean air, healthy food) and costs (pollution, toxicity) are distributed unevenly among humans, generally along lines of race and class. Equally, there are stark imbalances in terms of who is driving environmental change (e.g., contributing to climate change by emitting carbon dioxide) and who is experiencing the negative effects of those changes (e.g., experiencing extreme flooding associated with climate change). Much less attention is paid to these uneven distributions along species lines. What picture emerges if we add nonhuman beings to considerations of the distribution of resources and costs and benefits? Few tools are available. But the main measure for estimating resource distribution between humans and nonhumans is a measure of what is called human appropriation of net primary production, or HANPP, which calculates how much of the total carbon produced annually by plant growth is appropriated by humans—for example, for harvesting crops and consumption, and from land use change like converting forests to ranchland. What falls away from this measure is the unevenness among human consumption and among who is driving and benefiting from these land use transformations. Still, the results are important. A study from 2013 estimates that humans currently appropriate one-quarter of the earth's net primary production (Krausmann et al. 2013).

8 When I have presented my work or shared it with readers, people sometimes raise another potentially parallel structure: racial capitalism and, in
particular, people's historical and contemporary enslavement. There are
some structural similarities between how racialized people and nonhumans have been positioned within anthropocentric and racist capitalist
and colonial social relations. And there is excellent work in animal studies
and beyond that carefully examines the intersection of racism, colonialism, and anthropocentrism (see, e.g., Belcourt 2015; Kim 2015; Yarbrough
2015; Gillespie 2018b). But in this book I focus on animal captivity and do
not raise the enslavement of people alongside it. I do so for two reasons in
particular. First, the enslavement of people within racial capitalism is tied
to a dehumanization of people of color that is often enacted via their ani-
malization, or repeated comparison with animals. To place animal captivity and human enslavement side by side risks replaying that dehumanization, as many have noted. The second, related, reason is drawn from what
I have learned from Claire Jean Kim (2018) and Jared Sexton (2010), who
strongly caution against drawing parallels or especially analogies between
different kinds of oppression, particularly to antiblack slavery (a common
move among animal rights activists). This move, Kim and Sexton say,
denies the singularity of racial slavery and displaces the ongoing issue of
racial oppression, casting it as part of the past, relegating slavery to a historical condition—one that is now, the analogy suggests, only occupied by
animals. Sexton and Kim encourage us to forgo a comparative analysis in
favor of a relational one—to understand how variously oppressed subjects
are positioned or oriented in relation to each other. Lisa Lowe's book *The
Intimacies of Four Continents* (2015) exemplifies such a relational analysis of
differently positioned racialized subjects within the global colonial project.
9 As legal geographer Irus Braverman documents in her book *Zooland* (2012),
these time frames are subject to debate, especially among those who traffic
in "exotic animals" at an institutional level, like zookeepers. Moreover, as
the cultural geographer Kay Anderson (1997) has argued, our ideas about
domestication have as much, if not more, to do with the dominant conception of "the human" and the dualistic manner in which Western thought
positions "wildness" against "civilization." Rather than a universal and
apolitical process of humankind, Anderson wants us to see domestication
as both a physical transformation of nature into material that is more fixed
and enclosed, and a dominant means of defining and consolidating not
only humans' dominance over animals but also certain humans' dominance over other humans, especially along lines of race and gender.
10 K. Smith et al. (2017) provide these estimates, and see 't Sas-Rolfes et al.
(2019) for a summary of the range of estimates of illegal wildlife trade's
value. The exotic pet trade is part of a larger economy: global wildlife

trade, which includes dead wild animals traded for their parts, and includes plants. Prevailing estimates suggest that international legal wildlife trade is worth hundreds of billions of dollars per year (Warchol 2004; Engler and Parry-Jones 2007; Schneider 2008; Duffy, in White 2011; Sollund 2013)—possibly even as high as $300 billion annually (K. Smith et al. 2017). Interpol (the International Criminal Police Association) estimates that the illegal trade is the among the largest illegal industries in the world (Wyler and Sheikh 2008; Wyatt 2009; Barber-Meyer 2010; Rosen and Smith 2010).

11 The American Veterinary Medicine Association (AVMA) conducts US-wide household surveys of pet ownership, providing the data on bird and reptile ownership mentioned. The most recent data, from 2016, are published in the 2017–2018 AVMA Pet Ownership and Demographics Sourcebook. As the sourcebook notes, exotic pet ownership is "increasingly popular. More households than ever own specialty or exotic pets, such as fish, ferrets, rabbits, hamsters, guinea pigs, gerbils, turtles, snakes, lizards, poultry, livestock and amphibians. More than 13 percent of U.S. households owned a specialty or exotic pet at year-end 2016, a 25 percent increase from 2011" (see AVMA 2018). The American Pet Products Association (APPA) also conducts a US pet survey: the annual National Pet Owners survey. The most recent survey finds that 5.7 million households in the US are home to pet birds, an average of over two birds per household, bringing the total pet bird population in the US to over 20 million (APPA 2019). Other estimates of bird ownership in the United States place the number higher—a New York Times article published an estimate of 60 million owned parrots alone in the United States in 2010 (Lokting 2018). The statistic about more tigers living in captivity in the United States than in the wild worldwide is a common one to hear or read on news outlets like the BBC (Jeffrey 2018) and the Guardian (Hoare 2018) and in NGO reports, but tracking down the source is challenging. It is impossible to know how many tigers are kept captive in the United States because many states do not require permits and/or do not keep track of privately owned tigers. Brian Werner (2005) estimated there are 4,692 tigers captive in the United States. By contrast there are between 2,154 and 3,159 wild tigers in the world as of the most recent assessment in 2014 (Goodrich et al. 2015).

12 George Jennison (1872–1938), the superintendent of one of the first public zoos in England, Belle Vue Zoological Gardens, which his family founded in Manchester in 1837, reports in his history of exotic animal keeping, Animals for Show and Pleasure in Ancient Rome ([1937] 2005, xiii), that "almost without exception, a very fine zoological collection has marked the crest of power in every great nation and shrunk with it in its fall."

13 Sarah Whatmore's (2002) Hybrid Geographies and Marina Belozerskaya's (2006) The Medici Giraffe each examine in detail a different site of specta-

cle involving exotic animals—the gladiatorial games and the royal courts, respectively.

14 See Robbins 2002; Hanson 2004; Belozerskaya 2006; Simons 2012; also see Hoage and Deiss 1996 for discussions of nineteenth-century zoological parks in Europe and beyond.

15 For further discussion, see Simons 2012; also see Greenblatt 1991; Belozerskaya 2006.

16 For further discussion, see Mitman 1999; Burt 2000; Solnit 2006.

17 For more than a decade, NGO and academic experts have acknowledged the role of the internet and social media in facilitating the growth of the legal and illegal exotic pet trade (see IFAW 2008; Casey 2010; Lavorgna 2015; Siriwat and Nijman 2018).

18 *Finding Nemo* is a glaring example. The Oscar-winning Disney/Pixar animation from 2003, which garnered more than $864 million at the box office, tells the story of a boy clown fish who is captured on his way to school by a scuba diver. His father, Marlin, embarks on a mission to rescue him from a tank in a Sydney dentist's office. The film has a central message against keeping marine life in captivity, and following its release it became a favorite screening at snorkeling and diving hot spots around the world. But within months, the scuba diving industry was reporting a steep decline in sightings of clown fish, while pet suppliers reported rapid increases in sales. Clown fish are now facing extinction in many parts of the world. As parents whose children fell in love with Nemo at the cinema seek out the clown fish in ever-greater numbers, wild specimens have been overharvested—in the five years after the movie release, some populations plummeted by up to 75 percent, according to some marine biologists (in Alleyne 2008)—especially because clown fish are difficult and expensive to breed in captivity. For discussion of the role of film and video games in wildlife trade trends, see Doward 2010; Yong, Fam, and Lum 2011; Castro 2013; Nekaris et al. 2013.

19 For more information, see Laidlaw 2005; Nijman 2010.

20 For example, Trade Records Analysis of Flora and Fauna in Commerce (TRAFFIC), the international wildlife trade monitoring network, maintained a Twitter account (@TRAFFIC_WLTrade) that tracked wildlife trade news, mostly seizures and confiscations. In my monitoring of the feed until TRAFFIC stopped hosting the news archive in 2013, I observed a general media focus on Asian wildlife trade. The last entry from 2013 listed 196 stories in the category "in Asia" and only 9 "in Americas" and 34 "in Europe."

21 These estimates are found in Blundell and Mascia 2005; Pavlin, Schloegel, and Daszak 2009; K. Smith et al. 2009; Bush, Baker, and Macdonald 2014; K. Smith et al. 2017; Symes et al. 2018; Can, D'Cruze, and Macdonald

2019. The latter two most recent studies focus only on CITES-listed wild-life trade, which is a limited portion of the legal trade. Symes et al. (2018) analyze CITES trade data in mammals, birds, and reptiles between 2004 and 2013 to show global species and spatial trends. The data show that the United States is "by far the biggest importer" of CITES-listed mammals, birds, and reptiles, followed by Japan and the United Kingdom second and third for reptiles, the United Kingdom and Canada second and third for birds, and the United Kingdom and Germany second and third for mammals. Can, D'Cruze, and Macdonald (2019) also show the United States as the biggest importer of all CITES-listed live wild animals (based on CITES data from 2012 to 2016)—with China as the largest exporter of live mammals (94.8 percent of which were primates), Nicaragua the largest exporter of live amphibians, South Africa the largest exporter of live birds (93.2 percent of which were parrots), and Peru the largest exporter of live reptiles. In all, Can, D'Cruze, and Macdonald (2019) show that between 2012 and 2016, 11.6 billion CITES-listed individual live wild animals (of 1,316 different species) were exported from 189 different countries. These are only species listed under CITES, meaning that their trade is regulated because of concerns about its sustainability. In a reply to Can, D'Cruze, and Macdonald (2019), Eskew et al. (2019, 1) suggest that the trade volumes reported via CITES data are "almost certainly a vast underestimate" of the volume of international legal trade.

22 In their review of all trade records (CITES and non-CITES) globally from 2006 to 2012, Bush, Baker, and Macdonald (2014) find that demand for all taxa of exotic pets continues to be highest in the United States and Europe, but in recent years the Middle East has emerged as a large market for exotic pets, including birds, mammals, and reptiles.

23 In their review of live animal imports to the United States between 2000 and 2006, K. Smith et al. (2009) find that 69 percent of these imports originated in Southeast Asia.

24 Contributors to Sara Oldfield's (2003) edited book *The Trade in Wildlife: Regulation for Conservation* explore the various regulatory instruments associated with wildlife trade governance in a context of booming global trade and the trend toward trade liberalization. Particular challenges identified include weak enforcement of regulations, meager fines for illegal wildlife traders, and uneven resources for wildlife trade regulation between nations.

25 Canada additionally does not monitor non-CITES wildlife traded across its borders. Although the United States monitors wildlife imports of both CITES and non-CITES animals, studies have demonstrated significant discrepancies between CITES data and US data for CITES-listed species (Blundell and Mascia 2005; Thomas et al. 2006).

26 See K. Smith et al. (2017) for an overview of the zoonotic disease risks of

the exotic pet trade, focused on US imports. In Canada, the two major implementations of exotic animal regulation both came on the heels of lethal pet attacks: a man's Siberian tiger killed his girlfriend in northern British Columbia, and an escaped python killed two boys sleeping above a pet shop in New Brunswick. British Columbia's subsequent Controlled Alien Species regulation bans the ownership and sale of more than a thousand exotic animals. New Brunswick's regulation is currently underway.

27 In the Florida Everglades, so many owners have released their unwanted pet pythons into the area that a breeding population of pythons has established and is consuming and competing with many local animals, some of whom are endangered.

28 On the founding function of CITES, see Beissinger 2001, 182.

29 See Bush, Baker, and Macdonald 2014.

30 See Blundell and Mascia 2005; Mace, Masundire, and Baillie 2005; Sutherland et al. 2009; Bush, Baker, and Macdonald 2014.

31 See Adam 2010; D. Wilkie et al. 2010.

32 Yet, as Beissinger (2001, 184) explains, figures such as the CITES statistics for the number of live birds traded "greatly underestimate the numbers of birds extracted from the wild for the pet trade" by excluding mortality that occurs during capture, while confined by trappers, when transported within the country of origin, and while confined by the exporter before birds are granted CITES permits.

33 As Marx writes in *Capital* (1976, 163–164):

> A commodity appears at first sight an extremely obvious, trivial thing. But its analysis brings out that it is a very strange thing. . . . So far as it is a use-value, there is nothing mysterious about it, whether we consider it from the point of view that by its properties it satisfies human needs, or that it first takes these properties as the product of human labour. . . . But as soon as it emerges as a commodity, it changes into a thing that transcends sensuousness. . . . The mysterious character of the commodity-form consists . . . simply in the fact that the commodity reflects the social characteristics of men's [*sic*] own labour as objective characteristics of the products of labour themselves, as the socio-natural properties of these things. . . . The products of the human brain appear as autonomous figures endowed with a life of their own. . . . I call this the fetishism which attaches itself to the products of labour as soon as they are produced as commodities. . . . This finished form of the world of commodities . . . conceals the social character of private labour and the social relations between the individual workers, by making those relations appear as relations between material objects.

34 See, for example, classic work by Arjun Appadurai (1986) and Ian Cook et

al. (2004), as well as the relevant Polity book series Resources, which includes nineteen books and counting, each taking on a different commodity, from Coltan to Bioinformation (http://politybooks.com/serieslanding/?subject_id=2&series_id=20).

35 For example, as Michael Taussig (1980, 32) writes in his influential book on commodity fetishism, *The Devil and Commodity Fetishism in South America*: "Fetishism denotes the attribution of life, autonomy, power and even dominance to *otherwise inanimate objects* and presupposes the draining of these qualities from the human actors who bestow the attribution. Thus, in the case of commodity fetishism, social relationships are dismembered and appear to dissolve into relationships between mere things" (emphasis added). Theorists of commodities and commodity fetishism, from Marx to Taussig and others, in tending to presume inanimate objects, have *re-performed* another fetishism—animal fetishism.

36 There is a rich and extensive body of literature here, but see Dalla Costa and James 1973; Mies 1986; Fortunati 1995; Federici 2004; Fraser 2013.

37 Ahmed (2006, 41–42) writes: "Objects that I perceive as objects, as having properties of their own, as it were, are produced through the process of fetishism. The object is 'brought forth' as a thing that is 'itself' only insofar as it is cut off from its own arrival. So it becomes that which we have presented to us, only if we forget how it arrived, as a history that involves multiple forms of contact between others. Objects appear by being cut off from such histories of arrival, as histories that involve multiple generations, and the 'work' of bodies, which is of course the work of some bodies more than others."

38 If you keep to use value, Derrida (2006, 188) says, "the properties of the thing (and it is going to be a question of property) are always very human, at bottom, reassuring for this very reason. They always relate to what is proper to man, to the properties of man: either they respond to men's needs, and that is precisely their use-value, or else they are a product of a human activity that seems to intend them for those needs."

39 Spikes in consumer demand for various species frequently lead to large increases in the volume of trade, and in depleted wild populations of that species, as evidenced by the cases of clown fish (for whom demand spiked after the film *Finding Nemo* was released) and, at the time of writing, otters. K. Smith et al. (2017) and Bush, Baker, and Macdonald (2014) characterize the global exotic pet trade as demand-driven, and in their study of wildlife trade supply chains out of Madagascar, Robinson et al. (2018, 147) find that trappers collect animals to order—meaning they collect to fulfill orders "with specific information on number/species/sex [that is] transferred down the chain from exporter to local collector." Interviewed collectors stated they would be very unlikely to collect animals that were not ordered or

in larger quantity than ordered because no one would buy the animals or would only buy them for a lower price (Robinson et al. 2018). This demand-led quality suggests that curbing the exotic pet trade requires addressing demand. I'm not the first to suggest demand management as a response to the exotic pet trade, whether to address animal welfare concerns (Bush, Baker, and Macdonald 2014), risk of zoonotic disease transfer, depletion of wild populations (Courchamp et al. 2006; Challender, Harrop, and Mac-Millan 2015; Lunstrum and Givá 2020), or some combination of these issues (Moorhouse et al. 2017). Others have also noted the absence of demand management from international responses to the global exotic pet trade and wildlife trade more broadly (World Bank 2016; 't Sas-Rolfes et al. 2019).

40 The term "multispecies ethnography" was first used and popularized by Eben Kirksey and Stefan Helmreich (2010) in their introduction to their special issue of *Cultural Anthropology* on multispecies ethnography. Since then, many animal studies scholars have adopted the term. See Parreñas (2018) for an exemplary multispecies ethnography of orangutan rehabilitation in Borneo.

41 See Haraway (1991) and Agamben (2004) for critiques of this tendency to use animals as "mirrors" to derive and naturalize so-called universal human truths.

42 National and international governmental and intergovernmental campaigns frequently direct funding to supply management—for example, cracking down on illegal trappers and intercepting illegal shipments of animals. Meanwhile, demand reduction receives only a fraction of the funds to tackle wildlife trade (World Bank 2016).

Chapter One. An Act of Severing

1 See Wallace (2008) on spider monkey ranges.

2 See Ramos-Fernandez (2008) for a discussion of spider monkey sounds and communication.

3 Here I am following Levien (2013), who describes land enclosure as an "explosive" onetime act, a "massive and sudden change," following James Scott, and of course an act with lasting consequences. So, too, for enclosed animals: there is really no going back, once captured—especially if they leave their country of origin (see chapter 3).

4 For Marx, land enclosures were an act of original accumulation, necessary for the emergence of capitalism. Scholars since Marx, especially David Harvey (2007), have argued that enclosures are an ongoing part of capitalism, not merely a historical step within its development.

5 Not all people made landless even have access to a wage, though, as scholars such as Tania Li (2010) point out.

6 For Sevilla-Buitrago (2015), bodies cannot be enclosed because to be enclosed, something first must be a commons, and bodies are not commons. But what else are bodies other than commons? Bodies are lively forces held and shared in common with all the other bodies and lives they support and are supported by. Bodies take their shape in relation to each other, labor in common, and work for their communities. When these communities of bodies are separated from the conditions of their subsistence and autonomy, this amounts to a "profound remaking of their socioecological universe" (Makki 2014, 80).

7 For Watts, these two modes of enclosure—an animal's bodily enclosure and the enclosure of common land, which assimilates the peasantry into capitalist waged labor—are two threads woven together again and again throughout capitalist histories and presents. He argues that the demise of the peasantry involved not only the enclosure of space—lands held in common—but also the transformation of animals and their products into sites of accumulation. The exemplars of this transformation are, for Watts, the "alienated, lethargic elephant in . . . the zoo and the genetically modified sheep" and the industrial food system (M. Watts 2000, 295).

8 Researchers estimate that the number of parrots taken illegally from Mexico and imported to the United States declined from 150,000 a year in the late 1980s to about 9,400 by around 2003 (Guzmán et al. 2007). At the same time, Mexico has become a bigger player in the importation of exotic animals, especially birds. Between 2012 and 2016, Mexico was the top international importer of CITES-listed live wild birds (Can, D'Cruze, and Macdonald. 2019). This is in large part because the United States and the European Union have, since 1992 and 2007, respectively, had bans in place on international imports of wild-caught live birds.

9 See Sundberg 1998; Posocco 2008; Ybarra 2012.

10 See Hobson 2007; Dempsey 2010; Sundberg 2011.

11 I queried the CITES Trade Database (https://trade.cites.org/#) on August 23, 2019, for exports of any species for any purpose from Mexico to any country, 2010–2018.

12 Engebretson 2006, 272; see also Snyder et al. 2000; Wright et al. 2001; Michels 2002.

13 Poverty often marks many wildlife export regions, and some NGO, academic, and government reports tout the socioeconomic benefits that controlled wildlife trade can bring, namely, income from wildlife as a "renewable resource" ('t Sas-Rolfes et al. 2019, 14:34; also see Roe et al. 2002; Oldfield 2003; Nijman 2010). Yet few studies have been conducted on the actual benefits local people garner from wildlife trapping for international export, and an International Union for Conservation of Nature–sponsored review of these sparse studies is complicating the links between

wildlife trade and sustainable livelihoods. The potential of legal trade to work in favor of conservation varies substantially according to multiple factors, including the species being traded, the nature and persistence of demand for the species, and institutional structures in place, among others ('t Sas-Rolfes 2014). In the primary research conducted for this book, interviewees repeatedly confirmed that the poorest people involved in the trade, the capturers, receive the least amount of income from trading. This finding is corroborated by a recent study of the value chain of traded Malagasy animals, where Robinson et al. (2018) found that only 1.4 percent of value goes to collectors or trappers, while more than 90 percent of the value is captured by exporters. Little profit accrues at the local, rural level; instead, profit accumulates in urban areas for people who already have enough wealth and capital to be able to provide infrastructure, such as staff and animal shelter.

Chapter Two. Noah's Ark on the Auction Block

1   On contested commodities, see Radin 1996; on liminal commodities, see Parry 2012.
2   Kathryn Gillespie and I (2015) write about the common techniques of spatial and bodily control at both exotic animal auctions and farm animal auctions in our introduction to *Critical Animal Geographies*. Gillespie's (2018) book *The Cow with Ear Tag # 1389* elaborates in detail on the auction layout and the function of animal auctions for renewing and repurposing animals' commodity status (see her chapters 4 and 5).
3   In this sense, as Callon (1998) writes, the market itself is a coordination device with "the capacity to attach and shape some entities and disconnect others" (Callon 2002, 295). Muniesa, Millo, and Callon (2007, 2) thus refer more broadly to "market devices," which are "the material and discursive assemblages that intervene in the construction of markets." These market devices, including pricing tools, trading protocols, and so on, detach things from other things and attach them to new things, qualifying objects as marketable and enabling their movements. They make things into commodities. These attachments and detachments have strong spatial momentum, usually enabling or propelling movement within a commodity circuit, and the calculations that enable the exchange of commodities involve "detaching entities, bringing them together in a common space, and providing an assessment before circulating them elsewhere" (Barnes 2008, 1435).
4   The three other main auction types are the descending-bid auction; the first-price sealed-bid auction; and the second-price sealed-bid auction (see Klemperer 2004).

5 As discussed in the introduction, estimates of pet bird populations in the US vary from around 20 million (APPA 2019) to as many as 60 million (Lokting 2018).

6 African grey parrots are subject to extensive harvest for international pet trade. Since the 1980s, more than 12 million live parrots have been reported in international trade—62 percent of them reported as either wild-caught or of unknown origin (almost certainly also wild-caught) (UNODC 2016, 76). CITES (2016a) records indicate that between 1975 and 2015, 1.3 million wild African Grey parrots were exported from various range states. The numbers of birds exported is a fraction of the number of wild birds trapped, due to high pre-export mortality rates. In Cameroon, which accounted for almost half of exports from 1990 to 1996, as many as 90 percent of trapped birds died before reaching Douala Airport (BirdLife International 2018).

Chapter Three. Crafting the Unencounterable Animal

1 Success is usually measured by survival and reproduction—see Lunney et al. 2004; Teixeira et al. 2007; Guy, Curnoe, and Banks 2014; Moore and Wihermanto 2014.

2 Numbers of volunteers by nationality are provided sporadically in AR-CAS's annual reports, appearing in 2008, 2009, 2010, 2011, 2012 (based on total days worked, not total numbers of volunteers), and 2016. The reports are available to download at https://arcasguatemala.org/who-we-are/arcas -publications/ (accessed September 6, 2019).

3 "Brian" is a pseudonym for one of the ARCAS volunteers.

4 "Megan" is a pseudonym for one of the ARCAS primatologists interviewed for this research.

5 See Appadurai 1986; Gabrys 2011; Lepawsky and Billah 2011; Lepawsky and Mather 2011; Crang et al. 2013; Herod et al. 2013; Reddy 2013.

Chapter Four. Wild Life Politics

1 In some cases, if exotic animals can survive in the nonnative environ-ments to which they were accidentally or purposefully (and illegally) released, they can establish breeding populations that become invasive. The breeding population of Burmese pythons in the Florida Everglades is a classic case. The pythons, thought to be all former exotic pets or their descendants, are consuming native wildlife, including some endangered species (Dorcas et al. 2012).

2 The breeding population of Burmese pythons in the Florida Everglades (see preceding note) is one well-known example. Another example was

made famous by the best-selling book and award-winning documentary film of the same name *The Wild Parrots of Telegraph Hill* (Irving 2003; Bittner 2004). Since 1989, a colony of wild conures—medium-sized parrots—has lived in and around San Francisco, as is suggested by the title. While this story offers a glimmer of hope and indicates the resilience of wild animals, the conures are not immune to challenges unique to their urban and nonnative environment. Namely, since 1999 there have been reports of dozens of these parrots exhibiting a typically fatal neurological condition—one never observed in conure flocks in native environments. The condition manifests as ataxia, seizures, circling, and falling, which become so pronounced birds cannot self-feed, or die of injuries. A new academic study conducted in collaboration with Mickaboo Companion Bird Rescue (Van Sant et al. 2019) found that bromethalin, a common rat poison, is responsible for the birds' condition.

3 Kathryn Gillespie's (2018a) work also takes on these questions, without using these precise terms.

4 See McKenzie and Stoljar (2000, 11) for an extended critique of this long-standing formulation of autonomy.

5 In *The Open: Man and Animal*, Giorgio Agamben (2004) suggests that the figure of "the human" is formed through what he calls the "anthropological machine" in which a split is forged between the human and animals not only outside the body but also from the animal within.

6 This definition builds from Graeber (2009, 213), as well as Pickerill and Chatterton (2006) and Chatterton (2010), who see autonomy as a means and an end.

7 See McKenzie and Stoljar (2000) and Millar (2018) for two prominent but different examples of a relational approach to autonomy, which both term "relational autonomy."

8 As Pickerill and Chatterton (2006, 4) state, "Autonomy is a collective project, fulfilled only through reciprocal and mutually agreed relations with others."

9 See McKenzie and Stoljar (2000) for an elaboration of this relational conception of the self and how it shapes the idea of relational autonomy.

10 There are too many studies here to list, but on the racialized and colonial effects of wilderness discourses and practice in North America, see Baldwin, Cameron, and Kobayashi 2011; Thorpe 2012; Finney 2014; Davis 2019; and for more global examples, see Neumann 1998; Brockington 2002.

11 In North America, subsistence hunting was long vilified by colonists in the emerging model of wilderness conservation; see Tina Loo 2006; Eichler and Baumeister 2018. Wildlife management and animal rights efforts often still have disproportionately high costs for racialized and Indigenous people today; see, for example, the excellent film *Angry Inuk*,

by Inuk filmmaker Alethea Arnaquq-Baril, on the effects of seal hunting bans on Inuit, and Claire Jean Kim's (2015) book *Dangerous Crossings*, which tracks several high-profile cases of conflict between animal rights activists and the animal use practices of racialized people.

12 As noted in this book's introduction, social reproduction is a key, long-standing theme in feminist economic geography and feminist political economy. Feminists have observed that conventional economics and political economy tend to ignore the largely unwaged and unpriced realm of social reproduction, focusing on the so-called productive realm of the capitalist economy: waged work and commodities. A core, sustained feminist intervention into this literature suggests that the social reproductive realm is necessary to and devalued in capitalism (see, among many others, the work of Maria Mies, Cindi Katz, and Silvia Federici).

13 Feminist geographers Katharyne Mitchell, Sallie Marston, and Cindi Katz (2004) describe the work of social reproduction as "life's work."

14 Here I follow from Pickerill and Chatterton (2006), who suggest that both creation and resistance (or proposals and refusals) are part of practicing or working toward autonomy.

15 See Loo 2006; Kim 2015; *Angry Inuk* 2016; Eichler and Baumeister 2018.

16 David Harvey's (2003) concept of accumulation by dispossession speaks to the ongoingness of enclosure. Harvey argues that rather than enclosure forming a fundamental but temporary or passing moment in the history of capitalism, enclosure remains central to capital's functioning.

17 As Levien (2013, 365–366) describes, people attempt to intercede in the act of enclosure by engaging in sit-ins, blocking machines, and obstructing land surveys being conducted for the purpose of privatization. He emphasizes the importance of intervening before enclosure takes place, because of how difficult it is to undo once privatization is achieved and capital assumes possession of the means of (re)production. We can draw similar conclusions about the importance of intervening before animals are captured—enclosed—for the exotic pet trade. An added challenge of overturning enclosure for animals is their own sociobiological capacities, which tend to be weakened through capture and enclosure. Chapter 3 documents the immense challenge of rebuilding these capacities in enclosed animals.

18 Feminist theorists add that connections must also be drawn between a devaluation of animal life, global land enclosure processes, and capitalism's appropriation of female bodies in the service of reproducing and accumulating labor (Federici 2004).

19 See, for example, Courchamp et al. 2006; Baker et al. 2013; Challender, Harrop, and MacMillan 2015; Moorhouse et al. 2017; 't Sas-Rolfes et al. 2019; Lunstrum and Givá 2020.

20 See Veríssimo and Wan (2019) and 't Sas-Rolfes et al. (2019) for a review of demand-reduction campaigns and their characteristics.

21 Veríssimo and Wan (2019) and 't Sas-Rolfes et al. (2019) both observe that demand-reduction campaigns have tended to focus on Asia, and Margulies, Wong, and Duffy (2019) highlight a racist stereotype of the "Asian Super Consumer" in these demand management campaigns. Even if considering only funding to address wildlife trafficking in Africa and Asia, though, the majority (46 percent) of funding is directed to preventing "poaching," with an additional 19 percent for "law enforcement," including "intelligence-led operations and transnational coordination"; only 6 percent is allotted to "communication and awareness raising" (World Bank 2016, xi).

22 The EU ban on wild bird imports (enacted in 2005 and made permanent in 2007) reduced trade volumes to about 10 percent of their former levels. The ban also led to a redistribution of remaining trade volumes internationally, leading researchers to appeal for global bans (Reino et al. 2017).

REFERENCES

Adam, David. 2010. "Monkeys, Butterflies, Turtles . . . How the Pet Trade's Greed Is Emptying South-East Asia's Forests." *Guardian*, February 20. www.guardian.co.uk/environment/2010/feb/21/illegal-wildlife-trade.

Agamben, Giorgio. 2004. *The Open: Man and Animal*. Translated by Kevin Attell. Stanford, CA: Stanford University Press.

Ahmed, Sara. 2000. *Strange Encounters: Embodied Others in Post-coloniality*. Routledge: London.

Ahmed, Sara. 2006. *Queer Phenomenology: Orientations, Objects, Others*. Durham, NC: Duke University Press.

"Alex the African Grey." 2007. *Economist*, September 20. http://www .economist.com/node/9828615.

Alleyne, Richard. 2008. "Demand for Real Finding Nemo Clownfish Putting Stocks at Risk." *Telegraph*, June 26. http://www.telegraph.co.uk/news /earth/earthnews/3345594/Demand-for-real-Finding-Nemo-clownfish -putting-stocks-at-risk.html.

Anderson, Kay. 1997. "A Walk on the Wild Side: A Critical Geography of Domestication." *Progress in Human Geography* 21 (4): 463–485.

Angry Inuk. 2016. Directed by Alethea Arnaquq-Baril. Montreal: National Film Board of Canada. Accessed January 30, 2019. https://www.nfb.ca/film /angry_inuk/.

APPA. 2019. *2019–2020 APPA National Pet Owners Survey*. Stamford, CT: APPA.

Appadurai, Arjun. 1986. "Introduction: Commodities and the Politics of Value." In *The Social Life of Things: Commodities in Cultural Perspective*, edited by Arjun Appadurai, 3–63. Cambridge: Cambridge University Press.

ARCAS. 2010. ARCAS Annual Report 2009. Accessed August 29, 2013. http://www.arcasguatemala.com/en/about-arcas/arcas-publications.

ARCAS. 2012. ARCAS Annual Report 2011. Accessed August 29, 2013. http://www.arcasguatemala.com/en/about-arcas/arcas-publications.

Ashley, Shawn, Susan Brown, Joel Ledford, Janet Martin, Ann-Elizabeth Nash, Amanda Terry, Tim Tristan, and Clifford Warwick. 2014. "Morbidity and Mortality of Invertebrates, Amphibians, Reptiles, and Mammals at a Major Exotic Companion Animal Wholesaler." *Journal of Applied Animal Welfare Science* 17 (4): 308–321.

Aureli, Filippo, and Colleen Schaffner. 2008. "Social Interactions, Social Relationships and the Social System of Spider Monkeys." In *Spider Monkeys: Behaviour, Ecology and Evolution of the Genus* Ateles, edited by Christina Campbell, 236–265. Cambridge: Cambridge University Press.

AVMA. 2018. "Pet Ownership Is on the Rise." November 19. https://atwork.avma.org/2018/11/19/pet-ownership-is-on-the-rise/.

Baker, Sandra, Russ Cain, Freya Van Kesteren, Zinta Zommers, Neil D'Cruze, and David Macdonald. 2013. "Rough Trade: Animal Welfare in the Global Wildlife Trade." *BioScience* 63 (12): 928–938.

Bakker, Karen. 2003. *An Uncooperative Commodity: Privatizing Water in England and Wales*. Oxford: Oxford University Press.

Baldwin, Andrew, Laura Cameron, and Audrey Kobayashi, eds. 2011. *Rethinking the Great White North: Race, Nature, and the Historical Geographies of Whiteness in Canada*. Vancouver: UBC Press.

Barber-Meyer, Shannon. 2010. "Dealing with the Clandestine Nature of Wildlife-Trade Market." *Conservation Biology* 24 (4): 918–923.

Barnes, Trevor. 2008. "Making Space for the Market: Live Performances, Dead Objects, and Economic Geography." *Geography Compass* 2 (5): 1432–1448.

Bar-On, Yinon, Rob Phillips, and Ron Milo. 2018. "The Biomass Distribution on Earth." *Proceedings of the National Academy of Sciences of the United States of America* 115 (25): 6505–6511.

Barua, Maan. 2019. "Animating Capital: Work, Commodities, Circulation." *Progress in Human Geography* 43 (4): 650–669.

Baudrillard, Jean. 1981. *For a Critique of the Political Economy of the Sign*. St. Louis, MO: Telos.

Beissinger, Steven. 2001. "Trade of Live Wild Birds: Potentials, Principles, and Practices of Sustainable Use." In *Conservation of Exploited Species*, edited by John Reynolds, Georgina Mace, Kent Redford, and John Robinson, 182–202. Cambridge: Cambridge University Press.

Belcourt, Billy-Ray. 2015. "Animal Bodies, Colonial Subjects: (Re)Locating Animality in Decolonial Thought." *Societies* 5 (1): 1–11.

Bellinghausen, Hermann. 2012. "Commodification of Nature in Chiapas." *Compañero Manuel*, June 9. [Originally published in Spanish by

La Jornada.] http://compamanuel.wordpress.com/2012/06/09
/commodification-of-nature-in-chiapas/.

Belozerskaya, Mariana. 2006. *The Medici Giraffe: And Other Tales of Exotic Animals and Power.* New York: Little, Brown.

Benitez, Hesiquio. 2011. Director, Comisión Nacional para el Conocimiento y Uso de la Biodiversidad. Interview with the author. Mexico City, December 13.

Berger, John. 1980. *About Looking.* New York: Random House.

Bergman, Charles. 2009. "Wildlife Trafficking." *Smithsonian Magazine,* December. http://www.smithsonianmag.com/people-places/Wildlife -Trafficking.html.

BirdLife International. 2018. "*Psittacus erithacus*: The IUCN Red List of Threatened Species 2018." Accessed February 14, 2020. https://dx.doi .org/10.2305/IUCN.UK.2018-2.RLTS.T22724813A129879439.en.

BirdLife International. 2020. "Grey Parrot *Psittacus erithacus.*" Accessed January 31, 2020. http://datazone.birdlife.org/species/factsheet/grey -parrot-psittacus-erithacus/details.

Bishop, Greg, and Timothy Williams. 2011. "Police Kill Dozens of Animals Freed on Ohio Reserve." *New York Times,* October 19. http://www .nytimes.com/2011/10/20/us/police-kill-dozens-of-animals-freed-from -ohio-preserve.html?_r=0&adxnnl=1&pagewanted=all&adxnnlx =1368130111-hZoWymP/XLF/lH6OMfJv5w.

Bittner, Mark. 2004. *The Wild Parrots of Telegraph Hill: A Love Story.* New York: Three Rivers.

Blundell, Arthur, and Michael Mascia. 2005. "Discrepancies in Reported Levels of International Wildlife Trade." *Conservation Biology* 19 (6): 2020–2025.

Boyd, William. 2001. "Making Meat: Science, Technology, and American Poultry Production." *Technology and Culture* 42 (4): 631–664.

Bradshaw, G. A., Joseph P. Yenkosky, and Eileen McCarthy. 2009. "Avian Affective Dysregulation: Psychiatric Models and Treatment for Parrots in Captivity." *Proceedings of the Thirtieth Annual Association of Avian Veterinarians Conference with the Association of Exotic Mammal Veterinarians.* Milwaukee, WI, August 8–15. http://kerulos.org/wp-content/uploads/2018/07 /Bradshaw_Yenkosky_McCarthy_910_FINAL_8.13.09_AAV-TABLES.pdf.

Brantly, William. 1891. *Principles of the Law of Personal Property.* San Francisco: Bancroft-Whitney Company.

Braverman, Irus. 2012. *Zooland: The Institution of Captivity.* Stanford, CA: Stanford University Press.

Brockington, Dan. 2002. *Fortress Conservation: The Preservation of the Mkomazi Game Reserve, Tanzania.* Bloomington: Indiana University Press.

Brown, Sarah. 2009. "Gringo Politics." Master's thesis, University of British

Columbia. Accessed August 29, 2013. https://circle.ubc.ca/bitstream /handle/2429/13798/ubc_2009_fall_brown_sarah.pdf?sequence=1.

Burt, Jonathan. 2000. *Animals in Film*. London: Reaktion Books.

Bush, Emma, Sandra Baker, and David Macdonald. 2014. "Global Trade in Exotic Pets 2006–2012." *Conservation Biology* 28 (3): 663–676.

Butler, Judith. 2010. "Performative Agency." *Journal of Cultural Economy* 3 (2): 147–161.

Callon, Michel. 1998. *The Laws of the Markets*. Oxford: Blackwell.

Callon, Michel. 2002. "Technology, Politics and the Market: An Interview with Michel Callon." *Economy and Society* 31 (2): 285–306.

Campbell, Christina, and Nicole Gibson. 2008. "Spider Monkey Reproduction and Sexual Behaviour." In *Spider Monkeys: The Biology, Behavior and Ecology of the Genus* Ateles, edited by Christina Campbell, 266–287. Cambridge: Cambridge University Press.

Can, Özgün Emre, Neil D'Cruze, and David Macdonald. 2019. "Dealing in Deadly Pathogens: Taking Stock of the Legal Trade in Live Wildlife and Potential Risks to Human Health." *Global Ecology and Conservation* 17:e00515.

Cantu, Juan Carlos. 2011. Director, Defenders of Wildlife Mexico. Interview with the author. Mexico City, December 15.

Carey, Benedict. 2007. "Alex, a Parrot Who Had a Way with Words, Dies." *New York Times*, September 10. http://www.nytimes.com/2007/09/10 /science/10cnd-parrot.html?_r=0.

Casey, Michael. 2010. "Internet Is Biggest Threat to Endangered Species, Say Conservationists." *Guardian*, March 21. http://www.theguardian.com /environment/2010/mar/21/endangered-species-internet-threat.

Castro, Joseph. 2013. "Viral Videos of Cute, Exotic Animals May Harm Threatened Species." *NBC News Science*, August 14. http://www.nbcnews .com/science/viral-videos-cute-exotic-animals-may-harm-threatened -species-6C10913705.

Ceballos, Gerardo, Paul Ehrlich, and Rodolfo Dirzo. 2017. "Biological Annihilation via the Ongoing Sixth Mass Extinction Signaled by Vertebrate Population Losses and Declines." *Proceedings of the National Academy of Sciences of the United States of America* 114 (30): E6089–E6096.

Challender, Daniel, Stuart Harrop, and Douglas C. MacMillan. 2015. "Towards Informed and Multi-faceted Wildlife Trade Interventions." *Global Ecology and Conservation* 3 (January): 129–148.

Chatterton, Paul. 2010. "Symposium Autonomy: The Struggle for Survival, Self-Management and the Common Organiser." *Antipode* 42 (4): 897–908.

CITES. 2013. "What Is CITES?" Accessed January 31, 2020. http://www.cites .org/eng/disc/what.php.

CITES. 2016a. "Consideration of Proposals for Amendment of Appendices I and II: Proposal to Transfer from Appendix II to Appendix I of *Psittacus erithacus*." Adopted at CoP17, Johannesburg, South Africa. Geneva: CITES. Accessed February 14, 2020. https://cites.org/sites/default/files/eng/cop/17/prop/060216/E-CoP17-Prop-19.pdf.

CITES. 2016b. "Decisions 17.44 to 17.48 on Demand Reduction." Adopted at CoP17, Johannesburg, South Africa. Geneva: CITES. Accessed September 6, 2019. https://cites.org/eng/dec/valid17/81825.

CITES. 2017. "Demand Reduction: Report of the Secretariat." Geneva: CITES. Accessed January 31, 2020. https://cites.org/sites/default/files/eng/com/sc/69/E-SC69-15.pdf.

Collard, Rosemary-Claire. 2014. "Putting Animals Back Together, Taking Commodities Apart." *Annals of the Association of American Geographers* 104 (1): 151–165.

Collard, Rosemary-Claire, and Jessica Dempsey. 2013. "Life for Sale? The Politics of Lively Commodities." *Environment and Planning A: Economy and Space* 45 (11): 2682–2699.

Cook, Ian, et al. 2004. "Follow the Thing: Papaya." *Antipode* 36 (4): 642–664.

Cooper, Melissa. 2008. *Life as Surplus: Biotechnology and Capitalism in the Neoliberal Era*. Seattle: University of Washington Press.

Courchamp, Franck, Elena Angulo, Philippe Rivalan, Richard Hall, Laetitia Signoret, Leigh Bull, and Yves Meinard. 2006. "Rarity Value and Species Extinction: The Anthropogenic Allee Effect." *PLoS Biology* 4 (12): e415.

Crang, Mike, Alex Hughes, Nicky Gregson, Lucy Norris, and Farid Ahamed. 2013. "Rethinking Governance and Value in Commodity Chains through Global Recycling Networks." *Transactions of the Institute of British Geographers* 38 (1): 12–24.

Dalla Costa, Mariarosa, and Selma James. 1973. *The Power of Women and the Subversion of the Community*. Bristol: Falling Wall.

"Dark Blue." 2010. Radio Mundo, February 22. http://radiomundoreal.fm/Dark-Blue?lang=en.

Davis, Janae. 2019. "Black Faces, Black Spaces: Rethinking African American Underrepresentation in Wildland Spaces and Outdoor Recreation." *Environment and Planning E: Nature and Space* 2 (1): 89–109.

de la Maza, Javier, and Roberto de la Maza. 1985. "La fauna de mariposas de boca del Chajul, Chiapas, Mexico." *Revista de la Sociedad Mexicana de Lepidopterologia* 10:1–24.

DeLyser, Dydia, Rebecca Sheehan, and Andrew Curtis. 2004. "eBay and Research in Historical Geography." *Journal of Historical Geography* 30 (4): 764–782.

Dempsey, Jessica. 2010. "Tracking Grizzly Bears in British Columbia's Environmental Politics." *Environment and Planning A: Economy and Space* 42 (5): 1138–1156.

Derrida, Jacques. (1994) 2006. *Spectres of Marx: The State of the Debt, the Work of Mourning and the New International*. New York: Routledge.

Devine, Jennifer. 2014. "Counterinsurgency Ecotourism in Guatemala's Maya Biosphere Reserve." *Environment and Planning D: Society and Space* 32 (6): 984–1001.

Dirzo, Rodolfo, Hillary Young, Mauro Galetti, Gerardo Ceballos, Nick J. B. Isaac, and Ben Collen. 2014. "Defaunation in the Anthropocene." *Science* 345 (6195): 401–406.

Dorcas, Michael, John Willson, Robert Reed, Ray Snow, Michael Rochford, Melissa Miller, and Walter Meshaka. 2012. "Severe Mammal Declines Coincide with Proliferation of Invasive Burmese Pythons in Everglades National Park." *Proceedings of the National Academy of Sciences of the United States of America* 109 (7): 2418–2422.

Doward, Jamie. 2010. "Films Drive Trend for Keeping Pet Monkeys." *Guardian*, March 28. www.guardian.co.uk/world/2010/mar/28/primates-pet -monkeys-rspca.

Eichler, Lauren, and David Baumeister. 2018. "Hunting for Justice: An Indigenous Critique of the North American Model of Wildlife Conservation." *Environment and Society* 9 (1): 75–90.

Engebretson, M. 2006. "The Welfare and Suitability of Parrots as Companion Animals: A Review." *Animal Welfare* 15 (3): 263–276.

Engler, M., and R. Parry-Jones. 2007. "Opportunity or Threat: The Role of the European Union in Global Wildlife Trade." Brussels: TRAFFIC. June 1. https://www.traffic.org/publications/reports/opportunity-or-threat-the -role-of-the-european-union-in-the-global-wildlife-trade/.

Enríquez, Martha. 2011. "Conservation of the Montes Azules Biosphere Reserve, Chiapas: A Women's Issue." *Development* 54 (4): 473–479.

Eskew, Evan, Noam Ross, Carlos Zambrana-Torrelio, and William Karesh. 2019. "The CITES Trade Database Is Not a 'Global Snapshot' of Legal Wildlife Trade: Response to Can et al., 2019." *Global Ecology and Conservation* 18:e00631.

Estrada, Alejandro. 2014. "Reintroduction of the Scarlet Macaw (*Ara Macao Cyanoptera*) in the Tropical Rainforests of Palenque, Mexico: Project Design and First Year Progress." *Tropical Conservation Science* 7 (3): 342–364.

Federici, Silvia. 2004. *Caliban and the Witch: Women, the Body, and Primitive Accumulation*. New York: Automedia.

Finney, Carolyn. 2014. *Black Faces, White Spaces: Reimagining the Relationship of African Americans to the Great Outdoors*. Chapel Hill: University of North Carolina Press.

Fortunati, Leopoldina. 1995. *The Arcane of Reproduction Housework: Prostitution, Labor and Capital*. New York: Automedia.

References

Foucault, Michel. 1977. *Discipline and Punish: The Birth of the Prison.* New York: Vintage.

Fraser, Nancy. 2013. *Fortunes of Feminism: From State-Managed Capitalism to Neoliberal Crisis.* Brooklyn, NY: Verso Books.

Fraser, Nancy. 2014. "Can Society Be Commodities All the Way Down? Post-Polanyian Reflections on Capitalist Crisis." *Economy and Society* 43 (4): 541–558.

Gabrys, Jennifer. 2011. *Digital Rubbish: A Natural History of Electronics.* Ann Arbor: University of Michigan Press.

Galeano, Eduardo. 1997. *Open Veins of Latin America: Five Centuries of the Pillage of a Continent.* 25th anniversary edition. New York: Monthly Review Press.

Geismar, Haidy. 2008. "Alternative Market Values? Interventions into Auctions in Aotearoa/New Zealand." *Contemporary Pacific* 20 (2): 291–327.

Gillespie, Kathryn. 2018a. *The Cow with Ear Tag #1389.* Chicago: University of Chicago Press.

Gillespie, Kathryn. 2018b. "Placing Angola: Racialisation, Anthropocentrism, and Settler Colonialism at the Louisiana State Penitentiary's Angola Rodeo." *Antipode* 50 (5): 1267–1289.

Gillespie, Kathryn, and Rosemary-Claire Collard. 2015. *Critical Animal Geographies: Politics, Intersections and Hierarchies in a Multispecies World.* London: Routledge.

Goldstein, Jesse. 2013. "Terra Economica: Waste and the Production of Enclosed Nature." *Antipode* 45 (2): 357–375.

Gonzales, J. A. 2003. "Harvesting, Local Trade and Conservation of Parrots in the Northeastern Peruvian Amazon." *Conservation Biology* 114 (3): 437–446.

Goodrich, John, Anthony Lynam, Dale Miquelle, Hariyo Wibisono, Kae Kawanishi, Anak Pattanavibool, S. Htun, et al. 2015. "Tiger: *Panthera tigris.*" IUCN Red List. Accessed January 31, 2020. https://www.iucnredlist.org/species/15955/50659951.

Graeber, David. 2009. *Direct Action: An Ethnography.* Oakland, CA: AK Press.

Greenblatt, Stephen. 1991. *Marvelous Possessions: The Wonder of the New World.* Oxford: Clarendon.

Guy, Amanda, Darren Curnoe, and Peter Banks. 2014. "Welfare Based Primate Rehabilitation as a Potential Conservation Strategy: Does It Measure Up?" *Primates* 55:139–147.

Guy, Amanda, Olivia Stone, and Darren Curnoe. 2011. "The Release of a Troop of Rehabilitated Vervet Monkeys (*Chlorocebus aethiops*) in KwaZulu-Natal, South Africa: Outcomes and Assessment." *Folia Primatologica; International Journal of Primatology* 82 (6): 308–320.

Guzmán, Juan Carlos Cantú, Maria Elena Sánchez Saldaña, Manuel Grosselet, and Jesús Silva Gamez. 2007. "The Illegal Parrot Trade in Mexico:

A Comprehensive Assessment." Mexico City: Defenders of Wildlife. Accessed January 31, 2020. https://defenders.org/sites/default/files/publications/the_illegal_parrot_trade_in_mexico.pdf.

Hanson, Elizabeth. 2004. *Animal Attractions: Nature on Display in American Zoos.* Princeton, NJ: Princeton University Press.

Haraway, Donna. 1991. *Simians, Cyborgs, and Women: The Reinvention of Nature.* New York: Routledge.

Haraway, Donna. 1997. *Modest_Witness@Second_Millennium.FemaleMan©_Meets _Oncomouse™.* New York: Routledge.

Haraway, Donna. 2008. *When Species Meet.* Minneapolis: University of Minnesota Press.

Harfoot, Michael, Satu Glaser, Derek Tittensor, Gregory Britten, Claire McLardy, Kelly Malsch, and Neil Burgess. 2018. "Unveiling the Patterns and Trends in 40 Years of Global Trade in CITES-Listed Wildlife." *Biological Conservation* 223:47–57.

Harvey, David. 2007. *A Brief History of Neoliberalism.* Oxford: Oxford University Press.

Harvey, Neil. 2001. "Globalisation and Resistance in Post–Cold War Mexico: Difference, Citizenship and Biodiversity Conflicts in Chiapas." *Third World Quarterly* 22 (6): 1045–1061.

Heath, Chris. 2012. "18 Tigers, 17 Lions, 8 Bears, 3 Cougars, 2 Wolves, 1 Baboon, 1 Macaque, and 1 Man Dead in Ohio." *GQ*, February 6. http://www.gq.com/news-politics/newsmakers/201203/terry-thompson-ohio -zoo-massacre-chris-heath-gq-february-2012.

Herod, Andrew, Graham Pickren, Al Rainnie, and Susan McGrath-Champ. 2013. "Waste, Commodity Fetishism and the Ongoingness of Economic Life." *Area* 45 (3): 376–382.

Hoage, R. J., and William Deiss, eds. 1996. *New World, New Animals: From Menagerie to Zoological Park in the Nineteenth Century.* Baltimore: Johns Hopkins University Press.

Hoare, Philip. 2018. "More Tigers Live in US Back Yards Than in the Wild. Is This a Catastrophe?" *Guardian*, June 20. https://www.theguardian .com/environment/shortcuts/2018/jun/20/more-tigers-live-in-us-back -yards-than-in-the-wild-is-this-a-catastrophe.

Hobson, Kristy. 2007. "Political Animals? On Animals as Subjects in an Enlarged Political Geography." *Political Geography* 26 (3): 250–267.

Hoctor, Pat. 2013a. "Editorial." *Animal Finder's Guide* 29 (3): n.p.

Hoctor, Pat. 2013b. "Editorial." *Animal Finder's Guide* 29 (4): n.p.

IFAW. 2008. "Killing with Keystrokes: IFAW's Investigation into the European Online Ivory Trade." Yarmouth, MA: IFAW. http://www.ifaw.org/sites /default/files/FINAL Killing with Keystrokes 2.0 report 2011.pdf.

Irving, Judy, director. 2003. *The Wild Parrots of Telegraph Hill.* Pelican Media.

Jeffrey, James. 2018. "Does the US Have a Pet Tiger Problem?" *BBC News*, June 11. https://www.bbc.com/news/world-us-canada-44444016.

Jennison, George. (1937) 2005. *Animals for Show and Pleasure in Ancient Rome*. Philadelphia: University of Pennsylvania Press.

Kim, Claire Jean. 2015. *Dangerous Crossings: Species and Nature in a Multicultural Age*. New York: Cambridge University Press.

Kim, Claire Jean. 2018. "Abolition." In *Critical Terms in Animal Studies*, edited by Lori Gruen, 15–32. Chicago: University of Chicago Press.

Kimmerer, Robin Wall. 2015. *Braiding Sweetgrass: Indigenous Wisdom, Scientific Knowledge, and the Teachings of Plants*. Minneapolis: Milkweed Editions.

Kirksey, S. Eben, and Stefan Helmreich. 2010. "The Emergence of Multispecies Ethnography." *Cultural Anthropology* 25 (4): 545–576.

Klemperer, Paul. 2004. *Auctions: Theory and Practice*. Princeton, NJ: Princeton University Press.

Krausmann, Fridolin, Karl-Heinz Erb, Simone Gingrich, Helmut Haberl, Alberte Bondeau, Veronika Gaube, Christian Lauk, Christoph Plutzar, and Timothy D. Searchinger. 2013. "Global Human Appropriation of Net Primary Production Doubled in the 20th Century." *Proceedings of the National Academy of Sciences of the United States of America* 110 (25): 10324–10329.

Kretser, Heidi, McKenzie Johnson, Lisa Hickey, Peter Zahler, and Elizabeth Bennett. 2012. "Wildlife Trade Products Available to U.S. Military Personnel Serving Abroad." *Biodiversity Conservation* 21 (4): 967–980.

Laidlaw, Rob. 2005. *Scales and Tails: The Welfare and Trade of Reptiles Kept as Pets in Canada*. London: World Society for the Protection of Animals.

Latour, Bruno. 1987. *Science in Action: How to Follow Scientists and Engineers through Society*. Cambridge, MA: Harvard University Press.

Lavorgna, Anita. 2015. "The Social Organization of Pet Trafficking in Cyberspace." *European Journal on Criminal Policy and Research* 21 (3): 353–370.

Lepawsky, Josh, and Charles Mather. 2011. "From Beginnings and Endings to Boundaries and Edges: Rethinking Circulation and Exchange through Electronic Waste." *Area* 43 (3): 242–249.

Lepawsky, Josh, and Mostaem Billah. 2011. "Making Chains That (Un)make Things: Waste-Value Relations and the Bangladeshi Rubbish Electronics Industry." *Geografiska Annaler: Series B, Human Geography* 93 (2): 121–139.

Levien, Michael. 2013. "The Politics of Dispossession: Theorizing India's 'Land Wars.'" *Politics and Society* 41 (3): 351–394.

Li, Tania M. 2010. "To Make Live or Let Die? Rural Dispossession and the Protection of Surplus Populations." *Antipode* 41 (1): 66–93.

Lock, Margaret. 2002. "Alienation of Body Tissue and the Biopolitics of Immortalized Cell Lines." In *Commodifying Bodies*, edited by Nancy Scheper-Hughes and Lois Wacquant, 63–91. London: Sage.

Lokting, Britta. 2018. "The Pied Piper of Parrots." *New York Times*, January 17. https://www.nytimes.com/2018/01/17/nyregion/pet-parrot-trainer.html.

Loo, Tina. 2006. *States of Nature: Conserving Canada's Wildlife in the Twentieth Century*. Vancouver: UBC Press.

Lowe, Lisa. 2015. *The Intimacies of Four Continents*. Durham, NC: Duke University Press.

Lunney, Daniel, Shaan Gresser, Paul S. Mahon, and Alison Matthews. 2004. "Post-fire Survival and Reproduction of Rehabilitated and Unburnt Koalas." *Biological Conservation* 120 (4): 567–575.

Lunstrum, Elizabeth, and Nícia Givá. 2020. "What Drives Commercial Poaching? From Poverty to Economic Inequality." *Biological Conservation* 245: 108505.

Mace, Georgina, Hillary Masundire, and Johnathan Baillie. 2005. "Biodiversity." In *Ecosystems and Human Well-Being: Current State and Trends*, edited by Coalition and Trends Working Group of the Millennium Ecosystem Assessment, 77–122. Washington, DC: Island.

Mackenzie, Catriona, and Natalie Stoljar, eds. 2000. *Relational Autonomy: Feminist Perspectives on Autonomy, Agency, and the Social Self*. Oxford: Oxford University Press.

Mackey, Jeff. 2013. "Victory: Authorities Pull License from Tiger Tormentor!" *The PETA Files: PETA's Official Blog*, April 17. Accessed September 11, 2013. http://www.peta.org/b/thepetafiles/archive/tags/exotic+animals/default.aspx.

MacKinnon, J. B. 2013. *The Once and Future World: Nature as It Was, as It Is, as It Could Be*. Toronto: Random House Canada.

Makki, Fouad. 2014. "Development by Dispossession: *Terra Nullius* and the Social-ecology of New Enclosures in Ethiopia." *Rural Sociology* 79 (1): 79–103.

Margulies, Jared, Rebecca Wong, and Rosaleen Duffy. 2019. "The Imaginary 'Asian Super Consumer': A Critique of Demand Reduction Campaigns for the Illegal Wildlife Trade." *Geoforum* 107: 216–219.

Martinez, Fernando. 2011. ARCAS Director of Peten Program. Interview with the author. ARCAS Wildlife Rehabilitation Centre, November 16.

Marx, Karl. 1976. *Capital*. Vol. 1, *A Critique of Political Economy*. London: Penguin Classics.

McNab, Roan. 2011. Director, Wildlife Conservation Society—Guatemala. Interview with the author. Flores, November 1.

Megan [pseudonym]. 2011. ARCAS Primatologist. Interview with the author. ARCAS Wildlife Rehabilitation Centre, November 17.

Michels, Ann. 2002. "Global Parrot Smuggling Still a Problem." *Animal Welfare Institute Quarterly* 51 (4). Accessed September 10, 2013. http://awionline.org/pubs/Quarterly/fall02/parrot.htm.

Mies, Maria. 1986. *Patriarchy and Accumulation on a World Scale: Women in the International Division of Labour*. London: Zed Books.

Millar, Kathleen. 2018. *Reclaiming the Discarded: Life and Labor on Rio's Garbage Dump*. Durham, NC: Duke University Press.

Mitchell, Katharyne, Sallie Marston, and Cindi Katz. 2004. *Life's Work: Geographies of Social Reproduction*. New York: Wiley-Blackwell.

Mitman, Gregg. 1999. *Reel Nature: America's Romance with Wildlife on Film*. Cambridge, MA: Harvard University Press.

Moore, R., and K. Wihermanto. 2014. "Compassionate Conservation, Rehabilitation and Translocation of Indonesian Slow Lorises." *Endangered Species Research* 26:93–102.

Moorhouse, Tom, Margaret Balaskas, Neil D'Cruze, and David Macdonald. 2017. "Information Could Reduce Consumer Demand for Exotic Pets." *Conservation Letters* 10 (3): 337–345.

Morales, Alejandro. 2011. ARCAS Assistant Director. Interview with the author. ARCAS Wildlife Rehabilitation Centre, November 26.

Muniesa, Fabian, Yuuval Millo, and Michel Callon. 2007. "An Introduction to Market Devices." In *Market Devices*, edited by Michel Callon, Yuval Millo, and Fabian Muniesa, 1–12. Malden, MA: Wiley-Blackwell.

Myers, Norman. 1988. "Threatened Biotas: 'Hot Spots' in Tropical Forests." *Environmentalist* 8:187–208.

Myers, Norman. 1990. "The Biodiversity Challenge: Expanded Hot-Spots Analysis." *Environmentalist* 10:243–256.

Naranjo, Eduardo. 2011. ECOSUR professor. Interview with the author. RIBMA, October 29.

Nekaris, K. Anne-Isola, Nicola Campbell, Time G. Coggins, E. Johanna Rode, and Vincent Nijman. 2013. "Tickled to Death: Analysing Public Perceptions of 'Cute' Videos of Threatened Species (Slow Lorises–Nycticebus spp.) on Web 2.0 Sites." *PLOS ONE* 8 (7): e69215.

Nelson, Diane M. 1999. *A Finger in the Wound: Body Politics in Quincentennial Guatemala*. Berkeley: University of California Press.

Neumann, Rod. 1998. *Imposing Wilderness: Struggles over Livelihood and Nature Preservation in Africa*. Berkeley: University of California Press.

Nijman, Vincent. 2010. "An Overview of International Wildlife Trade from Southeast Asia." *Biodiversity Conservation* 19 (4): 1101–1114.

Nir, Sarah. 2012. "A Tighter Leash on Exotic Pets." *New York Times*, January 10. https://www.nytimes.com/2012/01/11/us/exotic-animals-business-faces-restrictions.html?pagewanted=all&_r=0.

Nordstrom, Nancy. 1997. *A Different Kind of War Story*. Philadelphia: University of Pennsylvania Press.

Ohio State Legislature. 2013. Senate Bill 310. Accessed September 11, 2013. http://www.legislature.state.oh.us/bills.cfm?ID=129_SB_310.

Oldfield, Sara, ed. 2003. *The Trade in Wildlife: Regulation for Conservation.* London: Earthscan.

Ontario Superior Court of Justice. 2013. *Nakhuda v. Story Book Farm Primate Sanctuary.* ONSC 5761. Accessed January 31, 2020. https://www.animal justice.ca/wp-content/uploads/2013/09/20130913091859258.pdf.

Palmer, Clare. 2010. *Animal Ethics in Context.* New York: Columbia University Press.

Parreñas, Rheana "Juno" Salazar. 2012. "Producing Affect: Transnational Volunteerism in a Malaysian Orangutan Rehabilitation Center." *American Ethnologist* 39 (4): 673–687.

Parreñas, Juno Salazar. 2016. "The Materiality of Intimacy: Rethinking 'Ethical Capitalism' through Embodied Encounters with Animals in Southeast Asia." *positions: asia critique* 24 (1): 97–127.

Parreñas, Juno Salazar. 2018. *Decolonizing Extinction: The Work of Care in Orangutan Rehabilitation.* Durham, DC: Duke University Press.

Parry, Bronwyn. 2008. "Entangled Exchange: Reconceptualising the Characterisation and Practice of Bodily Commodification." *Geoforum* 39 (3): 1133–1144.

Parry, Bronwyn. 2012. "Economies of Bodily Commodification." In *The Wiley-Blackwell Companion to Economic Geography,* edited by Trevor Barnes, Jaime Peck, and Eric Sheppard, 213–225. Malden, MA: Wiley-Blackwell.

Pavlin, Boris, Lisa Schloegel, and Peter Daszak. 2009. "Risk of Importing Zoonotic Diseases through Wildlife Trade, United States." *Emerging Infectious Diseases* 15 (11): 1721–1726.

Penrose, Jan. 2003. "When All the Cowboys Are Indians: The Nature of Race in All-Indian Rodeo." *Annals of the Association of American Geographers* 93 (3): 687–705.

Pepperberg, Irene. 2008. *Alex and Me.* New York: HarperCollins.

Pickerill, Jenny, and Paul Chatterton. 2006. "Notes towards Autonomous Geographies: Creation, Resistance and Self-Management as Survival Tactics." *Progress in Human Geography* 30 (6): 1–17.

Pires, Stephen. 2012. "The Illegal Parrot Trade: A Literature Review." *Global Crime* 13 (3): 176–190.

Pires, Stephen, and Ronald Clark. 2012. "Are Parrots CRAVED? An Analysis of Parrot Poaching in Mexico." *Journal of Research in Crime and Delinquency* 49 (1): 122–146.

Plumwood, Val. 1993. *Feminism and the Mastery of Nature.* London: Routledge.

Posocco, Silvia. 2008. "Zoning: Environmental Cosmopolitics in and around the Maya Biosphere Reserve, Petén, Guatemala." *Nature and Culture* 3 (2): 206–224.

Prudham, Scott. 2004. *Knock on Wood: Nature as Commodity in Douglas-Fir Country.* New York: Routledge.

Puig de la Bellascasa, Maria. 2010. "Ethical Doings in Naturecultures." *Ethics, Place, and Environment: A Journal of Philosophy and Geography* 13 (2): 151–169.

Radin, Margaret. 1996. *Contested Commodities*. Cambridge, MA: Harvard University Press.

Ramos-Fernandez, Gabriel. 2008. "Communication in Spider Monkeys: The Function and Mechanisms Underlying the Use of the Whinny." In *Spider Monkeys: Behaviour, Ecology and Evolution of the Genus* Ateles, edited by Christina Campbell, 220–235. Cambridge: Cambridge University Press.

Reddy, Rajyashree N. 2013. "Revitalising Economies of Disassembly." *Economic and Political Weekly* 48 (13): 62–70.

Reino, Luís, Rui Figueira, Pedro Beja, Miguel Araújo, César Capinha, and Diederik Strubbe. 2017. "Networks of Global Bird Invasion Altered by Regional Trade Ban." *Science Advances* 3 (11): e1700783.

Ritvo, Harriet. 1987. *The Animal Estate: The English and Other Creatures in the Victorian Age*. Cambridge, MA: Harvard University Press.

Robbins, Louise. 2002. *Elephant Slaves and Pampered Parrots: Exotic Animals in Eighteenth-Century Paris*. Baltimore: Johns Hopkins University Press.

Robinson, Jaine, Iain Fraser, Freya St. John, J. Christian Randrianantoandro, Raphali Andriantsimanarilafy, Julie Razafimanahaka, Richard Griffiths, and David Roberts. 2018. "Wildlife Supply Chains in Madagascar from Local Collection to Global Export." *Biological Conservation* 226:144–152.

Roe, Dilys, Teresa Mulliken, Simon Milledge, Josephine Mremi, Simon Mosha, and Maryanne Grieg-Gran. 2002. *Making a Killing or Making a Living? Wildlife Trade, Trade Controls and Rural Livelihoods*. London: International Institute for Environment and Development.

Rose, Nikolas. 2006. *The Politics of Life Itself: Biomedicine, Power, and Subjectivity in the Twenty-First Century*. Princeton, NJ: Princeton University Press.

Rose, Nikolas. 2008. "The Value of Life: Somatic Ethics and the Spirit of Biocapital." *Daedalus* 137 (1): 36–48.

Rosen, Gail, and Katherine Smith. 2010. "Summarizing the Evidence on the International Trade in Illegal Wildlife." *EcoHealth* 7 (1): 24–32.

Rosenberger, Alfred, Lauren Halenar, Siobhan Cooke, and Walter Hartwig. 2008. "Morphology and Evolution of the Spider Monkey, Genus *Ateles*." In *Spider Monkeys: Behaviour, Ecology and Evolution of the Genus* Ateles, edited by Christina Campbell, 19–49. Cambridge: Cambridge University Press.

Schneider, Jacqueline. 2008. "Reducing the Illicit Trade in Endangered Wildlife: The Market Reduction Approach." *Journal of Contemporary Criminal Justice* 24 (3): 274–295.

Sevilla-Buitrago, Alvaro. 2015. "Capitalist Formations of Enclosure: Space and the Extinction of the Commons." *Antipode* 47 (4): 999–1020.

Sexton, Jared. 2010. "People-of-Colour-Blindness: Notes on the Afterlife of Slavery." *Social Text* 28 (2): 31–56.

Shukin, Nicole. 2009. *Animal Capital: Rendering Life in Biopolitical Times.* Minneapolis: University of Minnesota Press.

Simons, John. 2012. *The Tiger That Swallowed the Boy: Exotic Animals in Victorian England.* Oxford: Libri.

Siriwat, Penthai, and Vincent Nijman. 2018. "Illegal Pet Trade on Social Media as an Emerging Impediment to the Conservation of Asian Otters Species." *Journal of Asia-Pacific Biodiversity* 11 (4): 469–475.

Smith, Charles. 1989. *Auctions: The Social Construction of Value.* Berkeley: University of California Press.

Smith, Katherine, Michael Behrens, Lisa Schloegel, Nina Marano, Stas Burgiel, and Peter Daszak. 2009. "Reducing the Risks of the Wildlife Trade." *Science* 324:594–595.

Smith, Katherine, C. Zambrana-Torrelio, A. White, M. Asmussen, C. Machalaba, S. Kennedy, K. Lopez, et al. 2017. "Summarizing US Wildlife Trade with an Eye toward Assessing the Risk of Infectious Disease Introduction." *EcoHealth* 14 (1): 29–39.

Smith, Neil. 2008. *Uneven Development: Nature, Capital, and the Production of Space.* 3rd ed. Athens: University of Georgia Press.

Snyder, Noel, Philip McGowan, James Gilardi, and Grajal Alejandro. 2000. "Parrots: Status Survey and Conservation Action Plan 2000–2004." Gland, Switzerland: International Union for Conservation of Nature and Natural Resources. Accessed September 10, 2013. http://www.parrots.org/index.php/ourpublication/papfiles/.

Sollund, Ragnhild. 2013. "Animal Trafficking and Trade: Abuse and Species Justice." In *Emerging Issues in Green Criminology: Exploring Power, Justice and Harm,* edited by Diane Westerhuis, Reece Walters, and Tanya Wyatt, 72–92. London: Palgrave.

Solnit, Rebecca. 2006. *River of Shadows: Eadweard Muybridge and the Technological Wild West.* New York: Viking.

Story Book Farm Primate Sanctuary. 2020. "About the Monkeys." Accessed January 18. http://www.storybookmonkeys.org/monkeys.htm.

Sundberg, Juanita. 1998. "NGO Landscapes in the Maya Biosphere Reserve, Guatemala." *Geographical Review* 88:388–412.

Sundberg, Juanita. 2011. "Diabolic Caminos in the Desert and Cat Fights on the Río: A Posthumanist Political Ecology of Boundary Enforcement in the United States–Mexico Borderlands." *Annals of the Association of American Geographers* 101 (2): 318–336.

Sunder Rajan, Kaushik. 2006. *Biocapital: The Constitution of Postgenomic Life.* Durham, NC: Duke University Press.

Sunder Rajan, Kaushik, ed. 2012. *Lively Capital: Biotechnologies, Ethics, and Governance in Global Markets.* Durham, NC: Duke University Press.

Sutherland, W. J., W. M. Adams, R. B. Aronson, R. Aveling, T. M. Blackburn, S. Broad, G. Ceballos, et al. 2009. "One Hundred Questions of Importance to the Conservation of Global Biological Diversity." *Conservation Biology* 23 (3): 557–567.

Symes, William, Francesca McGrath, Madhu Rao, and Roman Carrasco. 2018. "The Gravity of Wildlife Trade." *Biological Conservation* 218:268–276.

Taussig, Michael. 1980. *The Devil and Commodity Fetishism in South America.* Chapel Hill: University of North Carolina Press.

Teixeira, Camila, Cristiano Schetini de Azevedo, Mike Mendl, Cynthia Cipreste, and Robert Young. 2007. "Revisiting Translocation and Reintroduction Programmes: The Importance of Considering Stress." *Animal Behaviour* 73 (1): 1–13.

Thomas, Peter, Mark Albert, Arthur Blundell, and Michael Mascia. 2006. "Data on Wildlife Trade." *Conservation Biology* 20:598–599.

Thompson, Ginger. 2006. "Mexico Worries about Its Own Southern Border." *New York Times,* June 18. www.nytimes.com/2006/06/18/world/americas /18mexico.html?pagewanted=all&_r=0.

Thorpe, Jocelyn. 2012. *Temagami's Tangled Wild: Race, Gender, and the Making of Canadian Nature.* Vancouver: UBC Press.

't Sas-Rolfes, Michael. 2014. "Legal Rhino Horn: A Viable Conservation Alternative?" *BioRes* 8 (2): 4–5.

't Sas-Rolfes, Michael, Daniel Challender, Amy Hinsley, Diogo Veríssimo, and E. J. Milner-Gulland. 2019. "Illegal Wildlife Trade: Patterns, Processes, and Governance." *Annual Review of Environment and Resources* 44:14.1–14.28.

Tuan, Yi Fu. 1984. *Dominance and Affection: The Making of Pets.* New Haven, CT: Yale University Press.

UNODC (United Nations Office on Drugs and Crime). 2016. "World Wildlife Crime Report: Trafficking in Protected Species." Vienna: UNODC. Accessed February 27, 2019. https://www.unodc.org/documents/data-and -analysis/wildlife/World_Wildlife_Crime_Report_2016_final.pdf.

US Court of Appeals for the Fourth Circuit. 2001. *PETA v Doughney.* Accessed January 31, 2020. http://cyber.law.harvard.edu/stjohns/PETA_v _Doughney.html.

Vail, John. 2010. "Decommodification and Egalitarian Political Economy." *Politics and Society* 38 (3): 310–346.

Van Sant, Fern, Sayed Hassan, Drury Reavill, Rita McManamon, Elizabeth Howerth, Mauricio Seguel, Richard Bauer, et al. 2019. "Evidence of Bromethalin Toxicosis in Feral San Francisco 'Telegraph Hill' Conures." *PLOS ONE* 14 (3): e0213248.

Veríssimo, Diogo, and Anita Wan. 2019. "Characterizing Efforts to Reduce Consumer Demand for Wildlife Products." *Conservation Biology* 33 (3): 623–633.

Vick, Laura. 2008. "Immaturity in Spider Monkeys: A Risky Business." In *Spider Monkeys: Behaviour, Ecology and Evolution of the Genus* Ateles, edited by Christina Campbell, 288–328. Cambridge: Cambridge University Press.

Vrasti, Wanda. 2013. *Volunteer Tourism in the Global South: Giving Back in Neoliberal Times.* New York: Routledge.

Wadiwel, Dinesh. 2018. "Chicken Harvesting Machine: Animal Labour, Resistance, and the Time of Production." *South Atlantic Quarterly* 117 (3): 527–549.

Wallace, Robert. 2008. "Factors Influencing Spider Monkey Habitat Use and Ranging Patterns." In *Spider Monkeys: Behaviour, Ecology and Evolution of the Genus* Ateles, edited by Christina Campbell, 138–154. Cambridge: Cambridge University Press.

Warchol, Greg. 2004. "The Transnational Illegal Wildlife Trade." *Criminal Justice Studies* 17 (1): 53–57.

Watts, Michael. 2000. "Afterword: Enclosure." In *Animal Spaces, Beastly Places: New Geographies of Human-Animal Relations*, edited by Chris Philo and Chris Wilbert, 291–301. London: Routledge.

Watts, Vanessa. 2013. "Indigenous Place-Thought and Agency amongst Humans and Non-Humans (First Woman and Sky Woman Go on a European World Tour!)." *Decolonization: Indigeneity, Education and Society* 2 (1): 20–34.

Weis, Tony. 2013. *The Ecological Hoofprint: The Global Burden of Industrial Livestock.* London: Zed Books.

Weis, Tony. 2018. "Ghosts and Things: Agriculture and Animal Life." *Global Environmental Politics* 18 (2): 134–142.

Werner, Brian. 2005. "Distribution, Abundance and Reproductive Biology of Captive *Panthera Tigris* Populations Living within the United States of America." *Feline Conservation Federation* 49 (2): 24–25.

Weston, M., and M. Memon. 2007. "The Illegal Parrot Trade in Latin America and Its Consequences to Parrot Nutrition, Health and Conservation." *Bird Conservation* 9:76–83.

Whatmore, Sarah. 2002. *Hybrid Geographies: Natures Cultures Spaces.* London: Sage.

White, Rob. 2011. *Transnational Environmental Crime: Toward an Eco-global Criminology.* New York: Taylor and Francis.

Wilkie, David S., Elizabeth L. Bennet, Carlos A. Peres, and Andrew A. Cunningham. 2010. "The Empty Forest Revisited." *Annals of the New York Academy of Sciences* 1223 (1): 120–128.

Wilkie, Rhoda. 2005. "Sentient Commodities and Productive Paradoxes: The

Ambiguous Nature of Human-Livestock Relations in Northeast Scotland." *Journal of Rural Studies* 21 (2): 213–230.

Wilkie, Rhoda. 2010. *Livestock/Deadstock: Working with Farm Animals from Birth to Slaughter*. Philadelphia: Temple University Press.

World Bank. 2016. "Analysis of International Funding to Tackle Illegal Wildlife Trade." Washington, DC: World Bank. Accessed January 31, 2020. http://documents.worldbank.org/curated/en/695451479221164739/pdf/110267-WP-Illegal-Wildlife-Trade-OUO-9.pdf.

Wright, Tony, Catherine Toft, Ernesto Enkerlin-Hoeflich, Jamie Gonzales-Elizondo, Mariana Albornoz, Adriana Rodriguez-Ferraro, Franklin Rojas-Suárez, et al. 2001. "Nest Poaching in Neotropical Parrots." *Conservation Biology* 15:710–720.

WWF. 2018. *Living Planet Report 2018: Aiming Higher*. Edited by M. Grooten and R. E. A. Almond. Gland, Switzerland: WWF. https://wwf.panda.org/knowledge_hub/all_publications/living_planet_report_2018/.

Wyatt, Tanya. 2009. "Exploring the Organization of Russia Far East's Illegal Wildlife Trade: Two Case Studies of the Illegal Fur and Illegal Falcon Trades." *Global Crime* 10 (1–2): 144–145.

Wyler, Linda, and Pervaze Sheikh. 2008. "International Illegal Trade in Wildlife: Threats and U.S. Policy. Order Code RL34395 Congressional Research Service." Washington, DC: Congressional Research Service. Accessed January 31, 2020. https://fas.org/sgp/crs/misc/RL34395.pdf.

Wynter, Sylvia. 1995. "1492: A New World View." In *Race, Discourse, and the Origin of the Americas: A New World View*, edited by Vera Lawrence Hyatt and Rex Nettleford, 5–57. Washington, DC: Smithsonian Institution Press.

Yarbrough, Anastasia. 2015. "Species, Race, and Culture in the Space of Wildlife Management." In *Critical Animal Geographies: Politics, Intersections and Hierarchies in a Multispecies World*, edited by Kathryn Gillespie and Rosemary-Claire Collard, 108–126. New York: Routledge.

Ybarra, Megan. 2012. "Taming the Jungle, Saving the Maya Forest: Sedimented Counterinsurgency Practices in Contemporary Guatemalan Conservation." *Journal of Peasant Studies* 39 (2): 479–502.

Yenkosky, Joseph, G. Bradshaw, and Eileen McCarthy. 2010. "Post-traumatic Stress Disorder among Parrots in Captivity: Treatment Considerations." *Proceedings of the Thirty-First Annual Association of Avian Veterinarians Conference with the Association of Exotic Mammal Veterinarians*, San Diego, CA, August 1. http://citeseerx.ist.psu.edu/viewdoc/download?doi=10.1.1.462.5067&rep=rep1&type=pdf#page=27.

Yong, Ding Li, Shun Deng Fam, and Shawn Lum. 2011. "Reel Conservation: Can Big Screen Animations Save Tropical Biodiversity?" *Tropical Conservation Sciences* 4 (3): 244–253.

Youlatos, Dionisios. 2008. "Locomotion and Positional Behaviour of Spider

Monkeys." In *Spider Monkeys: Behaviour, Ecology and Evolution of the Genus Ateles*, edited by Christina Campbell, 185–219. Cambridge: Cambridge University Press.

Zapatistas. 2013. "What Is Zapatista Autonomy?" San Diego: Schools for Chiapas. April 3. https://schoolsforchiapas.org/blog-entry-zapatista -autonomy/.

Zelizer, Vivian. 2005. *The Purchase of Intimacy*. Princeton, NJ: Princeton University Press.

INDEX

Note: Page numbers followed by *f* denote figures, *m* maps, and *t* tables.

botflies, 49
Braverman, Irus, 144n9
buffalo, 74–75
butterflies, 40, 42–43, 49

cages. *See* enclosure
Callon, Michel, 53
Canada: animals as property, 2; animal trade, 14, 147n25; exotic animal regulation, 14, 71, 122, 138, 147n26; serval, escaped, 123–124
Cantu, Juan Carlos, 54–57
capital. *See* animal capital; lively capital
capitalism: anthropocentrism of, 22; human-animal relations in, 7–8, 21; and inequality, 7, 143n7; land enclosure enabling, 36, 135, 150n4, 155n16; nonhuman life, 8, 20–21; and patriarchy, 20–21; racial slavery, 144n8; reproductive labor, 20–21; super-exploitation, 21; unpriced work in, 19
capture: commodification, as enabling, 37, 53; as enclosure, 36–37, 52–53, 57–58; of infants, 34; lively capital, creating, 37, 57, 93, 103; and networks of relations, 52–53, 57; as open secret, 56; of parrots, 50–52; preventing, importance of, 138; private property, creating, 36; socio-ecological relations, severing, 29, 35, 37, 50, 89, 135–136, 138–139; of spider monkeys, 34, 37, 52; trauma of, 35–36, 79
Chiapas, Mexico, 39*m*, 40–41
Chiquibul National Park, 38
clown fish, 146n18, 149n39
commodification: of animal capital, 22–23; and animal fetishism, 16–18, 22, 25, 126; of animals, 4, 18, 29, 79, 111–112; capture enabling, 37, 53; and commodities, nature of, 35; and disentanglement, 53; in the exotic

pet trade, 22; feminist analyses of, 21; and making thinglike, 22–23; market devices enabling, 152n3
commodities: auctions legitimizing, 72; contested, 65, 71; creation of, 16–17; Darwin, the Ikea Monkey as, 20; and labor, 17–18; liminal, 65; lively, 35, 54; lives of, 18; sentient, 112; studies of, 17–18; value of, 17
commodity chains: analysis of, 17, 19, 26; exotic pets, 57, 149n39, 151n13; parrots, 55–57
commodity fetishism: and animal fetishism, 18–19, 25, 149n35; and auctions, 29, 64, 89; and exchange value, 17, 19, 25, 132–133; and exotic pets, 25; identifying, point of, 25; political responses to, 25, 126; production, concealing, 24–25, 125–126
conservation, 41–42, 151n13
controllability and animal value, 75, 77, 80–83, 88
Convention on International Trade in Endangered Species (CITES): overview of, 14; African greys under, 87; animal trade data, 15, 146n21, 148n32; and animal welfare, 15; and demand reduction, 137; parrots under, 48; as trade organization, 15

Darwin, the Ikea Monkey, 1–5, 20
decommodification, 94–95, 99, 111–112
defaunation, 4, 16, 87, 141n2
demand reduction, 26, 30, 137–138, 150n42, 156n21
Derrida, Jacques, 25, 133, 149n38
Devine, Jennifer, 41–42
domestication, 9, 144n9
Doughney, Michael, 68
drug trafficking, 45

El Colegio de la Frontera Sur, 42
empty forest syndrome, 15

enclosure: and animal fetishism, 19, 24–25, 57–58, 126, 135; of bodies, 151n6; bodily versus land, 36–37, 136, 150n3, 151n7; and capitalism, 36, 135, 150n4, 155n16; capture as, 36–37, 52–53, 57–58; finality of, 150n3; of land, 36, 135–136, 150n4, 155nn16–17; politics against, 135; resisting, 135–136, 155n17

encounters, 26–30, 35

encounter value: and auctions, 82–84; definition of, 6, 35, 142n6; lively capital, 6, 77, 82, 142n6

European Union, bird import bans, 49, 137–138, 156n22

exchange value: and animal fetishism, 132; and auctions, 84; and commodity fetishism, 17–19, 25, 132–133; Marx on, 17, 19, 132–133; versus use value, 132–133

exotic animal keeping, history of, 10–12

exotic animal regulation: anthropocentric, 14; Canada, 14, 71, 122, 138, 147n26; pet trade, 137–138, 150n42; United States, 69–70

exotic pets: bodily modification of, 53, 120–121; versus capital, 54; captive-bred, 9; captivity, problems in, 15; celebrity, 75; characteristics of, 58; as colonial subjects, 12; control over, 5, 7; and death, 7; debates over, 68; decommodification of, 111–112; demand for, 26, 137, 146n18, 149n39; encounter value of, 6, 58; escapes, 1–2, 14, 71, 122–124, 153nn1–2; human dependency, 125; infants, preference for, 34; life constraints, 124–125; as local environment threat, 14, 148n27; making thinglike, 5; mortality rates, 15; as object life, 6; as out of place, 9; owners of, 61, 68, 70–71, 88; permit requirements map, 64m; popularity of, 10, 145n11; property status of, 5, 141n1;

reproductive value, 77; risks of, 14; and sentience, 4–5; survival of, 53–54; as undomesticated, 9; use value of, 25; Victorian era, 11–12; welfare of, 14–15

exotic pet trade: animal circulation in, 3, 12; and animal welfare, 15; Asian, 13, 137, 146n20; colonial era, 11; commodification in, 22; commodity chains, 57, 149n39, 151n13; and defaunation, 16, 138–139; demand reduction, 137–138, 150n42; and encounter value, 142n6; flows of, 12–13; governing, 13–14, 147n24; growth of, 12, 146nn17–18; importers, top, 13, 146n21, 147n22; lively capital in, 6; love and violence in, 16; and making thinglike, 23, 139; mortality rates, 15, 51, 59, 153n6; multispecies approach to, 26–27; political responses to, 131–132; and poverty, 151n13; regulation of, 137–138, 150n42; resisting, 139; size of, 9–10; smuggling, 10; tracking difficulties, 26; wild-caught animals, 13; wild population extraction, 15. See also animal trade, American; auctions; bans

extinction, 8, 16, 52

fetishism: overview of, 23; analyses of, 25–26, 126; and defetishization, 25; historicization as countering, 23–24; political implications, 25–26, 126–127; and relations, erasure of, 23; stranger figures, 23–24, 126–127; and value, 23. See also animal fetishism; commodity fetishism

Fraser, Nancy, 21

freedom, 88–89

Gillespie, Kathryn, 35, 152n2, 154n3

Goldstein, Jesse, 71

Guatemala, 41–42, 58–59, 102. *See also* ARCAS

habitats, loss of, 3–4
Hanna, Jack, 70
Haraway, Donna, 6, 23, 35, 139, 142n6, 150n41
Harvey, David, 150n4, 155n16
histories of arrival, 24, 27, 84, 127, 149n37
Hoctor, Pat, 61
human appropriation of net primary production, 143n7
hyacinth macaws, 76t, 82, 86

iguanas, 97
Indigenous peoples: activism, 43, 135–136, 155n17; and autonomy, theories of, 128; as colonial subjects, 12; dispossession of, 12, 42, 44–45, 129–130, 134, 154n11; epistemologies, 130; life, views of, 134–135; and RIBMA, 44–45; trappers, 50; and ungovernable areas, 42; and wildlife management, 134, 154n11
individuality, value of, 77, 82

Jennison, George, 145n12

Kifaru Exotic Animal Auction. *See* auctions
Kim, Claire Jean, 144n8, 154n11
Kimmerer, Robin Wall, 133–134

Last Report on the Miracles at Little No Horse, The, 75
Latour, Bruno, 73
lively capital: versus animal capital, 142n6; animals, effects on, 120–121; animals becoming, 57, 111–112; and auctions, 65, 72, 84, 89; births of, 45; as capital, 6; capture creating, 37, 57, 93, 103; versus commodities, 6, 20, 142n6; and decommodifica-

tion, 111; detachment, 79; disposability of, 70; and entanglements, 57–58; framings of, 54; and human dependence, 93; making thinglike, 7, 53–54; rehabilitation unmaking, 93–94, 118; value of, 6, 77, 82, 142n6. *See also* auctions, animal valuation
living versus nonliving things, 142n5
Lock, Margaret, 53
Lolli Brothers Livestock Market Exotic Sale. *See* auctions

Mackey, Jeff, 61
MacKinnon, James, 3–4, 7
making thinglike: and animal fetishism, 23; animals, 5, 8; at auctions, 89; and commodification, 22–23; the exotic pet trade, 23, 139; lively capital, 7, 53; as process, 22–23
market devices, 152n3
markets, 71, 73, 152n3
Marx, Karl: on commodities, 17, 19, 125, 148n33; on commodity fetishism, 19, 25, 126; critiques of, 25; on exchange value, 17, 19; exchange versus use value, 132–133; on land enclosures, 135, 150n4
Maya Biosphere Reserve, 33
Maya Forest, 38, 45, 49
Maza, Javier and Roberto de la, 49
Mexico: bird imports, 49, 55; Chiapas, 39m, 40–41; Chiquibul National Park, 38; export reductions, 41, 49; exports versus imports, 41, 151n8; Guatemalan border, 58–59; local distributors, 56–57; parrot exports, 49–50, 55–56; Playon de la Gloria, 38–40, 42–43; political instability, 41–42; wildlife trade, 41, 49, 56
Mexico City, 54–55
Mid Ohio Alternative Bird and Animal Sale. *See* auctions
Mies, Maria, 21, 24, 155n12

Millar, Kathleen, 129, 132, 154n7
misanthropic humanism, 115–117
monitor lizards, 82–83
monkeys. *See* ARCAS, monkeys at;
    spider monkeys
multispecies encounters, 26–30, 94
multispecies ethnography, 26

Nakhuda, Yasmin, 2
Naranjo, Eduardo, 48–50, 54

object life, 6, 54, 57, 95, 132, 150n40
objects versus things, 142n5
Ohio, exotic pet regulation, 69–70
Ohio Association of Animal Owners,
    66
owls, 113–114

Parreñas, Juno Salazar, 92, 101, 130
parrots: African greys, 76t, 84, 86–87,
    153n6; at ARCAS, 47f, 103–104; at
    auctions, 76t, 82, 84, 86; captive,
    52, 87, 103–104; capturing, 50–52;
    commodity chains, 55–57; hyacinth
    macaws, 76t, 82, 86; Mexican ex-
    ports, 49–50, 55–56; prices, 55–56;
    red-lored, 51f; San Francisco es-
    capee colony, 153n2; scarlet macaws,
    45–48, 76t, 86; trade bans, 49, 55
Parry, Bronwyn, 71
patriarchy and capitalism, 20–21
Penrose, Jan, 63
People Eating Tasty Animals, 68
People for the Ethical Treatment of
    Animals, 68
Pepperberg, Irene, 86–87
pets, 4–5
plants, 133–134
Playon de la Gloria, 38–40, 42–43
Plumwood, Val, 131
political economy, feminist, 20–22,
    130, 155nn12–13
politics: animal owners versus activ-

ists, 66–68; at auctions, 61–62;
    commodity fetishism, 25, 126;
    against enclosure, 135; exotic pet
    trade, 131–132; of fetishism, 25–26,
    126–127; wild life, 26, 131–132,
    135–136. *See also* animal fetishism,
    political responses to

racial capitalism, 144n8
Radin, Margaret, 71
rationality, 128
rehabilitation, wildlife: and au-
    tonomy, 92; critiques of, 118; as
    decommodification, 94, 99, 112;
    dilemmas of, 118–119, 138; fetishism,
    undoing, 94, 118; goals of, 93–94;
    and human exceptionalism, 117–118;
    lively capital, unmaking, 93–94,
    118; and manual labor, 101; power
    relations, reperforming, 105–106,
    112–113; reflexive questions for, 119;
    unencounterability goal, 93–94,
    104–106; and voluntourism, 94.
    See also ARCAS
relationally autonomous animals,
    129–132, 137–138
Reserva Integral de la Biósfera de
    Montes Azules (RIBMA): overview
    of, 43–44; botflies, 49; Eduardo
    Naranjo, 48–50; establishment of,
    44; evictions, 44–45; Indigenous
    peoples in, 44–45; location of, 38,
    39m; photographs of, 44f; scarlet
    macaws, 45–46; ticks, 48–49
Ritvo, Harriet, 11–12
Rueben, 42–42, 45, 48, 54

scarlet macaws, 45–48, 76t, 86
servals, 83, 123–124
Sevilla-Buitrago, Alvaro, 36, 151n6
Sexton, Jared, 144n8
Shukin, Nicole, 19, 142n6
Shulz, Jurgen, 85–86

www.ingramcontent.com/pod-product-compliance
Lightning Source LLC
Chambersburg PA
CBHW070334270326
41926CB00017B/3866